# The Wisdom of Strategic Learning

## Second Edition

# The Wisdom of Strategic Learning

# The self managed learning solution

## Second Edition

## IAN CUNNINGHAM

Gower

First edition published 1994 by McGraw-Hill Book Company Europe

This edition published by
Gower Publishing Limited
Gower House
Croft Road
Aldershot
Hampshire GU11 3HR
England

Gower
Old Post Road
Brookfield
Vermont 05036
USA


Ian Cunningham has asserted his right under the Copyright, Designs and Patents Act 1988 to be identified as the author of this work.

**British Library Cataloguing in Publication Data**

Cunningham, Ian
    The wisdom of strategic learning: the self managed
    learning solution – 2nd edn.
    1. Organizational learning    2. Organizational change
    I. Title
    658.4'06
    ISBN 0 566 08079 6

**Library of Congress Cataloging-in-Publication Data**

Cunningham, Ian, 1943–
    The wisdom of strategic learning: the self managed learning
    solution / Ian Cunningham – 2nd edn.
        p.   cm.
    Includes bibliographical references and index.
    ISBN 0-566-08079-6 (hardback)
    1. Organizational learning.   2. Organizational change–Management.
    I. Title
    HD58.8.C857   1998
    658.4'06–dc21                                                           98–27582
                                                                                  CIP


Typeset in 10pt Palatino by Raven Typesetters, Chester and printed in Great Britain by MPG Books Ltd, Bodmin.

# Contents

List of illustrations                                             ix
Preface to first edition                                          xi
Preface to second edition                                         xv
Acknowledgements                                                 xix


**PART ONE**   INTRODUCTION

**1 Introduction: some basics**                                    3
   The basic issues                                                3
   Learning levels                                                 4
   Big picture and little picture                                  5
   Case examples                                                   5
   The active reader                                               6
   Strategic learning in a drinks business                         6
   Strategic learning in the public sector                        11
   Why 'strategic learning'?                                      13
   Progress of an organization                                    15
   Summary                                                        23
   Notes                                                          24


**PART TWO**   BIG PICTURE

**2 Strategic learning**                                          27
   Introduction                                                   27
   Background                                                     27
   Ineffective approaches                                         29
   Forecasting                                                    29
   White water                                                    30
   Planning and preparing                                         31
   Orders of change                                               32
   Luck                                                           33
   Pace of change                                                 34
   Discomfort in learning                                         34
   Pattern change                                                 35
   Feedback                                                       36

Truth vs maps                                      37
Maps for managing change                           38
Making learning stick                              41
Strategic excellence                               42
Conclusion: strategic questions about learning     43
Summary                                            44
Notes                                              45

**3  A learning business**                         **47**
Introduction                                       47
Learning and organizations                         49
The learning business                              54
Summary of issues                                  56
Who wants a learning business?                     56
The learning business culture                      58
Order and disorder                                 59
Diversity                                          61
Organizational types                               61
Creating a balance                                 65
Appraisal schemes                                  71
Summary                                            73
Notes                                              73

**PART THREE    GOOD LEARNING**

**4  Capability and wisdom**                       **79**
Introduction                                       79
Learning from all possible sources                 79
Learning and change                                80
Who learns?                                        82
Key concepts                                       85
Capability                                         89
Wisdom                                             96
Summary                                            99
Notes                                              100

**5  Holism**                                      **103**
Introduction                                       103
Feelings and emotions                              103
Connectedness                                      106
Centring                                           107
Grounding                                          113
Morality and ethics                                114
Summary                                            116
Notes                                              116

**PART FOUR**   SELF MANAGED LEARNING

| | |
|---|---|
| **6 Principles** | **121** |
| Introduction | 121 |
| Comments on SML programmes | 121 |
| Autonomy, responsibility, self control, choice | 124 |
| Some history | 128 |
| Self managed learning | 136 |
| Summary | 140 |
| Notes | 141 |
| | |
| **7 Strategy and designs** | **143** |
| Introduction | 143 |
| A model for SML strategy | 143 |
| Strategic learning and SML | 148 |
| Processes | 148 |
| Summary | 166 |
| Notes | 167 |
| | |
| **8 Tactics and practice** | **169** |
| Introduction | 169 |
| SML programmes | 172 |
| Nature of learning sets | 188 |
| Learning community | 194 |
| Assessment | 197 |
| Standards | 200 |
| Criteria | 200 |
| Evaluation | 201 |
| Summary | 202 |
| Notes | 202 |

**PART FIVE**   PRACTICE

| | |
|---|---|
| **9 Roles in learning and change** | **207** |
| Introduction | 207 |
| Learning theorist | 208 |
| Learning designer | 210 |
| Learning manager | 212 |
| Learning assistant | 213 |
| Four roles: pulling it together | 224 |
| Summary | 227 |
| Notes | 227 |
| | |
| **10 Developmental roles in practice** | **229** |
| Introduction | 229 |
| Developing from the four roles model | 229 |
| Selecting set advisers | 232 |
| Set adviser development | 236 |

Coaching and mentoring                                    246
The development adviser role                               247
On-line working and technology                            247
Summary                                                   248
Notes                                                     249

**11  The learner in context**                            **251**
Introduction                                              251
Self managing learner                                     251
Difference and diversity                                  254
Diversity and disadvantage: strategic learning issues     255
Cross-cultural issues                                     258
Summary                                                   261
Notes                                                     261

**12  Conclusions and directions**                        **263**
Introduction                                              263
Not self managed learning                                 263
Self managed learning going wrong                         268
Bandwidth                                                 269
Myths about SML                                           269
Real problems                                             273
Directions                                                274
Notes                                                     275

**Appendix I    Research into SML**                       **277**
Published papers – a selection                            277
Evaluation reports of specific programmes                 277
Studies internal to organizations                         278
Higher degrees                                            278
Related studies                                           278

**Appendix II    Selling SML**                            **279**
Dealing with misunderstandings of SML                     279
Research                                                  280
Users of SML                                              281
Why the above approaches may not work                     282
Conclusion                                                282

**Appendix III    The Fielding Institute MA**             **283**

**Index**                                                 **289**

# List of illustrations

**Figures**
1.1  Levels of learning                                              4
1.2  Spectrum of antagonistic/apathetic/reactive
     organizations                                                  14
1.3  Progression of an organization                                 16
1.4  Focus of learning                                              20
2.1  Managing change                                                39
2.2  Leadership                                                     41
3.1  The learning process (Western view)                            48
3.2  Change processes                                               64
3.3  Balanced development                                           65
3.4  Appraisal model                                                71
3.5  Developmental model                                            71
3.6  Focused development                                            73
4.1  Traditional change model                                       81
4.2  New change model                                               81
5.1  Extrovert–introvert mapping                                   109
5.2  Learning approaches                                           111
7.1  Strategy and tactics                                          144
7.2  Purposes, strategy and tactics                                145
7.3  U model                                                       146
7.4  Strategic learning: linking purposes and strategy             148
7.5  Preparing for SML                                             149
7.6  Organizational mapping: the organization chart                154
7.7  Strip map                                                     155
7.8  Balancing past and future                                     157
7.9  Planning learning in SML                                      159
7.10 Problem solving and learning: five questions                  159
7.11 Connection vs introjection                                    163
8.1  SML programmes in context                                     169
8.2  SML as strategy, not tactics                                  171
8.3  SML robust design                                             173
8.4  Strategic processes to tactical elements                      175
8.5  Learning contracts                                            180
9.1  Managing learning                                             212
9.2  The assisting role: a map                                     219
9.3  Support and stimulus                                          220

9.4   The four-leaf clover                                    224
10.1  Interacting with learners                                237
10.2  Development of set advisers                              237
11.1  Levels and differences                                   257
12.1  SML bandwidth: spectrum of possibilities                 269
A.1   Factors affecting leaders' decision making               282

**Tables**

2.1   Bureaucratic vs strategic                                 44
5.1   Connecting                                               106
5.2   Theory and practice                                      111
8.1   Robust design                                            173
8.2   Extract from questionnaire on basic strategic
      management ideas                                         176
8.3   Sets are not seminars                                    189
9.1   Learning assistant: roles                                215

# Preface to first edition

This book presents a number of arguments. I am making a case for a particular focus on organizational life which views learning as central to organizational and individual success. My case also includes the notion that 'success' is necessary but it isn't enough in the life of a person or an organization. Learning to *be* underpins learning to *do*. The book develops the idea that a *strategic* approach to learning is necessary. This is important for individuals *and* organizations. This point leads to the view that people with a strategic interest in themselves or their organizations ought to pay attention to learning issues.

I want to establish the concept of 'strategic learning' as an all-encompassing strategic approach to learning. It includes management development and training, but it is much more extensive. Also, strategic learning *starts* with strategic imperatives – the direction the organization is taking, its purpose, its vision, its mission, its strategic goals (or whatever language and approaches are used by the organization). Training programmes *may* then follow as tactics to use – but they may not (and it's not apparent that training *has* to be used). Also, *most* learning needs are not best met through training. This leads to the view that individuals need to consider their roles in assisting others to learn. The concept of 'assisting' is crucial to making organizations *good* places in which to learn. I shall weave into the text some ideas about what makes 'goodness', such as: good learning; a good learner; a good organization; a good learning assistant. I shall, as often as possible, draw on evidence from research (my own and others'). Each chapter is an overview of certain issues which, in some cases, are complex. Literary references in the text are idiosyncratic, as this is not a book that reviews other texts in the field. You may have a preference for classics that I don't mention: the choices are mine, and relate to the material being presented; that is, I want to refer you to texts that may add to what I have written rather than throw in references as a way of providing spurious credibility for what I have said. As well as being researched as far as ideas go, the methods and techniques suggested have all been tested in actual situations, so they are not the product of mere armchair theorizing.

## The reader

This book is intended for anyone who cares to read it. I recognize that it may appeal most to those interested in learning issues, and that might imply only those with a professional interest in the subject (for example, HR managers, trainers, educators). However, I hope that my argument that *everyone* in an organization needs to be attentive to learning is accepted. Hence the suggestion that it has a wider appeal than solely for the 'professional'. Assisting others to learn is part of what makes us human. Parents, as a natural part of their role, assist their children to learn, so the idea of assisting others at work to learn ought not to be entirely foreign.

## A strategic approach to learning

'Strategic' as a word has a hard bite to it, whereas 'learning' is often seen as a soft topic (flabby, psychological stuff removed from business realities). I want to combine hard and soft in this book – and in thinking about problems of making organizations work better.

I know that 'strategy' has a basis in a war metaphor: it belongs to a school of thought that sees organizations as competing aggressively in a hostile, difficult world. And, like so much in this book, it is both true and not true. Yes, organizational life is difficult – we live in turbulent, uncertain and complex times. Survival is high on many agendas for organizational action. Survival sometimes refers to the attacks of predators – that is, from takeovers or from competitors determined to drive a company out of business. I accept the warfare side of business, but I also want to balance this with a concern for organizations being *good* places for people to be, where it feels *good* for an individual to spend a high proportion of his or her waking hours. This is the soft side of strategic development and in many respects the soft side is harder to achieve and to maintain.[1]

As well as wanting a hard/soft balance in thinking about strategy, I also want a hard/soft balance in an approach to learning. The kind of learning I see as necessary for modern organizations is not some easy-going, sponge-like absorption of new knowledge, but a tough, searching and bone-deep personal change process. It is mostly accomplished through the struggle of adjusting to change or making change happen, rather than by absorbing ideas in a classroom. This does not, however, support the 'no pain, no gain' school of thought. Learning is sometimes pleasurable, and sometimes not. But learning is what has brought us to where we are – collectively and individually. Whatever abilities, skills, thoughts, beliefs and attitudes we possess, they have *all been learned*. We are as we are because it is either in our genes or it has been learned. Our genes provide us with the basis for learning, but we are not born with the knowledge and skills we all individually possess.

All this can seem pretty trite stuff if you accept my basic propositions. I am, nevertheless, amazed by the number of managers who seem to work on different assumptions – for example, when they bring in new systems or technologies and assume that these innovations will be implemented without people *learning* to use them. They seem to assume that by issuing instructions, or by just telling people, implementation comes naturally.

I also see this in the actions of consultants who produce erudite, rigorously argued reports for new structures or systems of working and assume that their implementation is no problem: it will just happen. They seem to have little or no sense of the learning necessary in their client organizations.

An old story concerns a grasshopper.[2] As he got older he found winters more difficult to cope with. His joints and bones ached so much that he went to the wise owl, the consultant of the animal kingdom, for advice. When the owl had heard his tale he recommended that the grasshopper change himself into a cricket. As the owl pointed out, crickets hibernate in winter, so his problems would be solved. The grasshopper was delighted with the proposed solution, but somehow could not implement it, try as he might. He went back to the owl to complain that he couldn't make this transformation. The owl replied 'Look, I come up with the solutions; it's your job to learn how to implement them.'

## Writing style

I shall be making a case for what I regard as 'best practice'. Sometimes I am challenged to be more accepting of other practices. My view is that if something is less than best, why accept it when there is something better? Toyota has a motto: 'Compromise is the enemy of achievement.' I agree; but that is only my view. Hence, in this book there are a lot of 'I' statements. That is because I want to own them as *my* views, *my* opinions. They are not truths or absolutes; it is just how I see the world. And if I were to write in a neutral way, it would be less honest and less authentic. I have also written about my reasons for coming to particular conclusions – for example, my personal experiences –

because you, as a reader, can then see the basis of my assumptions and make up your own mind about whether to accept them or not. So the book is something to argue with, or to disagree with. And I would rather have you angered by it than bored with it.

## Notes

1 The idea of the 'soft being hard' comes from, among others, Tom Lupton (former director of the Manchester Business School).

2 The story of the grasshopper and the owl is modified from one in Bennis, W.G., Benne, K.D. and Chin, R. (1970) *The Planning of Change* (2nd edn), New York: Holt, Rinehart and Winston, p 3. This is a fine book on the 1960s/early 1970s ideas about managing change. A lot of it is now dated and seems naïve, but there are some good papers in it (and in later editions of this text).

Ian Cunningham
1993

# Preface to second edition

The first edition of this book was written in early 1993. The feedback I have had since the book was published in 1994 has been largely positive. It has been especially gratifying to see the book being used in many countries around the world. However, readers and reviewers did identify some weaknesses that I have tried to rectify in this new edition. The descriptions in some places were too terse and needed more explanation. So some sections have been expanded and others rewritten to improve clarity. One new chapter (Chapter 10) has been added to give more practical elaboration to some key issues.

Also, I needed to signpost the reader better. Some reviewers felt that they had already accepted the case for the centrality of learning and so needed less of the opening argument. I would therefore urge readers who feel that they have a good grounding in the ideas about learning in the first three parts to skim these and get into the later material on self managed learning. On the other hand, there may be some readers who do not want to get into the detail of actual programmes and for whom the later parts may seem less relevant.

Some changes have not been dictated by the views of others but by developments that have occurred in the last five years. For instance, we have seen a continued growth in interest in the idea of a learning organization, and I have added some new evidence from this field. Also there have been more examples of the use of a more strategic approach to learning and more cases of the use of self managed learning. I have integrated some of this new evidence into the text. This has included taking out some old case material and putting in new cases. (One of the new cases includes the use of new technology and is also mentioned in a new Appendix III.) However, the developments over the last five years have not in any way changed the basic evidence I quoted in the first edition. Hence most of the quotes have stayed the same: they have stood the test of time and I see no reason to change them just to appear up to date. There have, however, been some refinements to the methods we use and these have been incorporated into this new edition.

One or two readers wanted more research evidence to be quoted and that has been done. (See Appendix I.) However, the research carried out in the last five years has not changed the basic principles. Rather, it has confirmed the previous research, so I have not gone overboard in deluging the reader with research references. There have been academic research projects such as that by Ross[1] which have raised issues about the differences between poor practice and good practice, and there have been independent in-company evaluations which have produced extremely positive results (for example, in Sainsbury's, Shell, Cable and Wireless and PPP healthcare). Some references to these studies are included in relevant chapters and in the new Appendix I.

Apart from not wanting to bore people, there is another reason why I have not gone heavily into the research. And that is that I have rarely seen anyone buy into the approach espoused in these pages because of research evidence. Despite the rhetoric of rationality about decision making in most organizations, the reality is that uncomfortable evidence about the need to change can easily be dismissed by those in power who feel threatened by it. (Chapter 3 has more on this issue and a new Appendix II discusses the issue of selling the ideas in the book.)

## Exemplars from the first edition

One pleasing feature of the first edition, in retrospect, has been the extent to which most examples I used there have stood the test of time. For instance, I praised Tesco and Lord MacLaurin for their learning orientation, and the results started to show when they went from second to first place in market share in their sector. Also I referred to Richard Branson and Virgin Atlantic, and again the success story has continued. I make no claims to be a good forecaster on this basis. My case is that learning well gives real advantage to individuals and organizations. In 1993 I was only commenting on what was happening at the time. They were more strategic in their learning than their competitors, and this has led to the growth we have seen. Whether this is sustained or not depends a great deal on whether the key people in these organizations continue to learn – and that is not guaranteed. At the time of writing it appears as though Branson and his colleagues have a lot to learn about running a rail company – and we will have to wait to see if they do.

Also Lord MacLaurin has moved from his Tesco role to trying to sort out English cricket. Having heard him talk about this at a recent dinner, I would say that he has taken his learning orientation into his new role, as I would expect, and I'm probably not the only one looking forward to seeing if he succeeds.

## Who's 'we'?

In the above I have referred to 'we'. I need to say who 'we' are. The term refers to colleagues in the consultancy Strategic Developments International, and names are mentioned in the Acknowledgements. Whilst I am happy to own the opinions expressed herein, I want to make it clear that we work as a team and that the evidence and ideas quoted often come out of our collective working.

I know that my colleagues join me in hoping that you find this text of value. We always welcome comments and ideas on our work and any reader interested can contact me via Gower or e-mail me at cunning@pavilion.co.uk

## Note

1 Ross, J. (1997) *How was it for you? Exploring the Learner's Experience of Self Managed Learning*, MSc Dissertation, University of Salford.

Ian Cunningham
February, 1998

# Acknowledgements

Although I take responsibility for all that the book contains, I want to acknowledge the help, support, advice and assistance of others. In no particular order of importance, these include:

- hundreds of managers and students with whom I've worked and from whom I've learned over the years
- colleagues in Strategic Developments International, especially Ben Bennett, Julia Colclough, Graham Dawes, Anne Gimson and Andre Mailer
- past colleagues too numerous to mention
- Julia Scott of Gower
- faculty and students of Pepperdine University's MS (Organization Development) program (especially Miriam Lacey, Chris Worley, Ann Feyerherm, Dave Hitchin and Gail Work)
- doctoral students of the Fielding Institute, especially Linda Honold and David Haddad
- colleagues in Finland, especially Pirjo Heikkinen, Pertti Kettunen and Leena Pukkala (Jyvaskyla University); Matti Pulkki (Jollas Institute) and Tuula Lillia
- people in organizations who have been innovating along the lines discussed in this book (and who have provided rich material for it), including Geoff Gaines (KPMG), Susan Wilson, Claire Pulley and Vivien Cook (Birmingham Midshires Building Society), Judith Evans, Nigel Broome and Sally Booth (Sainsbury's), Mark Aspinall and Anabel Adam (PPP healthcare), Rob Shorrick (formerly of PPP), Kathleen Bessos (Scottish Health Service Centre), Marcia Fellows and Jim Chitty (Arun District Council), Robert Lines, Alan Slater and Martin Springell (Ericsson), Simon Shellard (Debenhams), Jane Molloy (W H Smith), Ted Murphy (Abbey National) and Peter Kennedy and Ian Clark (ICL)
- a network of professional colleagues, most of whom have provided ideas and stimulus over many years, including Margaret Attwood, Richard Boot, Phil Boxer,

Tom Boydell, John Burgoyne, Charlotte Chambers, Magda Csath, Bob Garratt, Harry Gray, Roger Harrison, Vivien Hodgson, Peter Honey, Sarah Mann, Alistair Mant, Andrew Mayo, John Morris, Alan Mumford, Michael Pearn, Mike Pedler, Mike Reynolds, Bob Sang

● David Cunningham and Lucy Cunningham for their own brands of challenging thinking
● Caroline Cunningham for many things but, in the context of this book, for handling a whole range of problems from the computer to editing issues.

IC

# PART ONE    Introduction

The book is in five parts. This first part contains just one chapter and provides some opening thoughts. I introduce some themes to be explored later.

Chapter 1 provides clues towards understanding some key ideas I shall use. These include

- strategic learning
- self managed learning.

In Part Two I shall define more precisely what I mean by strategy in the context of learning and in Part Three I shall discuss what I mean by 'good learning'. Self managed learning is introduced as an idea in Chapter 1 and elucidated more fully in Part Four. Part Five looks at some issues of practical application.

In this edition, I have added three appendices to provide some more concrete detail on issues raised in the text.

# 1 Introduction: some basics

## The basic issues

René Fichant, the CEO of Michelin Tyre, once told a story which I shall modify here. Three men were shown a room with two doors. They were told that behind one door was wealth beyond their wildest dreams – gold, silver, priceless jewels. Behind the other door was a hungry man-eating tiger. They were each given the option of entering the room and opening a door. The first man refused the choice and left. The second man – a good strategic planner – hauled out his computer, analysed probability data, performed some risk analyses, plotted graphs, produced charts, created scenarios, and so on, and after much deliberation he opened a door and was eaten by a low-probability man-eating tiger. The third man (and, of course, the third one is always the winner) spent his time learning to tame tigers.

Learning in organizations makes sense. Indeed, organizations in which there is little learning, or the wrong kind of learning, do not survive in the modern world. Some, such as IBM, can survive a long time because of their size and monopolistic position. But even IBM's poor learning culture eventually caught up with it in the late 1980s.[1]

The trouble is that learning is not a very visible process. It is internal to people and often takes time. In a world that values the obvious, the immediate and the concrete, learning gets undervalued. Many organizations seem to have taken to heart the graffito I once saw which said '500 million lemmings can't be wrong.' And as they hurl themselves off the cliff shouting 'so far, so good' they take with them many innocents – into unemployment or impoverished jobs.

When I argue with top managers about the importance of learning – and the need to take a strategic view of it – I get a sense of how Kierkegaard felt in his dismay at how his words were received. As he said, he felt like a theatre manager who runs on stage to warn the audience of a fire. But they take his appearance to be part of the farce they are enjoying, and the more he shouts the louder they applaud.

Of course, it is not applause that is required, but another kind of action.

The situation may be changing, however. My modification of the 'Law of Revolutionary Ideas'[2] suggests that a new proposal goes through three stages of reaction:

1  'It's stupid and irrelevant – don't waste my time.'
2  'It's interesting, but not worth doing.'
3  'I said it was important all along.'

I believe many organizations are at stage 2, and a few are at stage 3. Although this comment is valid, it relates mainly to the English-speaking world. Japan is an example of a society that has taken learning extremely seriously for a long time, and its industries have reaped the benefits of its rapid learning.[3]

## Learning levels

While this book has its main focus on organizational life, I want to draw attention to wider issues. There are various levels at which we can pay attention to learning. These can be delineated, as shown in Figure 1.1.

Individual

|

Group/Team

|

Organization

|

Community

|

Society/Nation state

|

World

*Figure 1.1*    *Levels of learning*

While I believe that, strictly speaking, learning is done by individuals, there has been a growth of attention on 'learning organizations'. Usually this latter means creating a 'context for good learning' (and the latter will be explicitly addressed in Chapters 4 and 5). However, the other levels (that is, other than individual and organization) are also important. It's clear, for instance, that some work groups or teams seem rich in learning whereas others in the same organization are 'learning impoverished'. Also, particular communities within nation states seem to provide a better learning culture than others. In the UK, Wales and Scotland are significantly more learning oriented than the East End of

London. Working-class children in Cardiff and Glasgow are much more likely to gain qualifications and to enter post-school education than equivalent children in London's East End.

Issues of learning are of major significance to us all – in all the roles we play – as individuals; as members of groups, organizations and communities; as citizens of our countries and of the world. If the emphasis on learning in organizations de-emphasizes these other levels, then this is an unbalanced focus. If, on the other hand, learning to make organizations better places within which to learn helps us to focus on other contexts as well, then it must be a good thing. (Wider aspects of 'good learning' are discussed in Chapters 4 and 5.)

## Big picture and little picture

A famous 1960s writer, Baba Ram Dass, once said that when you're floating in inter-galactic ecstasy you need to remember your zip code. Somehow we have to hold together the big picture and the little picture. We have to integrate the visions for our organizations with day-to-day practice. Otherwise we have what we so often see in organizations: dead vision/mission statements devised through some detached bureaucratic process. They do not relate to people in their daily lives and hence become the butt of cynical banter from secretaries and shop-floor workers. ('Have you seen the latest nonsense to come from the top floor?')

## Case examples

I would like to introduce a few cases of learning-based approaches that address these and other problems, and this chapter will show some concrete examples that link the big picture and the little picture. They will provide a basis for what is to come in later chapters, and I shall signpost references for the reader who wants to leap ahead – or at least to know what follows the 'hors d'oeuvre'. This hors d'oeuvre provides small tasters of what follows – but please do not confuse it with the main meal.

At the core of this chapter are the outlines of two cases of strategic learning. The cases throw up a range of issues, a few of which will be addressed in this chapter. The remainder will emerge as the book progresses. I want to start with concrete examples so that the ideas and discussion that follow are grounded in real-life issues.

The two cases are presented fairly baldly. At first sight the aims of the programmes and the claims for their efficacy may seem familiar. After all, everyone in the business of promoting organizational learning claims that what they are doing is good. I hope in later chapters to demonstrate that there is genuinely something different, special and especially excellent about strategic learning and about the self managed learning method as part of this approach.

## The active reader

You will find examples of models, checklists, and other materials used in strategic learning approaches scattered through the text. I would encourage you to test them. Like clothes bought off the rail, they may not fit, but you'll only know this for certain by trying them on. And the process of 'trying them on' may help you to see what else you could use. Also, this kind of process is consonant with the self managed learning mode of operating that I shall emphasize in this book.

## Strategic learning in a drinks business

The first case presented here concerns the Wines and Spirits Division of Allied Domecq. The work started when the division was called the Hiram Walker group and was part of Allied-Lyons (before the company took on the Domecq business and changed its name).

The company distributes a wide range of wines and spirits (for example, Courvoisier brandy and Beefeater gin). The group was formed from a merger of well-established companies, and in its merger saw the need for significant change. Top management wanted to move the culture from the cosy, patriarchal model that had been common in the drinks business towards a faster-moving, more entre-preneurial culture. They also knew that they needed to change strategically to operate in a highly competitive marketplace. With increasingly sophisticated approaches to purchasing, especially from the large retail groups, they needed to develop highly capable managers to operate in these new environments. (Chapters 2 and 3 discuss the wider aspects of the environments and markets in which organizations operate.)

They decided that their entire management team needed extensive and coordinated development if the business was to compete effectively. However, the history of the companies that had merged into the new organization was one of fragmented management development. Also, the whole personnel/human resources (HR) function had had an 'industrial relations' attitude, rather than a developmental one.

When I was asked to talk with their human resources development director they had already decided that they wanted a management development approach that would put *all* their senior managers through a significant learning process over approximately a three-year period. They were also clear that they wanted something that responded to individual needs. I and my colleagues worked with them in designing a self managed learning programme that would take about 60 to 70 managers initially, expanding to cover all their senior people in the three-year timescale.

**Initiating the programme**

The first step was getting the buy-in of top management (at chairman and board level) to a process that was going to meet their strategic needs but would not look anything like a traditional management training course.

The company wanted to develop a culture that supported learning and change. Within this it realized that managers needed to take responsibility for their own learning, while the company needed to accept its responsibility to support managers in their learning. The self managed learning approach appealed because it met those needs and also allowed managers to work on job-related issues, hence overcoming transfer of learning problems.

The first stage was to put specific proposals to the board of the company, within the group, that handled the spirits business. They were to be the first part of the group to adopt the new approach.

The board recognized that they themselves needed to model this new approach. They had to give overt purposive support to the change, and they needed to learn better how to mentor and coach their senior managers (hence modelling a key aspect of the new culture). Therefore, in parallel with developing the self managed learning programme, the board members attended a workshop on mentoring and coaching.

In designing the senior management programme it was clear that the links between it and the strategic direction of the business had to be made explicit. Also, the programme needed to mirror the new culture being established. A more entrepreneurial culture needed more entrepreneurial managers. But managers would not become more entrepreneurial by sitting in classrooms listening to lectures, or by doing case studies. This would produce people who could *talk about* being entrepreneurial, but they would not necessarily *become* entrepreneurial.

**Self managed learning**

The self managed learning approach addresses this issue. For instance, it demands that managers manage their own learning. They negotiate their own objectives, decide how to achieve them, how to measure them and how to integrate their learning with organizational needs. As part of the programme individual managers joined 'learning sets' with five or six other managers. These sets met once a month for a whole day. In this programme they met over a period of nine months, which constituted the first phase of the work. The sets provided a place to negotiate learning objectives, agree a written 'learning contract' to carry out these objectives and get support to implement the contract. At the end of the nine months the individuals in their sets were required to assess themselves against the objectives they had set. (Chapters 6, 7 and 8 in Part Four explain more about self managed learning and how it works.)

The set is assisted in its working by a set adviser. This person's role is to help the set function. It is not a teaching role, nor is it the same as being a facilitator (as the term has come to be used in training and development circles). (This role is explained more fully in Chapter 9.) We initially chose 11 senior people from different departments of the company (mostly in the number two position in the department, just below board level) to act as set advisers. They attended a three-day workshop to develop their ability to fulfil the role, and they also received ongoing supervision and support from experienced set advisers (from outside the company) throughout the programme. This feature is important as it was part of our role to develop the strategic capability of the organization to continue to support this approach to learning. (Chapter 10 has more on the issue of developing set advisers.)

The first programme was launched with a two-day residential event. The role of external consultants (such as ourselves) was to stay as much as possible in the background to support the company people. So, for instance, explanations about the programme were delivered by board members, and the role of the company set advisers was stressed. During the two days the sets were formed, and emphasis was given to the fact that these groupings were not teams with a common goal, but were there to help individuals meet their own defined learning objectives.

The first three months of the programme were spent in developing and agreeing learning contracts, and the following six months were spent in meeting the requirements of these contracts. The contracts were drawn up by answering five questions:

1  Where have I been? (What have been my past experiences?)
2  Where am I now? (What kind of person/manager am I? What abilities do I possess? What are my strengths and weaknesses?)
3  Where do I want to get to? (What kind of

person/manager do I want to become? What abilities do I want to develop? What learning goals shall I set?)

4 How shall I get there? (What programme of learning and development do I need to undertake? What resources do I need to do it? How shall I overcome obstacles to my learning?)

5 How shall I know if I've arrived? (How do I measure achievement of goals? Who will provide measures of learning?)

The 'contract' was between the individual, their learning set and the organization (usually represented by their manager).

Learning sets were seen as a critical element in helping people to succeed in meeting their contracts. As evidence of top management commitment, and the strategic importance of the programme, people were not allowed to be taken out of set meetings (for example by their manager) unless sanctioned by the managing director. This ensured that short-term crises did not override the strategic imperative of the learning programme.

**The results**   A flavour of the programme is given by the comments of Ruth Harley, planning and inventory manager in the operations department. She was among the 66 managers on the first nine-month programme and she became involved in a second phase:

> Before I got involved in the programme, I didn't really know what to expect, as I hadn't heard of self managed learning before. I felt pleased that the company was making some provision for our development as managers. My phase one learning objectives were quite general: to improve my Lotus and PC skills in order to produce better management information reports, to build my confidence at doing stand-up presentations, and to broaden my knowledge of accounts and finance and depot operations.
>
> I liked the self managed learning process because I was the one that was identifying and taking responsibility for my own learning. You benefit from the knowledge and experience of your fellow set members, especially if you have a good cross-section of different departments with different viewpoints in the same set. It is a safe, supportive and challenging environment in which to learn.
>
> I felt that, as a result of self managed learning, people in the different departments involved started to work more closely together, both inside and outside the set environment. At first it was a very foreign process, and

it seemed odd to meet and talk in a group in such an unstructured way. The lack of structure makes you look to the set adviser for direction, but your questions are reflected back to you and the group, and you discover your own answers. It is definitely not the usual teacher/student relationship. I have achieved the learning objectives I set in phase one, and I am sure that the programme will bring further improvements as time goes on.

I am also linking my phase two learning objectives more closely into my work: as you become more experienced at self managed learning, you are able to focus more clearly on what you need. We are also setting some short-term objectives, as achieving short-term goals is very satisfying and spreads the development work more evenly across the year – and makes the end of the year less worrying.

This is only one view out of 66, but it is fairly representative. However, all the learning contracts were different. In essence there were 66 courses running in parallel, as people pursued their own needs. Learning sets, though, had some common patterns, including the technique of giving each person time to talk about personal needs and issues, and get support from others. Sometimes the support came through challenging questions, but the set's focus was always on how to assist good learning. (See Chapters 4 and 5 for a discussion on 'good learning'.)

Most of the learning activity, outside sets, took place in the company. People took the opportunity to learn from other managers in the organization. Participants also had a comprehensive handbook of materials on a wide range of topics. It was almost a mini learning resource centre for each person, providing diagnostic questionnaires, handouts, guidance to accessing other resources, and so on. Where needed, participants could get access to outside specialists, and this was supported by the company. (Chapters 6, 7 and 8 in Part Four give more information on these aspects of self managed learning.)

At the end of the programme there was an important phase of assessment. Individuals presented evidence of achievement to their peers in the set. They also met with the director responsible for their own division for a debriefing on the programme. The results of the assessment process were logged on individuals' personnel records, hence acknowledging the place of the programme in a person's career development. The company has evaluated the programme and identified a range of benefits, which include:

- Increased self motivation, self awareness and personal initiative
- Reduced departmental barriers and increased cohesion in the company
- Broadened skills and abilities in managers
- Greater understanding of roles (personal and other)
- Greater business awareness and strategic abilities
- Managers more open and receptive to change
- A positive attitude to learning and development.

The company has assessed the cost-effectiveness of the programme, which has proved to be the most cost-effective approach it has undertaken. As one director stated, in presenting the programme to participants, the company was not engaging in this management development for altruistic purposes. The ultimate benefit of the strategic approach to learning is more profit.

The first programmes were launched in 1991 and focused on the UK management population. Since then the company has expanded its self managed learning programmes to groups such as administrative and sales staff in the UK, project managers in Spain, international graduates across Europe and senior executives in Canada. Daniel Cloke, Corporate Human Resources Director, reported in 1998 that 'Self managed learning (SML) has been a key driver in cultural change.' He also commented that SML language was now used widely in the company, for example in project management through using the five questions of the learning contract. As well as seeing pay-off for their current managers and others, the company has found that the self managed learning approach provides a source of competitive advantage when recruiting – potential new recruits like to hear that the company is doing this kind of development work. Finally Daniel Cloke commented that 'The network of self managed groups has been a significant support for individuals during times of organizational change and business opportunities have been seized as a result of employees developing their skills and competences.'

## Strategic learning in the public sector

The National Health Service in Britain is one of the world's largest employers (with almost one million employees) and it has been going through massive strategic change. My colleagues and I worked in one region to support these changes through learning-based approaches. As with the previous example, our objective was to help the organization to be as self supporting as possible. For instance, we undertook development workshops for personnel and training staff throughout the region so that they could learn how to use a self managed learning (SML) approach integrated with other strategic initiatives. In some cases this meant new regional-level initiatives; in other cases districts within the region started programmes. The case I shall mention here was within one of the first wave of autonomous hospital trusts established.

The St Helier Trust was the largest hospital trust established in the region at the time. The chief executive wanted to develop his managers in a way that was congruent with the radical changes occurring in the health service in Britain. He specifically made a commitment to support an organization-wide strategic learning initiative as well as provide means for individuals to meet their own learning objectives.

The change process initially went through three phases. The first phase was based on 'focus groups' of managers developing ideas about what would be needed of managers in the new-style organization. Phase two consisted of setting up a managers' conference, which was attended by 70 of the 78 senior/top managers in the organization. This one-day conference was led by the chief executive, who gave personal backing to the proposal for a self managed learning (SML) programme for *all* the senior/top managers.

Prior to this conference, my colleagues and I had assisted in developing the set advisers who were to handle the SML programme, and in designing the programme. At the conference the SML approach was explained to the managers and 13 sets, with six managers in each, were formed. These sets then, in phase three of the initiative, met about once a month for four or five hours for six months. Twelve of the 13 sets were judged by the organization to have been successful.

This SML programme had similarities to the previous case, with the use of learning contracts and internal set advisers. The organization took this route for the following six reasons:

1  The SML approach reflected the change process in the health service.
2  SML mirrors the managerial process (in demanding of managers to set objectives, allocate resources, measure results, and so on).
3  It stresses learning and development rather than purely training.
4  It emphasizes career, personal and organizational development.

5 It breaks down internal professional barriers (a key issue in hospital settings) through the use of cross-disciplinary sets.

6 It is a 'learning umbrella', not an enforced learning style (people could use whatever learning methods suited them).

An independent evaluation of SML programmes at the regional level showed considerable success in the venture. A typical quote from the report was:

> All had found it an unfamiliar process on first acquaintance, using words like 'floundering', 'difficult', 'battled with it'. They described SML as causing them to think more, to be more reflective, to assess and look at themselves, to take responsibility, to take more initiatives, eg in choosing mentors, getting secondments, asking people for information. SML is seen as being both about career development and personal development.

## Why 'strategic' learning?

The two examples show a strategic approach to learning. I shall elaborate 12 criteria, or factors, that indicate that this approach is different from others. First, however, I shall give a brief outline of other approaches.

From research we conducted on a range of small, medium and large organizations in the public and private sector,[4] we identified four main organizational approaches to management learning, development and training. These, known collectively as the ARBS model, are summarized below.

### Apathetic/ antagonistic

These organizations were especially characterized by top management apathy or outright antagonism to supporting and resourcing training and development. Many small firms fell into this category. The boss was convinced that funding and giving time to such activity was either a waste of time or downright harmful. The latter position was taken by those who felt that supporting training and development would lead people to learn things that would make them more marketable (especially if they obtained qualifications) or raise their sights to look elsewhere for a job. The apathetic (the larger group) tended not to see learning as a priority. They felt that in difficult economic times their business survival was linked to other activities (for example, more aggressive selling) than to their employees learning new skills and abilities through organized development activity.

Organizations in this category not only didn't sponsor people for courses, they also didn't foster a learning environment. There was minimal coaching and mentoring, induction of new employees was haphazard and there were no rewards for learning.

**Reactive**    These organizations did provide support for learning, but purely (or mainly) on a reactive basis. If employees pushed their managers they might get funding for an external course. If individuals took initiatives they might find someone to coach them or, at the very least, to share knowledge and expertise. At one extreme, reactive organizations are close to apathetic. At the other extreme, they could be quite supportive of individual learning (see Figure 1.2). However, there was no strategic imperative guiding learning, and little or no evidence of attempts to evaluate courses or other developmental activity. Learning was hit-and-miss with no systematic planning (though there might be a designated training budget in the better examples of this type).

**Bureaucratic**    These organizations (typically relatively large) did have training budgets and either ran internal training courses or sent people on external courses (or both). Internal courses were highly standardized and often linked to particular grades or levels in the organization. In many organizations people had to go through a particular course when they reached (or were about to reach) a particular level in the hierarchy. The main overt commitment to learning in these organizations was through training. People were sent on courses if learning needs were identified (for example, in an appraisal interview). There was usually little emphasis on job-based learning (projects, secondments, mentoring, and so on), though this would often occur informally.

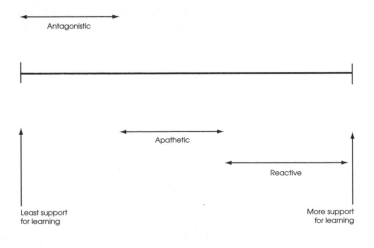

**Figure 1.2**    *Spectrum of antagonistic/apathetic/reactive organizations*

In large organizations with regional offices, we found considerable resentment towards head-office-driven training. The training department would carry out a mechanistic questionnaire-based training needs analysis and would design courses for the whole company based on an average of the identified needs. Managers outside head offices usually felt that the standardized offerings that resulted were unresponsive to their needs, and provided little value added to the business (and were certainly not cost-effective). However, the bureaucracy required that they conform to head office systems.

**Strategic**    These were the minority. They encompassed small, medium and large companies and were characterized by board-level commitment to learning and development. In the medium and large companies there was an active personnel/HR/ management development function which had access to the CEO. The people in HR/development were typically energetic, able, committed people who cared deeply about the business and its success. They were respected by senior managers and their expertise was regularly called upon. They sometimes directly supported line managers in coaching and counselling their staff. They were good networkers, well connected inside the organization and outside. They could readily access external sources of expertise as needed and were knowledgeable about current thinking on management, organizations and learning.

In taking a strategic approach to learning, these organizations would look for direct linkage between business needs and learning activity. They would pragmatically support learning methods that met specific needs. They were flexible and responsive to the differing needs of different parts of the organization.

# Progress of an organization

Figure 1.3 shows diagrammatically how an organization might progress through stages. Often a small business, as it grows, moves from an apathetic/antagonistic mode to a reactive mode. The directors have to start to react to demands from staff for development. (Only rarely does it seem that there is a direct jump to the bureaucratic.) This reactive approach could move then to a strategic or a bureaucratic approach, depending often on the views of top managers or a personnel/HR function. Too often the next stage has been the bureaucratic mode and the organization has stayed there. However, there are growing numbers of examples of organizations moving from this mode to the strategic.

A good example would be Birmingham Midshires Building Society. In the early 1990s this was a classic old-fashioned

**Figure 1.3**   *Progression of an organization*

mortgage lender that had a poor record of performance. The board brought in a new CEO, who espoused a more strategic approach to development, and other new senior appointments followed. Some of the changes on the people side included changing their HR/personnel function to a 'People Support Team', stopping most of the bureaucratic training activity and replacing it with flexible learning resources, coaches for teams in the business, and so on.

The next stage was to introduce learning contracts (they call them 'development contracts' but they are based on the same five questions used in Allied Domecq and St Helier NHS Trust). They did this from the top down. The CEO and his top team all carried out 360 degree feedback with the support of a development adviser (similar to a set adviser but working one to one) and then drew up development contracts as a basis for their learning. These were linked to both personal needs and to the strategic direction of the organization. The next stage includes linking the completion of development contracts to rewards, that is, attaching pay decisions to successful learning. Also in the next stage is the cascading down of this approach. (Some of these ideas are discussed further in later chapters. In keeping with the spirit of whetting your appetite for more

I'll leave further detail until then. Suffice it to say here that the organization has now become recognized as a high performer in its field, including winning awards for customer service, and so on.)

The last example of an organization that I want to mention here is J Sainsbury. This 128-year-old large food retailer realized that it needed to make changes from the bureaucratic to the strategic in its personnel function. This change was in keeping with the need in the company in general to be less bureaucratic and move towards creating more of a learning culture. The company went through a business process re-engineering project and this required the personnel function to work in a multi-functional mode where the personnel professionals operated more like internal consultants and less like narrow specialist personnel administrators. Judith Evans, their Director, Personnel Policy, picks up the story here.[5]

> We decided to use a self managed learning approach. In this way people would have to take responsibility for what they learnt and how they learnt it . . .
> After an introductory workshop, individuals worked in 'sets' or groups of around six people. From [a 360 degree assessment] they developed a learning contract that covered their objectives for the next six months. This was agreed with their colleagues in the set and with their manager. Each set had a [set adviser], a personnel manager who was at the same time a member of their own set. This was modelled from the top of the organization. The Retail Personnel Director and I had our own little set of two with an external [set adviser]; and we each had our own set which we were an adviser to.
> In the set in which I was an adviser, the initial assessments were very frank and honest, and it was easy for people to identify the areas they wanted to develop. The early learning came from sharing experiences and ideas with each other. What Bill found difficult, Jane found easy. The procedure Jane was trying to design, Kate had a manual for.
> But there were bigger issues people were struggling with: 'Why am I here?', 'What am I supposed to be doing?', 'What do I really want out of life?' There was some deeper self-analysis and struggling with personal choices. 'Do I want to move location to further my career, or do I want to stay here and spend more time with my family?'
> Everyone has discovered more about themselves; what they want out of life, what their strengths and

limitations are and who they can call on for support. Discussing where they stand has given them greater confidence to tackle situations, to learn new skills and to take on the full remit of their new roles.

So self managed learning has given us much more than a traditional training course. As well as people with more skills, it has given us more confident and able individuals who have the courage to tackle the many tough issues brought about by a changing organisation.

Some of what Judith Evans described above is elaborated in other chapters. Some points that are important to raise here, though, include:

1  The learning was strategic for the individual *and* for the organization. People comment that self managed learning helps them become more strategic in their careers through exploring some fundamental questions in depth and over time.
2  The development was holistic. Judith Evans quotes people becoming more courageous, for instance. 'Developing courage' isn't usually part of a business school curriculum but there is no doubt that it is important in working in changing environments.

What Judith Evans did not say was that this SML programme went right through the almost 700 professional staff in the personnel function, and evaluations of the programme have shown significant benefits not only to individuals but also to the business.

## Strategic learning

In order to exemplify further the strategic approach, I shall again refer to the examples outlined above, and suggest 12 reasons why the specific initiatives were consonant with strategic learning.

### 1. Organization-wide commitment

The examples were high-profile, centrally resourced, across-the-board developments. They were in no sense marginal or peripheral 'extras'. All managers knew of the programmes, and all were to be involved (in the Allied Domecq case, in stages). The programmes were seen as a collective responsibility, and there was widespread commitment to their success.

### 2. Top management giving demonstrable support

This support was demonstrated by top-level involvement in learning. In the St Helier case, the CEO had just completed an executive MBA by action learning, and he made certain that all his top team entered fully into the SML approach.

### 3. Linked to strategic direction and cultural change

The learning approach was directly integrated into the change process at all levels. As the organizations wanted to be more customer oriented, more outgoing and more entrepreneurial, the *process* of learning had to match this.

Standardized training courses teaching how to be responsive to customers are a nonsense. People on a course are 'internal customers'; if their requirements are ignored in the course design, that is the message transmitted even if the content of the course says otherwise.

A classic example of process/content mismatch was when I attended a lecture by an eminent psychologist. Near the end of one and a half hours of non-stop lecturing he mentioned some research evidence which showed that people's ability to concentrate in a lecture diminished rapidly after 45 minutes. He saw no incongruence between the process (a long lecture) and the content (long lectures are bad).

## 4. Large-scale development

In the examples *all* relevant managers were going to experience the programme. It was not a case of selecting managers to go on a course, but rather an integrated, strategic initiative.

Figure 1.4 shows how, over time, the focus of learning has changed. The model is crude as there have been many exceptions, but as a generalization for the English-speaking world it holds up.

Up to the 1960s and 1970s the emphasis of management development (and most other training/learning activities in organizations) was on the course as the unit of analysis. Managers attended courses either on a reactive or a bureaucratic basis. During the 1970s and 1980s two challenges to this emerged. On the one hand organizations saw that small numbers of people going through expensive courses was of limited value. These organizations opted for a 'mass' approach, and began to use some of the methods indicated in Figure 1.4.

One example was distance learning, which is an update of the old correspondence course method. It promised cheap, mass training to large numbers of managers with no necessity for them to leave the workplace. Where this was attached to a degree, such as an MBA, it proved attractive to managers who wanted the qualification. The problem with this approach, as with other 'mass' methods, was that it was usually detached from work issues and had a rigidity and lack of responsiveness to individual needs that was worse than the standard taught course. At least on courses there was interaction with tutors which allowed questions to be asked by learners in order to pursue some of their own interests.

In pure distance learning the learner receives material through the post (print based as well as possibly audio and/or video tapes) and is restricted to responding to this.

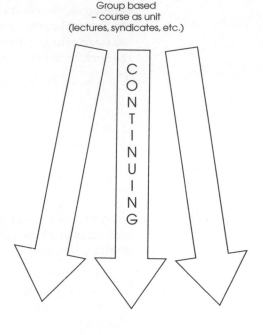

1960s/1970s

Group based
– course as unit
(lectures, syndicates, etc.)

1970s/1980s

Mass (examples)
● Distance learning
● Open learning
● Compulsory mass training
● Computer-based training
● Learning resource centres

Individual (examples)
● Self development
● Action learning
● Self managed learning
● Individualized learning
● Independent study

**Figure 1.4**   *Focus of learning*

Some tutor contact has been added to many programmes to alleviate the problem, but it is usually limited. There are also wider issues about the kind of learning that can occur on such courses. (This is discussed more fully in Chapters 4 and 5 in Part Three.)

There was another kind of reaction against the taught course in other organizations, who saw the need to respond to individual differences, and to promote a more holistic approach to learning. Hence self development (see Figure 1.4) became popular.

Learners on self development programmes have usually welcomed the freedom and responsiveness of such programmes. However, concern has grown that they may become detached from the organizational mainstream and that the small numbers of people going through programmes had limited impact on organizational development.

In the late 1980s and early 1990s there was an effort to develop ideas evolved in self development and cultural change work, into a more sophisticated learning organization/learning company model (to be discussed in Chapter 3). Hence, we are now seeing the need to deal with large numbers across whole organizations, together with responsiveness to individual differences and a desire to promote a particular kind of learning. The mass and the individual approaches are merging in best practice. Interestingly, action learning, in the hands of most practitioners, became (in the 1980s) very individual or small group focused, but when Revans evolved the ideas of action learning from the late 1940s to the 1970s he was already clear that there was an organizational- and a societal-level focus. His work in Belgium, for instance, was not just linked into organizational change but, for him, was designed to impact on the Belgium economy. (It is doubtful if it did, but the orientation is interesting, none the less.)

Self managed learning started off in the late 1970s as a heavily individually focused approach. While my colleagues and I were always clear that we wanted both a basis for learning in organizational issues and a pay-off for the organization, at that time we had not developed a way of engaging with large numbers across an entire organization. This only came in the mid- to late 1980s. (SML programme designs are discussed in Part Four.)

## 5. Not a one-off project

In some cases, the initial activity is called 'a project', but I am always looking to see the long-term developments. I am, by and large, unhappy with the idea of programmes being 'experimental' or 'pilots'. I appreciate that some practitioners see a strategic choice:

(a) a pilot or experimental scheme leading later to a full-blown organization-wide programme
(b) big bang – going for a full-scale programme immediately.

My experience is that while (a) looks like a sensible option, it usually is not. Experiments tend to stay experiments. If they succeed it is still seen as 'in the lab', but not necessarily suitable for others (for example, if a learning programme is for an élite high-flying group, it may be assumed that it is not right for ordinary mortals).

While organizations also might talk of 'initiatives' or 'programmes' (which is the usual language of an organization), I always want to stress that these terms do not imply one-off action. SML programmes may last for, say, six to nine months (as in the case examples) but they are a prelude to continued lifelong learning for the people on the programme, and activities initiated on the programme often continue beyond its end date (for example, particular projects or ongoing work with a mentor).

*6. Development of organizational capability*

Developing set advisers and mentors is often a start point for widespread development of organizational capability to support and foster learning. (I shall discuss other factors in Chapter 3 and in Part Five.) Also, when managers have been in a set for nine months they know how it works, and they have learned how to assist their peers in their learning. With the growth of flatter organizations (and the concomitant reduction in time that leaders can spend with people who report to them) peer group support for learning is starting to loom larger as a priority in strategic learning.

In the Allied Domecq case there was, from the beginning, an explicit plan to use managers from the first programme as set advisers for the next level down in the organization. Their experience in sets can accelerate their learning to become effective set advisers.

*7. Multi-functional development*

The first two case examples showed the value of bringing together people from different functions in the organization to address learning issues. In a learning set people get to know each other in depth and learn how to support learning across different departments and disciplines. This encourages an integrated approach to learning across the organization through networking. This is not just a spin-off from a programme (as is often the case on training courses). Self managed learning encourages the open exploration of live issues, and this is infinitely superior to telling 'war stories' in the bar between sessions on a training course as a way of getting to know people in other departments.

A strategic approach to learning has to encompass the development of a learning culture across the whole organization. It may seem paradoxical to focus on the personal learning needs of individuals, but when people in a learning set start to see the similarities of some of their problems, this enhances the in-depth development of a learning culture. People feel less isolated and more able to be open with colleagues.

*8. Long term, not quick fix*

First, self managed learning programmes usually need to last at least four or five months to show real, significant benefits. But as people continue their normal work throughout this time, the programmes do not become an intolerable intrusion into their jobs. However, by continually looping between live action, and then reflection and analysis in sets, people's learning is greatly enhanced.

This is different from the 'quick fix', where you go to a two-day seminar and learn all you need to know about X (which can be TQM, performance management, or any technique you care to mention). Someone on an SML programme may attend such a two-day seminar, but they will do it as part of an agreed learning contract with agreed learning objectives, and report back to their learning set on what they have learned.

Another element of long termism is the overall commitment to the continued use of SML. The organizations in the case examples did not see SML stopping at the end of the first programme. As we so often hear in evaluations of SML: 'It becomes a way of life.'

*9. Cascading down the organization*

Strategic learning means involving everyone in appropriate learning. SML approaches need to cascade down the organization, involving other staff. In further cases I shall mention in later chapters we have used SML with secretaries, technicians and clerical staff. Strategic learning does not stop with managers, but as it usually needs to start there, much of my discussion will focus on managers.

*10. Part of the organization's competitive advantage*

Strategic learning is becoming a key part of an organization's competitive advantage. Top managers are realizing that unless their organization is learning better and faster than ever before, they will be at a disadvantage. Organizations are starting to make this more explicit.

*11. Visibility*

Strategic learning is being made visible outside as well as inside the organization. It is recognized as part of the strategic direction of an organization, and is something organizations feel proud of.

*12. Integrating strategy and tactics*

Strategic visions and missions are unhelpful without a link to tactical action. The long and short terms need to be synchronized. Motivation to stick with long-term goals can come from short-term pay-off (which is seen as part of a bigger picture). (This is discussed further in Chapters 2 and 3 in Part Two, as are other aspects of the points covered above.)

## Summary

In this chapter I have made a case for learning in organizations, discussed some case examples and indicated how this use of self managed learning (SML) is part of a strategic learning approach. Issues alluded to here will be covered in more depth in subsequent chapters.

## Notes

1 Pascale, R.T. (1993) 'The benefit of a clash of opinions', *Personnel Management* (October), 38–41, specifically criticizes IBM, for example for its lack of self questioning (comparing it unfavourably with Honda and Nordstrom).

2 See Clarke's Law of Revolutionary Ideas on p. 20 of Peers, J. and Bennett, C. (1981) *1,001 Logical Laws*, London: Hamlyn.

3 My reference here is *only* to Japan's general ability to learn. I am not implying that Japan is a Utopia – far from it. In areas where Japan is weak (for example, the political and financial arenas) people have not learned as well. Peter Wickens, reviewing a research study from the perspective of his experience of working for a Japanese company, commented on how Japanese companies had been more systematic in their development activity than UK companies. The UK business culture has been too dominated by fads and fashions, he suggested, though he did recognize the downside of the Japanese approach in producing more risk-averse managers. (See Wickens, P. (1997) 'Study reveals fickle fate of British management', *People Management*, 28 August, 53–4. The research study he reviewed is Storey, J., Edwards, P. and Sisson, K. (1997) *Managers in the Making: Careers, Development and Control in Corporate Britain and Japan*, London: Sage.)

4 Cunningham, C. (1991) Report on Management Development and Training in Central Sussex, Sussex TEC.

5 Comments here are extracted from Evans, J. (1997) 'Key skills for tomorrow's world', *Capability*, **3** (2), 11–14.

# PART TWO   Big picture

This part of the book develops the idea of strategic learning (Chapter 2) and concepts of a learning business (Chapter 3). It attends especially to 'big picture' issues. Later parts move into specifics.

As with other parts of the book, I make an idealized case for a learning business. Few organizations approach the ideal, though many show significant aspects of the ideal and many more clearly want to move in this direction.

The style of treatment of issues here is discursive and exploratory. I am not trying to make neat tight definitions, but rather to sketch out a territory that will be defined in more detail later. As it is probably impossible to prescribe universal models to fit all organizations, my objective is to make a case for a way of thinking that can be shaped to the needs of an individual or an organization

# 2 Strategic learning

## Introduction

In this chapter I want to elaborate the case for strategic learning; that is, learning that is strategic for individuals, groups, organizations, communities and whole societies. In Chapter 1 I gave some examples of what I see as strategic learning: here I want to present a backcloth to later chapters which will delve more deeply into methods and approaches. I want to say something about the environment in which organizations are operating which justifies a strategic approach to learning. I shall then look at what is going on inside organizations which impacts on learning issues, and mention the needs of managers within modern organizations. The focus of the chapter is thus mainly on organizations and managers. I shall also present a model for balanced development in organizations and indicate the kind of strategic questions that need to be addressed in developing learning in organizations. All this will be a prelude to Chapter 3, which discusses the idea of a 'learning business'.

## Background

In 1987 a colleague and I wrote a list of things we saw going wrong in organizations. The list is as follows:

- Training and development activity is not cost-effective
- Lack of linkage between individual development and organizational needs
- Managers who are intelligent and potentially able, but do not make things happen
- Too much work pressure to allow managers to take extended time off the job for training and development
- Lack of internal training and development resources to meet needs
- Managers who have learning needs that cannot be met on standard courses
- Lack of responsiveness to change by middle managers
- Managerial stress due to changed work requirements
- Younger managers who need more experience – and quickly

- Too much emphasis on the latest fad or gimmick – little long-term evaluation of development activity.

You could write the same list today. And it could have been written ten years before it was. There is perhaps now more rhetoric about *training* than there used to be, but serious concern about *learning* is still patchy.

The situation is not helped by governments and educational bodies assuming that the only really meaningful learning goes on in courses (in the training or the educational arena). For example, the British government's proposals on lifelong learning prompted one reviewer to argue that something needed to be done about the 40 per cent of those in the post-16 age group who were 'non-learners'. The assumption was that if the person was not in formal education or training, they were not learning. This is totally bizarre! People learn all the time and in all sorts of contexts. Some learning might be relatively trivial (there is a new form to fill out so I have to learn how to do that) through to moderately complex (there is a new piece of software on the computer that I have to learn how to use) to the quite difficult (the company is going into new markets and I have to learn to work with people from different cultures). Whatever change occurs in an organization it requires learning on the part of some or all the people. *It is impossible to bring about any change that does not require learning.* Yet this ubiquitous and essential process is very poorly understood by most organizations.

One hopeful trend is that organizations are starting to do things like appoint 'directors of learning' instead of training managers. Another trend has been the learning organization movement, which I shall comment on further in the next chapter. However, there are still too many managers who do not recognize the importance of learning. Just to take an example that I experienced recently. A senior and experienced manager was having difficulties with some of his staff. They were not performing well and he was concerned. I asked him what he was proposing to do about it. He struggled to come up with any ideas, seeming to feel that it was almost intractable. When I suggested that he talk to the development people in his organization (whom I knew to be able and respected practitioners), he seemed genuinely surprised that there could be a learning solution to his problem. Once we'd talked a bit he readily accepted the point and he could see that his staff might improve if they *learned* to be more effective.

This may seem a trivial example – but in my experience it is all too common. And hence it isn't trivial. Organizations have performance problems which managers either decide to accept or try to find ways of avoiding a learning solution (by cracking the whip or by exhortation or by some of the other ineffectual approaches I shall discuss in this chapter).

## Ineffective approaches

The following sections cover some approaches that are ineffective in dealing with change as well as pointing the way to approaches that work better. The main problem is that many organizations try to find ways of dealing with change while avoiding learning-based approaches. The approaches that are most common include:

1 **Forecasting the future** The attempt here is to predict the future so that change can be anticipated and dealt with. I shall argue that this crystal ball gazing is inadequate.
2 **Treating change as a one-off event and not a process** This approach often uses the 'Unfreeze–Change– Refreeze' model as though 'change' is a thing that has a finite life. I shall suggest that this is an erroneous model for modern organizational life.
3 **Treating change as all one process** I shall argue that change is a complex phenomenon and not susceptible to the simplistic nostrums of 'change management' consultants.
4 **Relying on luck** I know that most managers would not say explicitly that they rely on luck – but implicitly a fair few do.
5 **Relying on textbook knowledge or the advice of management gurus** My concern is that many managers want some simple truths by which to manage their organizations (and I shall suggest that there may be some maps to help people on their way but they are not comprehensive truths that give unambiguous advice to suit all circumstances).

The first issue to be tackled is that of forecasting.

## Forecasting

Most strategic planning, forecasting, futurology and predicting is an attempt to introduce a façade of certainty into an uncertain world. We know that economic forecasts do not work. If you track back projections made by government forecasters, by academics, by independent researchers and by company economists, you find that the rare person or group who makes an accurate projection – for example, of GDP growth, unemployment, balance of payments deficits/surpluses (or whatever) – does so by chance, because they do not tend to repeat their 'successes' in subsequent years. And many of their colleagues get it wrong all the time.

Let me take one concrete example. The *Guardian* newspaper, in a leader of 31 December 1997, mentioned that 'the

*Financial Times* asked a panel of six leading City pundits to predict where the FTSE index would be at the end of 1997. At the time, it was standing at 4,118 points. One forecaster said 3,200 and all the others were between 4,000 and 4,400. If the highest forecast of 4,400 had come true, it would have meant that the index would have risen by 6.8 per cent. In fact, the FTSE index closed yesterday at 5,132.3 points. This was a rise of 24.6 per cent over the year: an increase nearly four times higher than the most optimistic forecasts.'[1] The *Guardian*'s leader writer went on to show how these forecasters had been even more wrong about the situation on Wall Street and that 'virtually no serious forecaster accurately predicted the meltdown of the markets in East Asia, the single biggest economic event of the year'.

World political events in the late 1980s and early 1990s have proved to be equally unpredictable. One week before the Berlin Wall was knocked down you could get odds of 15 to 1 from a bookmaker against the Wall coming down *this century*. I know of *no* political commentator of the mid-1980s who was remotely accurate about what has happened in Central and Eastern Europe, including the unification of Germany and the break-up of Yugoslavia and the USSR. Even a few weeks before the invasion of Kuwait no one predicted it – or the ensuing Gulf War.

The point of raising these issues is that forecasting and predicting will not allow us to escape from the need to *learn* to deal with an ever-changing world. The trouble is that many managers will still read these forecasts and still try to avoid the nuisance of solutions that involve them learning new ways of thinking and acting.

## White water

Vaill[2] has suggested the metaphor of permanent white water to describe modern organizational life. The metaphor can be described as follows. In the past we have assumed that the way organizations changed has been comparable to the flow of a river. The river has calm periods when it flows smoothly and clearly. Then there may be a period of turbulence – rapids or waterfalls – which produces white-water conditions. The river then resumes its normal sedate progress. This metaphor is matched by the common prescription in change literature that in order to manage change you first unfreeze the organization, then change it, then refreeze it in a new state. Both metaphors assume that change occurs in between two steady states. Vaill and others argue that even if this was a sensible metaphor in the past (which is dubious), it certainly is not today. He suggests that we have conditions of permanent, unremitting turbulence: permanent white water.

When I first went white-water rafting down the Arkansas river in Colorado it was comparable to the way Vaill sees things. In the morning we went down a stretch of river which was mainly calm, with periods of white water intervening (and not too turbulent, either). During the morning our guide taught us how to survive in the conditions we would meet in the afternoon. First you had to learn to survive if you came out of the inflatable raft. Basically, you float on your back, going down the river feet first. If you go on your front you can catch your foot in a rock and drown, or beat your face on the rocks. If you're on your back the most that can happen, usually, is a bruised bottom.

The second thing you learned was how to support and help each other. If someone goes into the water you must learn how to get that person back into the raft as quickly as possible – without capsizing or overturning what is a flat-bottomed vessel. The basic technique is to grab the person by the shoulders of their life jacket and haul them in, the person doing the hauling being held by someone else to ensure that the 'hauler' doesn't go into the water too.

In the afternoon of our trip we put on our helmets and went down a stretch of very turbulent water, which called on what we had learned in the morning as one person *did* fall in when we hit a rock at the bottom of a short waterfall. The link to organizational life seemed quite real. We have to learn how to operate on our own *and* with others in conditions of unpredictable turbulence. Personal (selfish) survival is not enough – because we do need others to make an organization work. Personal survival skills are necessary but not sufficient.

## Planning and preparing

What you also learn in white-water rafting is the general value of being prepared. Preparation is about learning relevant skills, about learning to think in the right way, about developing emotional resilience (there is no benefit from panicking in situations of real danger), about learning to value your colleagues, and so on. This 'preparational planning'[3] seems to me infinitely superior to other planning modes currently used by organizations. Crudely, I can identify three main competing modes:

1 *Extrapolation.* This mode assumes that the world of the future will be an extrapolation from the past. There might be odd 'blips' on the graph, but broadly the organization will grow at X per cent per annum for the next Y years in a relatively smooth curve. (And if it is not too smooth, a little creative accounting will soon adjust matters.)

2 *Discontinuous change*. Here planners may assume quantum leaps in performance (never quantum drops) due to some discontinuity. Often such plans come from fantasized futurological scenarios. While Schwartz[4] and others argue that scenarios (as used in Shell) are for learning purposes, managers often come to believe in them as 'real' predictions of the future (and scenario builders also may slip into this).

3 *Short termism*. This mode says that the quarterly figures are as far ahead as we look. We don't concern ourselves with strategic planning; we just get on with earning money. We shall respond to the market and hope for the best.

*Preparational planning* is a challenge to all three modes. It is essentially a *learning-based* approach. It is at the heart of a strategic learning stance. It responds to the challenges made by Stacey[5] and others from evidence from Chaos Theory. Chaos Theory shows that the future is logically and scientifically unpredictable in the kind of modes in which organizations operate. But Stacey shows that a learning-based approach can lead to a redefinition of traditional approaches to strategic planning.

## Orders of change

However, we need to think differently about the nature of change in order to determine our learning needs. Much of the change literature seems to imply that change is all one thing. Changing the paper clips we use is assumed to be the same process as changing strategic direction. Clearly this assumption is unhelpful. A superior assumption is prompted by the work of Bateson[6] and others. In this way of thinking we separate first-order change from second-order change. First-order change is change within defined and accepted parameters: it is about incremental change, which is often doing more of (or better than) what we have done in the past. First-order change might mean producing more widgets than last year – or to a modified design. But they are still widgets.

Second-order change occurs when we move outside existing parameters and frameworks. It can mean changing the way we change. For example, in an airline with which I was consulting, they shifted their thinking from the idea that they were flying aircraft to the idea that they were flying people. So a technical/financial orientation switched to a marketing/customer care focus. In the process the airline became a different kind of organization with a different strategic direction. And the kind of *learning* needed to make this shift was totally different from anything they had experienced previously. It is not simple incremental learning. As the saying goes, 'you can't leap a chasm in two jumps'.

Unfortunately some organizations seem to have an in-built first-order-only change mode, whereas others seem able to operate more broadly. One difference is between

- *the palm tree organization* and
- *the redwood organization.*

Palm tree organizations grow by first-order change only. Like the palm tree they add to their height, but make no other changes. Eventually there is fatal collapse, as the trunk cannot support itself.

Redwoods are different: they not only grow upwards but also add girth and bulk. They can then last for thousands of years and grow to great heights.

## Luck

Many managers come to reject strategic planning approaches (reasonably, given their failures) and to rely on what they term 'luck'. The assumption is that if forecasting and linear old-fashioned planning do not work, we simply have to be fatalistic. If we obtain a large order for a product, it is luck. If a competitor gets the order, we were unlucky. These assumptions support prevailing cultures which undervalue learning and change.

I see this every time I go into a park on a Sunday morning to watch soccer. Someone takes a shot at goal and the ball slices wide. Immediately colleagues shout 'Unlucky'. Now, as far as I can see, luck played no part in this. The person shot at goal and failed. I don't want to berate someone for failure, but unless people realize that they've *failed* in what they were trying to do, will they ever *learn* to improve?

The greatest football player I have ever seen, George Best, *learned* to be great by using direct feedback from his play. For instance, when practising as a youngster, he took out a football to improve his shooting. However, he became bored with kicking the ball into the goal and having to retrieve it, so he practised hitting the ball against the crossbar so that it rebounded to him. If he failed, he had the tedious task of retrieving the ball. George Best, like every great sportsperson, *learned* to be great. He was not born that way, despite misguided journalists talking about people being born as great players. All great sportspeople and athletes practise, and *learn* from practice. When they do great things, it's not from luck. I'm told that after he had won a golf tournament, Gary Player was once confronted by a so-called fan. 'It seems as though you're a lucky golfer,' said the fan. 'Yes,' said Player 'and isn't it interesting that the more I practise the luckier I seem to get.'

My former chairman, when I was a CEO, once chided me for saying that we had been lucky in getting a new contract. 'Luck is preparation meeting opportunity,' he said. And I could not disagree with him. We had *prepared* well and when the opportunity came, we could take it. If we had not done the preparational planning we would not have won the contract.

## Pace of change

Will Rogers is reputed to have said that 'even if you're on the right track, if you sit still you'll get run over'. One of the issues in a white-water world is living with the pace of change and, indeed, welcoming it. There is an African story about the lion and the antelope. The issue in life for the lion is that it needs to be faster than the slowest antelope; otherwise it does not eat. The issue for the antelope is to be faster than the quickest lion; otherwise it does not survive. But it doesn't matter if you're a lion or an antelope, when you wake up in the morning you wake up running.

This world of 'hot action'[7] is even more complex. Any study of managerial work shows that managers have to make multiple decisions in real time with inadequate information and to imposed deadlines. This 'hot action' world is totally different in pace, style of thought and activity from the 'cool action' world of the academic, the researcher and many trainers and developers. These latter often have the luxury of working sequentially on problems and recommending others to take action (that is, take the risks) based on their cool, detached analyses. Training programmes are structured on this basis. Subjects are taught sequentially: case studies are analysed separate from 'real world' action, and participants in case analyses do not have to take the risks of implementing their recommendations (and hence really learning what works and what does not).

## Discomfort in learning

British managers sometimes seem to me to be quite prone to blame ill luck (and therefore be unprepared to learn). The Australians have a joke: 'How do you know if an aircraft is full of Poms? Because when the engines are switched off the whining continues.'

Facing up to the need to change (and therefore to learn) is often painful, and this first stage – opening up to new learning – is usually more difficult than the new learning itself. The problem is, therefore, complacency and 'hedgehog management' – that is, faced with an oncoming juggernaut, roll into a ball and pretend you can cope.

Acquiring new knowledge, skills and competences will be irrelevant if managers do not change fundamentally their mind sets, their mental frameworks.

You might like to try an exercise I have often used with groups of managers. Please fold your arms. Now fold them the other way – for example, if you have your left hand with fingers up and your right hand tucked in, reverse it (that is, right hand fingers up, left hand tucked in). Some people find this almost impossible to do; others can do it, but feel uncomfortable or strange. This is an example of new learning. If you did it you have quite possibly never done it before in your life, so you have learned something new. In itself, of course, it is quite useless learning. My object in suggesting the exercise was to draw your attention to your own habits (this being one of them), and that changing habits or patterns of working can be uncomfortable.

## Pattern change

You may also notice in this exercise that you have not learned something that could sensibly be labelled 'knowledge' or 'skill' or 'competence'. I prefer to call it 'pattern change' – that is, you previously had a pattern of folding your arms one way and I've asked you to change that pattern (or habit).

Much of strategic learning concerns pattern change. It is about people in organizations reshaping what they already have. A term to describe a certain kind of pattern change is 'reframing'. The metaphor here is that we look at the world through a frame – through the lenses of spectacles or through a camera's viewfinder. We 'see' what we frame, and we cannot frame the whole world. A classic story of reframing is of the two shoe salesmen who, many years ago, went to an African country. The first one wired back that no one was wearing shoes in this country, there was no market for the product and he was returning home immediately. The second salesman wired back: 'No one is wearing shoes here. An immense market for our product. Ship every shoe you can find.'

Each shoe salesman faced 'reality', but each framed it differently. The key learning for the first salesman was not selling skills, product knowledge or whatever; it was how to look at the world around him in the most appropriate way: how to change his mental patterns.

The kind of change indicated here is within the realm of the second-order change already discussed. Hence pattern change can be seen as part of a second-order learning – it moves up out of an approach which adds on knowledge and skills (first-order learning). It can be characterized as 'metalearning' because typically when this kind of learning occurs, people learn about how to learn for themselves. Experience of pattern change can shift a person's mental frameworks and awareness of this can provide the basis for continued 'self managed learning'.[8]

Let me take another marketing/selling example. In 1961 when I first went to live in London I used to enjoy wandering around the Soho district. In a small, unprepossessing side street a man called John Stephen opened a small men's fashion shop. There were no other shops around as this street was tucked in behind the main shopping areas. However, the shop thrived and was part of a revolution in men's fashion business in the 1960s. The street became famous, and Carnaby Street (for this was its name) became a tourist attraction.

Why was this so? One key element was that John Stephen did what no one else in the trade did: he *looked* at his customers, he *learned* from them and he *responded* to what he had learned. He noticed that the young men coming into his shop were pulling down on the ends of the shirt collars to make them longer, so he ordered shirts with longer collars, and this became a major fashion item in the 1960s. He also noticed that his customers were pushing their trousers further down on their hips. So he made the hipster trousers that also became popular at the time. This was real strategic learning, which required a combination, among other things, of

- *Visual acuity* (really seeing what was going on)
- *Recognition* of the value of this data
- *Linking* this data to a strategic vision
- *Integrating* that with practical action
- *Continual monitoring* of the results.

**Feedback**       Visual acuity is an important point as it is linked to the concept of 'feedback': a term that has been horribly misused in management. Leaving aside the distortion of this term from cybernetics (a separate problem), feedback has become associated with someone expressing a view about something to another person – as in the opening gambit 'Let me give you some feedback' (meaning the person is about to jump on you from a great height). This kind of feedback is what I call 'secondary feedback'. It may be based on data, but it is not primary data. It is someone's view/perspective/opinion on something. It often occurs in appraisal interviews where a boss might 'pass on' feedback to a subordinate. For example: 'Feedback from your staff suggests you're not good at ...' or 'Feedback from other departments says they like X about you.'

There are prescriptions for cleaning up feedback – for example:

- Make it timely
- Do not allow it to be highly generalized – make it specific
- Keep it non-evaluative.

The last point is not possible in absolute terms. Any decision to pick something out of the stream of events and activities in an organization and draw someone's attention to it is an evaluation of that activity (positive or negative).

'Primary feedback' is sensory-based data – it is something you see, hear or feel. John Stephen worked off primary feedback (what he saw), not the views or opinions of his customers (secondary feedback). Good salespeople and presenters work off primary feedback. If, as a presenter, I tell a joke and people laugh, I can *see* it (facial changes, body movement, and so on) and *hear* it. I don't need someone to say 'that was a good joke'. A tennis player or a golfer can see and feel when the ball has been well hit. They know without being told when they have done well.[9]

## Truth vs maps

Strategic learning is ideally based on primary feedback. One factor that supports this is the shaky nature of generalizations, theories and ideas about management. As soon as someone promulgates a generalization or proposition about good management, counter-evidence readily emerges. For example, 'sticking to the knitting' was popular due to Peters and Waterman.[10] However, companies that did this often performed badly (for example, IBM and DEC in the computer business). Creative, innovative companies are supposed to be unbureaucratic and flexible with flattened pyramids. So how has Sony (which defies these generalizations) been one of the world's most innovative companies?

In running self managed learning programmes we have suggested that introducing learners to theories, generalizations and ideas is useful, but that they cannot be taught as truths. We tend to talk of a mapping process. Maps help you find your way around, but they are not true (in the sense we normally use the term – that is, direct correspondence to reality). Maps may help you plan a journey, but they won't tell you what the traffic will be like, or if there will be road works, or if the weather will affect your journey. They are limited in what they can represent and they are static. They do not respond to a changing world. But we shouldn't throw them away. In our use of maps we just need to recognize their limitations. So with all 'secondary data': any generalizations about management and organization are just that – generalizations that could prove untrustworthy.

In discussing this case about the nature of knowledge in a seminar on SML one eminent (but sceptical) professor turned to another (whose subject was accounting and finance) and said: 'Well, isn't there some certainty in the knowledge in your field? You deal with numbers and money. Isn't that real?' The other professor said: 'If you note at the bottom of a set of accounts it says that this is "a true and fair view of the state of the company's affairs". The operative word here is "a". This is "a" view – there are many views.' And we know from the literature on creative accounting what can be done with figures (see, for instance, Griffiths[11]).

## Maps for managing change

In this book I shall offer models and generalizations. I offer them only as maps, not as rigid truths. However, I have been particularly interested in developing 'process maps' rather than 'content maps'. The former are, as much as possible, content free – that is, they can help you shape up data and ideas, but they do not offer 'content generalizations'. Let me demonstrate two examples, the first of which is from Revans.[12]

Revans has developed ideas on change from his work on action learning. He suggests that a 'coalition of power' that can implement change would be made up of the people in the organization

1  who know about the problem/issue;
2  who care about it;
3  who can do something about it.

This is a process model. The content can be added in the precise circumstances of a particular planned change. We could take a specific change we want to see happen and write the names of people against each of 1, 2 and 3.

I believe that learning to use process models like this is another important aspect of strategic learning. Note that the learning I am suggesting is how to think in a particular way, how to use data, how to sort it, and so on. I am suggesting that the *content* issues are less important (from a learning point of view). Knowing how to solve problems (process) is more important than knowing the solution to one particular problem (content).

My own basic process model on managing change is built up, like Revans's, from a series of questions. My thesis is that in managing change we need to balance aspects of organizational processes, and that strategic learning is in part learning to do this 'balancing'. I suggest that we need to attend to four basic questions:

1 *WHY?* Why do we want to do it and in what way do we want to do it? This question throws up issues about our values and beliefs, and addresses matters concerning the fundamental purposes of the organization.
2 *WHAT?* What do we want to do? This raises issues of strategy, tactics, operations, tasks, and so on.
3 *HOW?* How do we want to do it? This indicates matters of organizational culture, structure, processes, procedures, and so on.
4 *WHO?* Who do we want to do it? The answer to this question relates to the people in the organization. Who are they? How should they be recruited, selected, promoted, developed, and so on?

Figure 2.1 shows diagrammatically the linkage of these four basic questions. The 'Why?' question feeds into the other three: values and beliefs underpin decisions about 'What?', 'How?' and 'Who?'.

This, then, is a clear process model. Learning to use it gives managers a series of key questions with which to fill in content. The model is crucial in strategic learning because it postulates that, for instance, individual learning (in the 'Who?' box) has to be linked to

- strategy, tactics, tasks (answers to the 'What?' question);
- culture, structure, processes, procedures (answers to the 'How?' question);
- values and beliefs (answers to the 'Why?' question).

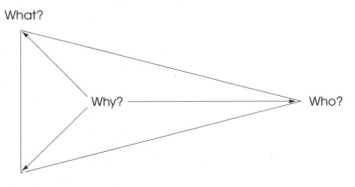

*Figure 2.1*   *Managing change*

Let me take an idealized case to show the linkages of the four fundamental questions as they affect learning.

**Example – an ideal organization**

- *Why?* The organization values learning. People are assumed to be able to learn and to change. People are assumed to be trustworthy and be able to make sensible decisions about their own learning.
- *How?* The culture supports learning. People are given freedom to apply new learning. People are challenged to perform better and given support to learn new ways of working. Organizational rules are at a minimum and any structures are designed to assist people in their development. Failures are seen as learning opportunities.
- *What?* The strategic direction of the organization is clear. People know what they are to achieve and they feel committed to it. Strategic goals are linked into day-to-day action. There is congruence and coherence between strategy and tactics. Tasks that people carry out are stretching – causing them continually to learn. But tasks are not so demanding as to cause undue stress.
- *Who?* The organization selects good learners and helps each individual to learn to their maximum potential. Individuals learn things that are of value to them and to the organization (there is no mismatch).

*Real life*   In real organizations there is usually a lack of coherence between these four areas. You may like to address these questions to your own organization. Would the answers be different from those in the idealized case above? There would probably be a difference. This can be a starting point for considering action needed to bring strategic coherence to learning activity.

*Leadership*   An important aspect of developing strategic coherence is strategic leadership. By 'strategic leadership' I mean leadership that is based on integrating the four dimensions I've mentioned and is involved with the broad sweep of strategic change. This is different from 'team' or 'supervisory' leadership, which may be more focused on implementing, on task performance and on maintaining interpersonal relationships. Shop-floor supervisors and team leaders will have an important implementation role and may also put in ideas at the strategic level, but in a normal hierarchical organization their role will be more oriented to *supporting* strategic leadership than being strategic leaders themselves. The dimensions of strategic leadership are shown in Figure 2.2.

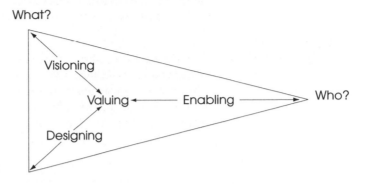

How?

**Figure 2.2** *Leadership*

The four processes of strategic leadership – namely, valuing, visioning, designing and enabling – are linked to answering the four questions Why? What? How? and Who? The ideal strategic leader:

- *values* learning and believes in its importance;   (WHY?)
- *visions* strategies, tasks and activities which need learning – and which are learnable;   (WHAT?)
- *designs* processes, structures, cultures which support learning;   (HOW?)
- *enables* individuals to learn.   (WHO?)

In real organizations all of this will not happen perfectly and easily. Part of the art of leadership can be struggling with and/or coping with mismatches. Such leadership is usually not the responsibility of one individual; leading a strategic learning approach mostly requires the collaboration of a number of key people in power positions. Revans's model (Who knows?, Who can?, Who cares?) can help to identify these crucial people.

## Making learning stick

Strategic leaders are important not just in initiating effective learning, but also in making it stick. Often a new CEO will initiate changes which require new learning, but when the CEO goes and a new person takes over, much of this change may be reversed. The concept of hysteresis is helpful here; it is used in physics precisely to indicate the propensity for reversibility. If a piece of metal is magnetized and remains magnetized when the magnetizing field is withdrawn, the metal has high hysteresis. If the magnetism is rapidly lost, it has low hysteresis. Organizations can exhibit analogous properties. What seemed like a fundamental change can prove readily reversible. A new leadership can develop a trusting, supportive, healthy culture; but if the leadership goes, the market turns sour and destructive organizational politics become rife, then the culture can rapidly cease to be trusting and supportive.

Ideal strategic learning would provide a basis for second-order change with high hysteresis (low reversibility). Unfortunately this seems not to be the norm. In the next chapter, on the 'learning business', I shall try to indicate approaches that could improve the chances of high hysteresis.

## Strategic excellence

Much of what I have discussed is part of strategic excellence. Note that I am interested in excellence, not competence. I do not support the idea that strategic advantage comes from developing core/strategic competences in an organization. Competence is about being averagely good: at worst it means mediocrity; at best keeping up with the pack. Excellence is about moving beyond the pack. It is a holistic concept – you cannot speak about 'excellences' in the same way as you can about 'competences'. Competence is a reductionist notion. It is assumed that if we learn all the parts well, this will add up to something good. But organizational and business life is not like that. Organizations exist in order to *integrate* individual activity – and integrative learning has to be a facet of strategic learning. The random accumulation of lots of 'competences' will not necessarily produce excellence. (See Chapter 4 for an elaboration of this issue.)

Excellence also has an aesthetic quality. It is about providing products and services which have a particular quality. I remember David Potter, the founder of Psion, which makes personal organizers and produces computer software, saying that he wanted his products to be compared to fine Italian glass. Each personal organizer was from a template that he wanted to compare with the template of beautiful Italian glass. He was not saying that his products had the *same* beauty; the aesthetic quality was different. But there had to be an aesthetic dimension to make him feel satisfied about what he was doing.

In sport you find similar notions. The finest sportspeople seem not only to want to win, but to do it in style. They comment on how, in moments of supreme performance, their abilities fuse in a transcendent quality that is well beyond the norm.

## Issues for managers

This can seem heady, even unreal, stuff for managers. Yet given the demanding climate of modern management, individual managers do have to face issues of personal excellence. The average (competent) performers with no special talents are the most vulnerable in turbulent times – vulnerable to losing their jobs and, worse, vulnerable to not finding new jobs.

In Chapter 1 I related examples of self managed learning. In these programmes we have heard managers saying that this is the first time in their lives that they have thought strategically about their own careers. Really strategically. They may have made naïve assumptions in the past about a smooth progression up the organizational hierarchy, but through the rigour and challenge of SML they have had to examine seriously how well prepared they really were for different eventualities. They often had, at an individual level, mirrored the fallacies of organizational planning – for example, simplistic extrapolations from the past to the future, or highly short-term target setting.

Strategic learning, then, needs to accommodate individual and collective action. In Chapters 4 and 5 I shall say more about the kind of learning required of individual managers, and about ways of connecting individual and organizational learning.

## Conclusion: strategic questions about learning

To make some of the ideas expressed here more concrete, it can be helpful to answer a series of questions specifically about learning activity. This can provide the basis for a link between strategic thinking and operational activity (a link which will be developed further in Chapter 3). The questions, with some issues they raise, are:

- *Who?* Who is to learn? Is it everyone in the organization? Will top management give the same commitment to their own continued learning as junior staff? Will age count against people – that is, will it be assumed that, say, those over 50 are not worth further investment? Will women get the same opportunities as men?
- *How?* How will learning occur? Is it to be organized or just expected to happen? Will there be a focus on team-/ group-based learning as well as individual learning? How will learning be measured? How will learning methods be chosen?
- *Where?* Where will learning take place? On the job? Off the job and in the organization? Off the job and outside the organization? Also, how will the different modes be integrated?
- *When?* When in a person's career will there be particular emphases on learning (for example, new entrants, those being promoted, and so on)?
- *How much?* How much will be spent on learning? What resources will be allocated to organized learning activity?

- *What?* What is to be learned? What constitutes 'good learning'? What learning needs will be identified? What will constitute 'quality' in learning? What strategic changes are needed in learning activity?

Table 2.1 suggests a contrast between a typical bureaucratic training-oriented organization and a strategic-learning-oriented organization.

***Table 2.1***   *Bureaucratic vs strategic*

| Strategic questions | Bureaucratic training oriented | Strategic learning |
|---|---|---|
| Who? | Most resources go on younger white able-bodied males. Top management may ask to be briefed on what training is being given to others, but it would not dream of going through such training itself. | Everybody learns. There is a strong commitment to maximizing everyone's potential. And it is assumed that *everyone* has potential to improve. |
| How? | It is assumed that day-to-day tasks are learned on the job. Training courses are the main *organized* learning activities. Courses are trainer-led with imposed curricula. | A wide range of learning approaches is made available – secondments, projects, study visits, packaged learning resources, and so on. All managers act as mentors/coaches to their staff, and take the role seriously. Courses, when used, respond to the needs of those attending – they are not trainer-controlled. (This issue is more fully discussed in Chapter 5.) |
| Where? | Off-job and on-job learning unintegrated. 'Transfer of training' problems. | Integrated approach. Off-job learning planned to integrate with job needs. No transfer problem. |
| When? | Main emphasis on training for qualifications for younger staff plus remedial short courses for middle managers. | Throughout a person's career. |
| How much? | Designated training budget – assumed to cover all costs. | Learning is resourced through a variety of sources. |

## Summary

This chapter has made a case for strategic learning, and has considered some ways of developing a strategic approach to learning.

I wanted to show how people try to avoid learning, for example by relying on simplistic forecasts that imply a relatively unchanging world, by relying on luck, and other ineffective approaches. I have suggested that change is not 'all one thing' and that the responses to change need to balance the answers to some fundamental questions. I have also argued that strategic leadership is crucial in developing a strategic approach to learning. The next chapter moves these ideas on and postulates the need for 'learning businesses'.

Notes

1  The quotes are from the second leader in the *Guardian* of 31 December 1997.
2  Vaill, P. (1990) *Managing as a Performing Art*, San Francisco: Jossey-Bass.
3  For a fuller discussion of planning modes, see Cunningham, I. (1984) 'Planning to develop managers', *Management Education and Development*, **15**, 2 (Summer), 83–104.
4  Schwartz, P. (1991) *The Art of the Long View*, New York: Doubleday.
5  Stacey, R.D. (1992) *Managing Chaos*, London: Kogan Page.
6  Bateson, G. (1973) *Steps to an Ecology of Mind*, London: Paladin.
7  The distinction between hot and cool action was made by Michael Eraut, a colleague at Sussex University.
8  For further discussion on 'pattern change' and 'second-order learning' see Cunningham, I. (1988) 'Patterns of managing for the future', *Industrial Management and Data Systems* (Jan./Feb.), 18 22; also Cunningham, I. (1988) 'Learning to learn', in Hodgson, V., Mann, S. and Snell, R. (eds) *Beyond Distance Teaching: Towards Open Learning*, Milton Keynes: OU Press.
9  Tim Gallwey in his writings on 'The Inner Game' is helpful in showing how to work off primary data. The field of neurolinguistic programming is good at showing the needs for sensory-based data, and Richard Bandler and John Grinder's writings are particularly stimulating in this respect (better usually than the more mechanistic writings of their followers). Specific references regarding the above include: Gallwey, W.T. (1974) *The Inner Game of Tennis*, New York: Random House; Bandler, R. and Grinder, J. (1982) *Reframing*, Moab, UT: Real People Press; Bandler, R. and Grinder, J. (1979) *Frogs into Princes*, Moab, UT: Real People Press.
10  Peters, T.J. and Waterman, R.H. (1982) *In Search of Excellence*, New York: Harper & Row.
11  Griffiths, I. (1986) *Creative Accounting*, London: Firethorn Press.
12  Reg Revans's books and articles on action learning are

not always an easy read, but they are stimulating and highly relevant. Some possible texts to check out include: Revans, R.W. (1966) *The Theory of Practice in Management*, London: MacDonald; Revans, R.W. (1971) *Developing Effective Managers*, London: Longman; Revans, R.W. (1980) *Action Learning: New Techniques for Management*, London: Blond & Briggs.

# 3 A learning business

**Introduction**

In the early 1970s Peter Drucker wrote some marvellous insightful stuff on Japan and its then growing success.[1] He made specific reference to the Japanese emphasis on learning, including:

- the idea of 'continuous learning'
- *every* employee (including top managers) attended regular training sessions
- learning was seen as part of regular, scheduled work
- training sessions were not, as a rule, run by trainers but by the employees
- experts (for example, industrial engineers) would *assist* in learning sessions but not take the lead or dominate
- learning did not focus on just one skill at a time – people learned about all the work in a unit: they did not focus on one person or one job but on the *whole* unit or the *whole* plant
- training sessions were oriented to developing new, creative ways of doing things.

This approach made the entire workforce in a company receptive to change and innovation.

Drucker's writing on this topic covered diverse issues, including many of the problems in the Japanese approach. It still stands today as an excellent analysis. Why, then, has he been largely ignored given that:

1 Drucker is probably the world's most respected management writer;
2 his analyses were based on solid data;
3 his analyses were extremely valid;
4 his analyses were clearly and unambiguously expressed?

Only recently has there been any significant interest in these methods of working, and this has largely been because Japanese companies have moved into North America and Europe and shown that the indigenous workforce can learn in similar ways to Japanese employees.

Part of the problem is described by Drucker himself. He argued that the Japanese tradition had a Zen basis which saw learning as a perpetual process of self improvement. Japanese people understood the concept of a learning curve to mean unending learning – ever-growing visions and abilities. The Western view of a learning curve is an upwards movement followed by a plateau (see Figure 3.1), while the Japanese model allows for plateaux, but assumes that they are only temporary resting places before the next learning phase. In Western management, there is often reference to a new employee or a newly promoted person 'being on a learning curve'. It is assumed that this learning is a temporary nuisance soon to be cured by the person 'plateauing' into competent performance (and, by implication, ceasing significant learning until the next promotion, unless for remedial reasons).

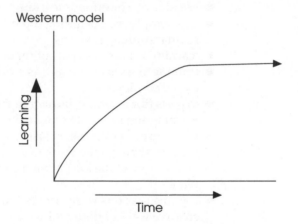

**Figure 3.1**   *The learning process (Western view)*

As Drucker points out, we need to learn about learning in a different way. This is analogous to the difference between first-order and second-order change discussed earlier. Bateson[2] shows that we need to realize that first-order and second-order learning are different. In the Western model, first-order learning is via the 'learning curve' model. In order to release ourselves from that way of thinking we have to learn about learning itself, to understand that there are different models. There is also a problem with the Japanese culture in that it is superb at continuous first-order learning but not good at second-order learning. This leads to great efficiency within existing ways of thinking, but problems in dealing with second-order change (which requires second-order learning). It seems that all cultures have the problem of dealing with second-order learning. This should not be surprising as I explored in the previous chapter how there is a tendency to want to avoid the discomfort of moving away from existing paradigms and mind sets. (These issues are more fully discussed in Chapters 4 and 5.)

Getting organizations to become places within which good learning can take place is, therefore, a tricky task. We are faced with the potential paradox that if an organization is not a good place within which to learn, how can it learn to be better (given that it does not learn well)? There are some ways out of this apparent dilemma. A classic one is to bring in new people at the top to make these changes. A more open approach is to rethink the value of the 'it' that I refer to as needing to learn. Most of the literature on 'learning organizations', 'learning companies' and 'organizational learning' assumes that there is an 'it' called an organization that can itself learn. I doubt that this use of language makes sense. Learning for me is most easily attached to a process that individuals undertake. I shall use the concept of a 'learning business' in this chapter, and say something initially about what I mean by that. I shall continue by sketching a definition of a learning business, before launching into more specific points about how a learning business can operate.

Fundamentally a learning business makes strategic learning work. So the ideas discussed in Chapter 2 can be made visible and practical in such a business. A learning business is one in which the internal and external pressures can be addressed in a learning mode.

Some of the issues that organizations face today include:

- a tougher world
- lean organizations – flat pyramid, more fluidity, more pressure
- tensions between centre and periphery: centralize vs decentralize
- faster change
- more demands on managers
- global/international environment
- quality demands
- innovation/speed to market
- customer service demands
- impact of IT
- need for strategic leadership.

All these issues need to be addressed within a learning 'frame'. If organizations are to deal with them effectively, learning has to take place. There is no option.

# Learning and organizations

The idea of a 'learning business' is about integrating 'soft' (learning) with 'hard' (business). I fear that today much of what is supposed to constitute a 'learning organization' is a rehash of 1960/70s 'organization development' (OD). The excellent OD practitioners have always seen the need for integration. They have worked with 'touchy/feely' ideas (truth and love) and methods (T-groups). They have also paid attention to profits, new technology, quality production, and so on. However, often OD practitioners have been trapped (or trapped themselves) in marginalized, semi-subversive roles.[3] They have undermined existing power and authority relationships with paradoxical insensitivity. They have adopted 'holier than thou' postures with barely concealed disdain for engineers, accountants and others whom they see as crass, narrow minded and hard nosed.

Again paradoxically, they have paid little attention to learning issues. They have assumed that if people relate to each other more effectively, the organization will automatically improve. Often, though, team-building (to take one method as an example) can create inwardly focused teams that then compete with other teams in the organization (because that is the *raison d'être* of a team in sport – to compete: if there is no competition there is no need for a team and, conversely, if a team is to exist it needs other teams to compete against). Teams can then become places with poor learning cultures where ideas that challenge the status quo are rejected.[4]

All this need not happen, of course. Teams do not have to end up as closed, set cultures. But I believe that unless a more sophisticated approach is taken towards developing the organization, this is a real danger.

The worst kind of OD is an example of what I would call a 'closed' approach to the problem of organizational learning. Other closed approaches include the following two examples (mentioned here because of their particular popularity at present – and not because they are the only examples).

## Knowledge management

The issue here is not that knowledge management is a bad idea. Far from it. The problem of closed approaches to knowledge management is that they become mechanistic IT-driven initiatives. Organizations accumulate masses of information and assume that this constitutes knowledge management. The best examples (ones I would label as 'open' approaches) recognize that the core of the issue is learning – learning how to share knowledge effectively, learning what is useful and what is not, learning how to use sources of knowledge (Intranets, web sites, libraries, and so on), and learning how to utilize knowledge for commercial advantage and the like.

Nonaka and Takeuchi's book on the subject of knowledge management[5] has been seen by many as a sophisticated approach to the issue – and their use of notions such as the difference between tacit and explicit knowledge is a great leap forward from the purely IT-driven approaches. They show how tacit knowledge can be inside the person and not susceptible to easy sharing. A salesperson can learn the tricks of the trade over many years and not be able to articulate them to a newcomer. It is also well known that effective leaders are often quite unable to say what makes them effective. The books on leadership often capture what leaders can say about themselves to an interviewer. But such information may be the least relevant in explaining their performance. As Bateson points out,[2] as someone becomes more effective at something their actions become based on unconscious processes. The great artist can say technically how they painted a picture but a novice could not copy their work from their words. By definition, if their actions stem in part from unconscious processes they may not be able to raise these unconscious elements into consciousness.

In Chapter 4 I shall suggest that qualities such as wisdom are vital – and that pinning down wisdom in a mechanistic model cannot work. Nonaka and Takeuchi do use the very Japanese approach of equating knowledge with wisdom and including 'ideals, values and emotions' in their definition of knowledge. (These issues are discussed more fully in Chapters 4 and 5.) However, they seem to underestimate the kind of learning that is needed to work in the ways they espouse. They make reference to learning issues, but they do not seem to recognize that adopting their proposals requires a sophisticated second-order learning.

**Communities of practice**

Galagan,[6] quoting Linde, defines a 'community of practice' as 'a naturally occurring and evolving collection of people who together engage in particular kinds of activity and who come to develop and share ways of doing things – ways of talking, beliefs, values and practices – as a result of their joint involvement in that activity'. The idea of communities of practice as a basic social unit for learning has been especially promoted by Xerox's Institute for Research on Learning, the key research being that of Orr[6] on how copier technicians share their mutual learning with each other and how such learning is often not in keeping with company manuals. Another aspect of their research has been to show how company training courses tend not to reflect the realities of how work in a community of practice is carried out and how people in such a community help each other learn through the telling of stories about their work, sometimes sharing ways of solving problems and sometimes inducting new members into the community. A useful conclusion of the research and writing from the Institute has been the recognition that learning and working are inseparable. They have also shown how such communities can be creative social units which get round corporate bureaucracies in order, for instance, to serve customers better.

The positive features of this work are, therefore, very evident. They can show that head office manuals and bureaucratic training approaches are not just wasteful, but often run counter to the real needs of those who have to carry out the work (as in the example of copier maintenance people). The research has shown how inept some of the control methods used in organizations really are.

An interesting feature of this work is in taking such a community of practice as the basic unit of analysis rather than the organization. This has prompted some writers to go overboard in their enthusiasm for such communities (and develop what I am labelling a closed approach). For example, Brown and Duguid[6] suggest that the main role for company providers such as trainers is to support the naturally occurring communities of practice. They suggest that organizations should see themselves as communities of communities (p. 53 in Brown and Duguid) and that communities of practice need to be supported but not intruded on.

Communities of practice can undoubtedly be powerful bases for learning, whether they are street gangs, medical practitioners or IT consultants. Whilst communities of practice are not necessarily coterminous with organizational departments, they often reflect functional differences. The danger of the community of communities model of an organization is that it can be highly conservative. As in the Galagan article,[6] there is some recognition from workers in this field that communities of practice can exclude people who do not fit (women, ethnic minorities, disabled people, and so on) and that their closed nature can inhibit productive change, locking such a community into solely first-order learning.

One example from my own research on organizations came from work in the old Department of Health and Social Security in the UK. In offices in central London a classic community of practice operated in sections which had to pay out benefits. They had developed their own way of working which did not conform to the manuals. They indoctrinated new members into the culture very effectively and operated quite autonomously. The problem was that their error rate was around 50 per cent, that is, claimants had only an even chance of getting the right money.

The community of practice had evolved ways which were, for them, highly functional in dealing with their many complaints – they lied systematically to members of the public ('We are just dealing with your case' when they weren't and had no intention of doing so). One person, when interviewed, said that the lying was so ingrained that it never felt like lying. It was just what you did, as everyone else did it. I would contend that this kind of situation is one which requires changing – and it requires a focus which comes from outside the community of practice. The evidence of problems of 'groupthink' also points to the dangers of closed, inward-looking communities.

Interestingly, most writers and researchers in this field seem to be unaware of European research, especially that of Revans (see earlier references to his work). Revans was using the community of practice of coal mine managers to get together and learn from each other as long ago as the 1940s. Where Revans is more useful than many of the Institute for Research on Learning people is in his recognition (a) that you can intervene and improve the process of learning, (b) that often one should do that because learning in such communities is frequently inefficient (as he found), and (c) that you can devise effective ways of doing it. His action learning approach has been shown to be effective in getting people to move their practice beyond current modes of working and his books have examples of projects he has fostered around the world. Our self managed learning approach has built on Revans's ideas and Chapters 6 onwards describe in more detail how we have addressed such issues. Others have promoted coaching and mentoring methods to move a community of practice on. What all these approaches have to recognize is that the subcultures defined by communities of practice need first to be understood before one can do anything to progress the situation.

A problem in some writing on communities of practice, then, is the implicit (or sometimes explicit) presumption that such social units always work well as learning vehicles. They often do not, as Revans's work has shown. All in all, therefore, I would argue for a more open stance on this issue. The social nature of learning needs to be recognized but we also need to be aware of the ways in which we can foster effective second-order learning and that such learning needs to respond to moral imperatives (see Chapter 5).

## The learning business

The closed approach to developing organizations is one reason why I prefer the concept of a learning business. The term 'business' can be applied to activity on a larger scale than the organization; for instance, we talk of 'the oil business' or 'the airline business' and we mean by this the entire sector. It seems eminently sensible to look at learning issues across an entire sector. At the time of writing, the airline business is in turmoil: many companies are losing money and there are major issues about state support for airlines and deregulation (in Europe especially), dirty tricks activity in taking passengers from competitors, safety issues, terrorist activity, and so on. Learning to deal with these issues is a global problem affecting the whole airline business. And it also affects passengers: their safety is threatened if airlines and manufacturers do not learn from accidents; and their comfort is affected if airlines do not learn best practice in customer care. In interviewing the cabin crew manager at British Airways in 1986 it was clear to me that his ability to learn from the experience of other airlines was a major contributory factor to British Airways' improved standing with passengers at that time.

Porter[7] has argued (very convincingly) that whole industries in particular countries have benefited from a kind of internal competition and collaboration. Japan is most often quoted in relation to its car industry, consumer electronics industry, and the like. Japan has large companies competing against each other in home markets and in export markets, and this has a positive effect on their success. Hence, again, the business sector becomes an important unit of analysis at the country level. This, then, also points to treating countries as 'businesses', as has happened with Japan. Learning at the level of a whole society clearly benefits that society/nation, and it benefits organizations.

In the UK, employers have come together in regional/local groupings (as Training and Enterprise Councils) in order to foster better learning in their locality. At one meeting involved in the setting up of one of these bodies I heard a representative of a public sector body ask why industrial and commercial companies would want to work together on these issues when they might be in competition. There was an immediate response from company representatives that everyone benefited from a more capable, trained workforce. Those involved in purchasing saw the importance of their suppliers *learning* to be better (because they would get better-quality goods). Some competitors argued that, as people moved across businesses, it was in everyone's interest to have able people moving through this fluid labour market. These and other benefits point to the need for 'learning societies' and 'learning communities' (in the latter case I mean in this context communities such as whole villages and towns or districts of cities).[8]

It is also conceivable to talk of a learning business at the global level. We are aware that the world has to learn together to deal with environmental issues. Richer countries have to learn to use less energy, and poorer countries that cut down tropical forests to make money need to learn new ways of wealth creation. But we all need to support each other in this learning process.

One area in which the term 'business' might not appear to be suitable concerns public organizations and other non-profit-making bodies. Here, however, the need to be more business-like is becoming accepted. Tax-payers in many countries are unhappy with the service they get from public organizations and are demanding to be treated with greater respect. Also, the term 'business' has only recently become associated with commerce (its etymological root is from 'busy') and my *Concise Oxford Dictionary* defines business-like as 'systematic, practical, prompt, well-ordered' which, while not covering all the facets of business that I want to discuss, is a fair starting point.

Charles Handy makes an excellent case for renaming 'voluntary' or 'non-profit' organizations as 'social businesses'. As he says, 'they are businesses in most senses of the word. They are concerned to turn inputs into outputs as efficiently as possible for the benefit of their clients – not a bad definition for any business.'[9] Sir Duncan Nichol, the former CEO of the National Health Service in Britain, has commented:

> We run a business which has a vision, some strategic objectives, plans and priorities which feed into these and are discharged down an executive structure which is clear. We may not have a profit motive but we are concerned with the productivity, quality and motivation of the people who work for us. So there are similarities between us and other businesses.[10]

In the industrial sector the Rover car company created the 'Rover Learning Business' as part of its organization. They say that it works for the 'Extended Enterprise', that is, including suppliers and dealers as their 'business partners'. The company insists that a key part of the successful turnaround of the business has been due to its emphasis on creating a better learning environment. And Paul Kirk, the MD of Rover Power Train, used all the right language when he argued for a learning focus in the following terms. 'Training is something you have done to you. Learning is something you have to do for yourself.'[11] Rover has clearly made great progress in its work in this field, and the emphasis on a 'learning business' is apt. However, in the context of this book the term is used to cover a whole organization rather than an organization within an organization (which is the Rover model).

## Summary of issues

I do not want to use the term 'learning organization' in this book. I accept that some of what I shall cover is also linked by others to the idea of a learning organization. Much, however, is not. I want to leave aside the idea of focusing on organizations to the detriment of wider concerns.

I have also signalled that I am unhappy with aspects of 'organization development' as the term has been used. Much of the literature in this field uses the metaphor of a human body for an organization as if it were not a metaphor – as if organizations really were living organisms and needed to be treated as such. However, I am comfortable with the body metaphor, as long as it is used in a limited sense. Like most metaphors, it has its strengths and weaknesses. On the down side, ideas of 'organizational health' are overplayed, and can justify 'slimming down/shedding fat' as a nice euphemism for sacking people. Organizations that claim to have become 'leaner and fitter' may not be. Also, organizations that, from a societal point of view, may have outlived their usefulness are made to survive (because killing off an organization is equivalent to murder, if you take the body/organism metaphor too seriously).

Having made these points, I shall be discussing most issues in this book at the organizational level, but I want to locate all that I say within the wider framework that I have postulated.

## Who wants a learning business?

I shall make a generalized and perhaps crude distinction between people who set up and/or run businesses. First, I want to distinguish between *seekers* and *makers*.

Seekers in business are usually of two kinds:

- power seekers
- status seekers.

(There are many other 'seeker' modes, for example knowledge seekers, but they are less relevant in business.)

Both kinds of seeker want something from a business, but are less interested in the business itself. Power seekers want to be in positions of power for the ego pay-off that power brings. Politicians are usually strong on power seeking. Status seekers enjoy being in the news, being recognized, gaining titles, and so on. Power and status seekers use the business arena to get what they want. They learn because they must if they are to get what they want. They are, however, less interested in the learning of others around them, and are not too interested in developing learning businesses.

Makers in business are also usually of two kinds:

- money makers
- business makers.

They both want to *make* something in relation to their businesses and so are different from seekers. However, money makers are interested in businesses only as a means to an end: to make money. They are often in the financial sector, but also may be at the top of conglomerates and even manufacturing companies. They tend to be short-term oriented, looking for rapid cash acquisition. They usually have a narrow view of their work and take little interest in wider social issues. As might be expected, they also have little interest in developing learning businesses.

Business makers are in it for the long term. They care about what they make or provide. Many family businesses have this trait and each generation is brought up to identify with the business. Clarks, as a shoe company operating for a number of generations, was noted for its directors putting the word 'shoemaker' on their passports. In Europe, the German family businesses, often not large companies, are strong on business making, as are most Japanese companies.

Business makers may, of course, use power to achieve what they want, but they don't *seek* power for its own sake. Also status may come as a by-product of their business success. They may enjoy such status as they attain, but they do not see status seeking as a basic goal.

Business makers are the prime groups interested in creating learning businesses, though that does not guarantee that they will make a success of it. Also, many top managers are a complex mix of aspects of each type; hence, it is not actually a simple matter to put a person or a business into one slot. That being said, the distinctions do seem to help in, for instance, seeing whether it is worth trying to make a business more of a learning business. My experience is that if top management is dominated by the other three types, then it may be pointless to spend time and effort trying to effect a change (unless you can persuade them to alter their basic orientation).

## The learning business culture

In writings on learning organizations culture is usually seen as a core determinant of the 'goodness' of the organization. Criteria for a good culture for learning are often commonly agreed in the literature – trust, openness, support, teamworking, and so on. While not disagreeing with these criteria, I want to start in a different place. I want to look at three factors (from Sathe[12]) which impact on the strength of a culture and the relevance of these for a learning business.

1 *Thickness.* Thick cultures have many shared values, beliefs and ways of working (thin cultures have few). Hence thicker cultures exert a stronger influence on employees.
2 *Extent of sharing.* If values and ways of working are widely shared, this makes the culture stronger.
3 *Clarity of ordering.* If there is clarity about the relative importance of particular values, this makes the culture stronger.

If the culture is strong on learning,

● it would have a shared value for learning and a shared belief in its efficiency *(thickness)*;
● these values and beliefs would be widely shared *(extent)*;
● these values and beliefs would be rated as important (compared with others) *(clarity)*.

Strong cultures have become highly valued as a factor in business success. However, my experience of consulting and researching in strong cultures shows that there can be a downside to this strength. Strong cultures often become arrogant and closed. Competitive advantage may be seen to come from the organization's uniqueness and its strong culture. This can lead to isolationism. This is not to imply that the organization is cut off from its markets, but it can come to deal with its customers in a 'take it or leave it' mode.

Computer companies, such as IBM and Digital, suffered from this syndrome, and this was a factor in the problems they experienced as they entered the 1990s. They did pay attention to learning, but it was largely first-order learning; that is, they worked hard at improving what they were doing, but they did not learn to make the big changes that were necessary (second-order learning). Digital's strong engineering culture was a great strength in its early days, but it needed to learn to deal with its markets and customers in a different way – and did not. There were those in Digital in the late 1980s who felt that they were working hard to fix their problems. But that was the problem (second-order) – attempting to fix problems (first-order). Thus the solution became the problem. The organization was in need of major surgery and was bleeding to death, and top management continued to try to put band-aids on severed arteries, all the time believing it was doing a good job.

In all this, Digital's strong culture was a major negative factor. The arrogant belief in its own ways of working caused it to reject the solid, incontrovertible evidence that it needed major change. Strong cultures can find it difficult to deal with mistakes and with major market changes, unless they have in-built second-order change/learning capability. (This issue will be a feature of some of the solutions analysed in this and later chapters.)

## Order and disorder

One aspect of fostering second-order change is the need for organizations to accept and even encourage disorder *en route* to creating new kinds of order (to respond to changes in the environment[13] of the organization). Let me quickly summarize an idealized simplified sequence of events.

1 The world/environment is changing – but initially the signs/signals are weak.
2 The signals need amplifying – comparable to the way an amplifier works in a radio or hi-fi system. The organization needs to foster this.
3 The organization needs to allow a variety of messy amplified signals to enter into the business such that they disorient current thinking – like loud-speakers booming out different sounds.
4 This disorienting produces disequilibrium – it knocks the organization off balance.
5 The disorder produced needs to be tolerated. The organization needs to be prepared for it and resilient enough to live with it.
6 Out of the disorder come new shapes, new kinds of order which are better suited to the organization's environment.[14]

I shall give a simplified example of this process at work showing second-order learning. In the English 'new towns' created after the Second World War there was a heavy emphasis on town planning, usually of a rather rigid, centralized, authoritarian nature. One thing planners did was to include open spaces in the new towns and also paths to cross them. Often they would get clever and make the paths run in different shapes, for example curves rather than straight lines. These looked fine and elegant on plans, but in practice people would take short cuts, subverting the planners' aim to keep people to the paths. Hence the grass would get worn in places, or fences had to be erected to stop people doing these unauthorized anarchic things. Practice was less elegant than the plans.

One enlightened new town did it differently. Instead of first-order change (putting paths in different places) they did a creative piece of second-order change: they didn't put paths in at all (at first). They grassed over the open spaces and let people walk where they liked. Gradually the grass wore down in places, and in wet weather parts of these spaces would get quite muddy. This was the disorder phase.

To create appropriate order the authorities only had to observe the location of the muddy parts and put paths in those places. So order was created around how people actually behaved, and there was no need for unsightly and wasteful fencing. This sequence follows (approximately) the sequence of amplify signals – create disorder – create order (at a higher level) that I outlined above. It is usually the ideal way for learning businesses to introduce structures and procedures. That is, get on with doing things in a poorly structured, unsystematic way and then, where the messy bits occur, put in procedures and structures – but only in those places. This avoids bureaucracy, which tends to be focused on structuring and proceduralizing for the sake of the structurers and proceduralizers (not customers and suppliers).

I would urge you not, though, to over-focus on the 'disorder to order' sequence. This does not work if the original amplification process is inadequate. The organization needs to be

- prepared to amplify weak signals;
- open to data from the environment;
- non-defensive in its response to amplified data (for example, welcoming bad news – the best learning businesses *encourage* complaints);
- resourceful – that is, full of resources that are able to respond to amplified signals;
- one which allows considerable freedom in sub-units – these latter, for example sales teams, must be free to gather unwelcome data and spray it around the organization at will;
- reflective – able to ponder on, wallow in, and struggle with new information;
- open to changing beliefs – about itself, its products and services and its markets.

Note: here a distinction is being made between 'beliefs' (what we hold to be true, what we assume the world is like, and so on) and 'values' (what we care about, what we feel is worth while or desirable). Values may be fixed and rooted, while beliefs change. Indeed, a key value may be that we value change at the beliefs level: we accept that beliefs we have held in the past may be unhelpful and need changing. A Taoist metaphor suggests that we need to be like a young sapling. The sapling's strength and resilience comes from its being

- well rooted in the earth – solid and fixed
- flexible, so that it can bend in the wind.

The Taoists contrast this with the old dead tree that stands firm, but when a strong wind blows it snaps and breaks. The message is that organizational resilience comes from a firm solid base in values and ideals, with an ability to bend and move above ground in our contacts with the world.

## Diversity

One of the ways to encourage continued fluidity and flexibility in the organization is to value internal diversity. This links to the resourcefulness criterion mentioned above. Diversity provides a variety in the eyes and ears of people in the organization. For instance, people from different cultural or class backgrounds pay attention to different things in their environment.

Organizations lose a great deal by trying to be comfortably homogeneous (usually by hiring young, white, able-bodied, middle-class, heterosexual males for managerial positions). It makes superficial communication easier, but the reduction in the organization's learning capability through this strategy is enormous. Women have shown how they bring a different perspective to organizational life and other discriminated-against groups have become more vocal about equal opportunity issues. And, of course, the often illegal, discriminatory practices of organizations are wrong and need to be stopped. However, my case here is to put the positive benefits for organizations in welcoming difference and diversity.

(In Chapter 11, I shall discuss more fully ways of using diversity positively.)

## Organizational types

Another way to approach the issue of recognizing a learning business is to consider organizational types. Like typologies I have already used, the one following is a crude generalization which I offer as a useful map, not as a truth.

*Static organizations* are classic lumbering bureaucracies. Organizational dinosaurs. But dinosaurs existed for a long time before they expired, and so have the rigid, old-fashioned, staid organizations. However, they are recognizably poor learning businesses.

*Pendulum organizations* move from one side to the other in an illusion of change. Pendulums are, in reality, fixed and allow only a limited movement over a defined territory. Classic pendulum swinging occurs when organizations oscillate across some of the following variables:

| | | |
|---|---|---|
| Centralized | – | Decentralized |
| Corporate/strategic | – | No planning; |
| long-term planning | | short termism |
| Tough management | – | Tender management |
| Diversify | – | Stick to the knitting |

Pendulum organizations lurch from side to side across these variables with seemingly no way out of the continual wasteful movement.

*Organic organizations* use the body/organism metaphor, as earlier described – and, as I indicated earlier, there are limitations to this metaphor. For example, people moving in and out of organizations would be analogous to swapping limbs or organs with other bodies (organizations). Hence 'organic' organizations can be very conservative ('we don't want to lose or add a limb'). They are what an ex-boss of mine described as 'cosy wrap' organizations – 1960s-style pseudo-communes imagining that peace and love can prosper within their boundaries while keeping the world out. They are, therefore, rare in a pure form, but the ideal still permeates much of organization development consultancy.

*Chaotic organizations* are becoming more recognized, though references to organizations as 'organized anarchies' are quite old.[15] Static and pendulum organizations have their own kind of chaos, but the chaotic type is particularly seen as a response to a chaotic, crazy world. The most popular proponent of chaos (in the sense the term is used here) is Tom Peters.[16] He and others encourage the notion that specific kinds of chaos are of value in producing innovative organizations with high levels of responsiveness to markets. Chaos Theory has given a specialized theoretical justification to chaotic organizations, but Chaos Theory has a specific technical way of using the term 'chaos'. In its more common-sense use, unremitting chaos can lead to organizational collapse. Let me side-track to some ideas of Robert Pirsig to help us make sense of this issue.[17]

**Dynamic and systematic**

Pirsig makes a distinction between two concepts: Dynamic and static (he deliberately uses a capital 'D' for Dynamic and a small 's' for static). The distinction is elegantly simple and highly usable, but I do not like 'static' as a term, as it implies a fixedness which is not part of Pirsig's argument, so I shall use the term 'Systematic' (with a capital 'S') in my analysis.

Broadly, the idea of the 'Dynamic' is linked to second-order change and disorderly leaps – often into the unknown. In artistic movements it is the creative leap into a new mode – often initially rejected by 'Systematic' society, as in the outrages over the first exhibitions of the Impressionists, Surrealists and others. Dynamic processes amplify deviations from the norm and provide what in cybernetics is technically called 'positive feedback'. This can enhance deviation to the extent of producing destructive, chaotic situations. As we have seen in such creative individuals as Van Gogh or Nietzsche, this 'chaotic' condition can lead to madness – an inability to live in the world of others. This is where the Systematic forces can apply. They dampen deviations (provide 'negative feedback' in the technical terms of cybernetics) and create homoeostasis (as in the well-known example of the thermostat preventing a house from over-heating).

However, if there is only the Systematic dimension, this, in organizations, produces a static organization and eventual bureaucratic death. We need Dynamic leaps to increase choice and versatility while adding the Systematic elements to provide stability and control over hostile forces. Dynamic change produces the creative new ideas, but innovations that work in the marketplace need Systematic procedures to make them work. As Pirsig points out, Dynamic quality is necessary for growth, Systematic quality is necessary for survival. Therefore, in the world of Total Quality Management (TQM), we find organizations that overemphasized putting in systems and procedures (such as ISO 9000) and produced stasis. Other organizations over-emphasize creativity and new ideas (for example, in the computer industry) without the right systems to launch in the market and make profits.

Figure 3.2 shows the problem of the Dynamic leap without 'locking-on' devices, and compares this with balanced Dynamic/Systematic progress.

Pirsig likens the lock-on effect to a ratchet mechanism. There is Dynamic movement upwards which, if it looks right, is prevented from falling back by Systematic procedures. Then there is another Dynamic advance followed by another Systematic 'latch'.

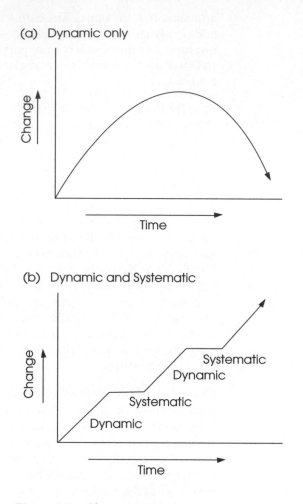

(a)  Dynamic only

*Figure 3.2    Change processes*

The issue that Pirsig raises is how we disentangle, from all the Dynamic changes, those that are worth having. The person, or group, promoting a seemingly crazy new idea could actually be crazy, or criminal, or both. Cults that seem to promise Dynamic spiritual change usually end in violent disasters, producing the horrors of Jonestown, the Rajneesh organization in Oregon and Waco. In Chapters 4 and 5 I want to address the issues of 'good learning' that can allow us to make good choices, but here I want to signal the importance of these choice issues for organizations. In hiring a new CEO as a saviour with dynamic (Dynamic) new ideas, we have to ask if the person is a con-man in disguise? Learning businesses need to address this.

If, for a moment, we return to the 'chaotic organization', we can say that, as this correlates with high Dynamic, low

Systematic, it can be an unproductive option. My preferred option is for a learning business, which is a mix of organic and chaotic. It provides for the Dynamic disjunctures and Systematic procedures, but it does not allow procedures and rules to block Dynamic change. The procedures and rules evolve organically to respond to need, as in the example of the paths across open spaces that I discussed earlier.

## Creating a balance

If we return to the triangle model used in Chapter 1, we can see how the kind of balance I'm suggesting can work (see Figure 3.3).

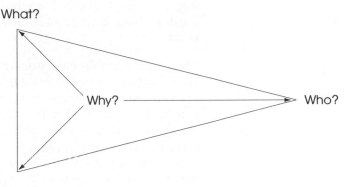

What?

Why?

Who?

How?

**Figure 3.3**  *Balanced development*

## How

If we take the 'How?' corner as an example, the Systematic dimension of this constitutes

- organization structures/organization charts;
- rules for how to do things (for example, fill in expense claims, do budgets, and so on).

The Dynamic dimension is about culture and cultural change. Culture cannot be pinned down neatly, like charts and structures. Indeed, someone once suggested that 'culture', used as a variable in explaining organizational performance, is a word given to what is left when all other explanations have been used. So you could find two organizations with the same technology, same kind of employees, same structure working in the same market providing the same product. If one is better than the other you might have to fall back on saying that one culture is better than the other.

The separation of Dynamic and Systematic is important when we consider learning and change. Dynamic change, such as cultural change, is nothing like Systematic change. It cannot be achieved using the same technology. This is the first thing that must be learned *before* any learning can take place as to how to change Dynamic and Systematic dimensions.

Here is an example. The BBC personnel function over time had gradually been seen as providing interpretations of rules for line managers on such issues as how to discipline someone, when it was possible to dismiss someone, and so on. They had volumes of rule books sitting on shelves, and the personnel manager's main job was to react to line management requests for help in interpreting and implementing the rules. Systematic change was the order of the day: changes occurred mainly in terms of modifying rules.

Then there was a decision from the top to change. Personnel would become more proactive in working in a consultancy mode with line managers on cultural/business change. The rule book would be de-emphasized, and decision making would be the responsibility of line managers as often as possible. This was a Dynamic (second-order) change. It required a changed mind set in everyone, and personnel managers had to engage in Dynamic (second-order) learning to make this work. In Part Four I shall outline the programme the BBC chose – a self managed learning programme for new personnel managers.

**Who**  Returning to the triangle model in Figure 3.3, I would now like to comment on the 'Who?' corner. A learning business needs to develop people policies and strategies that will help to lock-on the changes needed. It will assist organizational hysteresis (the ability to hinder reversing 'good' change).

I shall present a modification of the Birkbeck model[18] as a way of showing an approach. In this model you can distinguish between tactics and methods for

- aligning people with roles, and
- aligning roles with people.

*Aligning people with roles*  Under *'aligning people with roles'* the main approaches are:

- recruitment and selection
- career guidance
- learning and development.

Activity under these headings helps to get the right people in the right positions. These approaches start with an assumption of a role or roles that are defined, and then work on the people dimension to meet needs.

A learning business is one which addresses each of these in the following ways:

### Recruitment/selection

The business looks to recruit people who can learn. Learnability is a key criterion at selection. Indeed, often people with lesser abilities/experience are selected over better qualified applicants because the former show higher evidence of learning capability.

### Career guidance

People are assisted in choosing career paths from a learning point of view; that is, they are helped to choose options that will enhance their learning and development.

### Learning and development

This is oriented towards a learning, not a teaching, frame as discussed in Chapters 1 and 2.

*Aligning roles with people*

These tactics and methods reverse the assumptions of the previous category. Roles, tasks and methods of working are adjusted to fit people: people are taken as the defined element (for example, the capabilities of those already in the organization or available from the labour market). Some of the specific activities available include:

- organization design
- role/job design
- methods design
- design of reward systems
- equipment design and the design of hardware and software
- environment design.

I shall discuss these activities in turn.

### Organization design

The key issue is designing the organization for learnability. This is the area of overlap with the 'How?' question as it affects culture and structure issues. It is clear that a learning business will pay attention to learning factors when engaging in organization design and specifically consider how real people can use the organization for learning purposes. It may be, for instance, that a matrix structure with floating project teams promotes more learning of the right kind than a classic pyramid structure with fixed jobs.

### Role/job design

This follows from the above. If jobs are tightly defined, for example by rigid job descriptions, this inhibits learning. My preference is for no job descriptions, but rather to have loose role specifications. By this I mean simple specifications which delineate different roles in the organization. So it may be useful to specify roles such as 'marketing manager' or 'personnel manager' and provide enough information about the person's role in order to inform other role holders. Also, by avoiding detailed descriptions of duties and responsibilities (as in job descriptions) you avoid constraining people's freedom of movement. It is clear from the available research that if the activities of people are restricted, they do not learn as well and they find more problems in applying new learning.[19]

This whole area is an example of bringing the Dynamic and the Systematic together. The Dynamic forces need freedom, but if people's roles overlap extensively, the level of chaos induced can cause organizational breakdown. Hence some Systematic role specification is necessary, but always with an in-built capacity for change.

### Methods design

This is a subset of the above. Methods of working can be constraining and anti-learning, as in the archetypal paper-shuffling methods of bureaucracies, or they can be liberating and open as in an ideal learning business. This is one of the attractions of self managing teams where individual employees have freedom to develop methods of working to suit themselves (provided, from the Systematic standpoint, that the organization is properly served by the team).

### Design of reward systems

This is a crucial area in an organization. From a learning business point of view, the key question is: Is learning rewarded properly? Rewards are, of course, not just monetary. There are perks and there are psychological rewards, for instance. However, I shall refer to money specifically, as it is the baseline for reward strategies.

My starting point is that people should be rewarded for new learning that is significant and of value to the business. This should be the main (or only) criterion for getting pay increments, given that there may be elements in pay increases to cover inflation/market forces. Given this – that is, if inflation is $x$ per cent, give $x$ per cent pay rise – then any other increment on pay (for someone in the same role) should be because of what they have learned. (Obviously, if someone is promoted, that is another matter; here I am discussing a situation of no promotion and the decisions to be taken in an annual pay review.) I believe that increases in performance which have come from hard work but not from new learning should be rewarded with bonuses (either individual or collective, or both). A person or group may work less hard next year and therefore warrant less of a bonus. Learning is evidenced by the person

- showing new capabilities and ways of working which provide irreversible changes in performance
- taking on a wider role due to new learning.

These both enhance hysteresis (that is, irreversibility) and provide a more resourceful person for the business.

The point about a wider role provides a link back to organization/role design issues. It is crucial that individuals, and groups, have a chance to enlarge their roles, so that learning can be enhanced and people rewarded for it.

### Equipment design and the design of hardware and software

The equipment people use may inhibit or enhance learning. A good example is IT/computer systems. Some systems liberate people's energies and encourage learning. Others constrain and limit people. In developing IT systems, learning criteria need to play more of a role than they usually do. IT managers are often blinkered in the way they think about the potential for people using the systems they design and the hardware they buy.

### Environment design

Some working environments encourage useful interaction between people and enhance learning. This does not necessarily mean open plan offices (and often, if poorly designed, open plan offices fail to fulfil their potential). It can mean areas where people can chat over a coffee, or outdoor space (patios and courtyards) where, in good weather, people can meet and talk. Some organizations have creatively located different departments on the same office floor in order to encourage new interactions.

*Integrating alignments*

In the above analysis, the danger is that managers focus on one or two areas for change. However, usually all the above choices for action are available, and they overlap and interact extensively. Let me quote one example I experienced in the early 1970s. An English local authority received complaints about the quality of road sweeping and about accidents caused by their drivers. They also discovered that repair bills were high due to these accidents, and that poor driving contributed to increased maintenance costs. Further, government legislation now demanded that drivers of road sweeping and other local authority vehicles gain a Public Service Vehicle (PSV) licence, which is at a significantly higher level than the standard driving test. (Most of the authority's drivers did not have a PSV licence.) The local authority recognized a range of learning needs here, and, at considerable expense, hired an experienced trainer and set up a training programme (with training vehicles and a training area off the road). In considering the factors in 'aligning roles with people' and 'aligning people with roles', the following occurred.

*Selection*

Drivers had been selected who were not good learners: most of them struggled in the training programme and the failure rate was high.

*Job/method design*

The jobs the drivers did and the methods they used were inherently likely to produce accidents. They had to drive around all day at a standard, slow speed in areas with many parked cars.

*Equipment design*

The vehicles they drove were user unfriendly. For instance, the noise levels were above the permissible values, thus causing hearing problems.

*Rewards design*

Drivers were not rewarded for learning new skills successfully. Hence the good ones (who got their PSV licences) left to work in the private sector where wages were higher.

A good learning business would have recognized the interaction of these factors and acted accordingly. They would have taken a strategic approach to the issues, and looked at the overall picture rather than just one facet of it.

Some specific things that needed doing included:

- making learning capability one of the criteria for selection – and using it
- devising a development approach which responded to the actual working conditions that the drivers faced – and this needed to involve the drivers in the design of it, as opposed to imposing a standardized training course
- reconsidering the vehicles used by the drivers
- reconsidering the rewards system, for example rewarding drivers who obtained their PSV licence.

These are just some examples of the need to pull together aspects of the situation in a more systemic way.

## Appraisal schemes

Appraisal schemes are one aspect of the 'Who?' category (the people dimension) that is perhaps worth mentioning as a specific method which is claimed to help people learn. So often, however, appraisal schemes are poorly used and do not seem to be cost-effective. One reason for this is the negative/punitive dimension of appraisals. I want here to indicate, in simplified form, what traditional appraisal schemes are like, and what a development approach, as part of a learning business, looks like. The two modes are summarized in Figures 3.4 and 3.5.

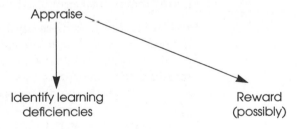

*Figure 3.4*   *Appraisal model*

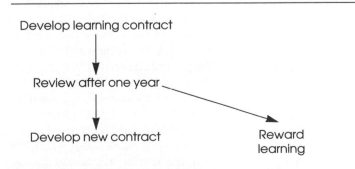

*Figure 3.5*   *Developmental model*

The traditional model (Figure 3.4) starts with an appraisal which identifies learning needs. This is a negative, deficiency-based approach. People so often leave an appraisal with the identified weaknesses uppermost in their minds. Learning in this model is associated with something negative: a way of remedying weaknesses.

The developmental model (Figure 3.5) starts differently. People are encouraged to look at themselves, using the Five Questions approach outlined in Chapter 1. They then draw up learning contracts which provide a basis for learning and development activity. This is agreed with the person who will conduct their annual reviews (one year later). When the reviews take place they are based on documents written by the individuals to which they are committed. As the individuals will have been working on the issues in the documents, the object of the review will be to assess how they have done. A good reviewer will acknowledge first the achievements (and these may feed into rewards decisions) and then help each learner to identify any new learning that is needed in the following year.

The developmental method is significantly fairer than the traditional model. To appraise people *before* they have had a chance to learn is unfair. They have not been given an opportunity to change and are therefore being judged or advised from the wrong base. This is another factor in the failure of traditional appraisal schemes.

In a learning business there would also be greater attention on developing people as good learners than on developing appraisers to check on this. I am not arguing against providing development for those doing performance reviews (appraisals), but if an organization is to use appraisals the appraisees need an opportunity to learn how to make the process work to the advantage of themselves and the organization.

The benefit of this is that it encourages more self responsibility and meets the needs for individuals to manage their own learning and development. One organization conducted research on why their annual appraisal scheme was not working. They found that with the pace of change in the company, either the appraiser or the appraisee was likely to have moved in the interval between appraisals. In less than 50 per cent of cases were individuals appraised by the person with whom they had set objectives and written a development plan one year earlier. The only sensible way to deal with this situation is to help the learner (appraisee) manage the process, and de-emphasize the power of the appraiser.

**Focused development** One way of describing a learning business is that it focuses a range of issues so that learning is developed in a coherent way. This metaphor is shown diagrammatically in Figure 3.6. The learning business is here compared to a convex lens: various strands that can run in parallel (and therefore may never meet up) are brought to a single-point focus, so that learning integrates all these dimensions.

In Figure 3.6 only some of the parallel strands are indicated. The objective of using this diagram is only to show the idea of 'focusing', not to be all encompassing.

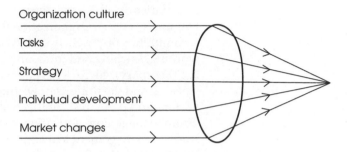

Organization culture

Tasks

Strategy

Individual development

Market changes

*Figure 3.6   Focused development*

**Summary** In this chapter I have moved around the field of learning businesses and I have used a variety of models (maps) to say something of the territory. I have also tried to present a case for the importance of learning businesses as the organizational implementation of the strategic learning discussed in Chapter 2.[20] I have raised some concerns about how learning in organizations is seen and I have suggested that some kinds of organization are more congenial than others for developing strategic learning. I have suggested that organizations need to consider how they align people with roles and roles with people – and how these two dimensions themselves need integrating. In Chapter 4 I shall consider these issues in describing 'good learning'.

**Notes**
1  The most accessible summary of Drucker's views is 'Drucker on Japan', *Management Today*, June 1974, 89–92 and 138–48.
2  Bateson, G. (1973) *Steps to an Ecology of Mind*, London: Paladin. (See references to Deutero Learning in this collection of readings – not an easy, fun read. Indeed, Bateson can be heavy going if you are not used to his style.)
3  McLean, A.J., Sims, D.B.P., Mangham, I.L. and Tuffield, D. (1982) *Organization Development in Transition*,

Chichester: Wiley is an excellent research-based text showing some of the problems with OD.

4  Janis, I.L. (1971) 'Group think', *Psychology Today* (November) is a neat summary of some key issues on poor team learning.

5  Nonaka, I. and Takeuchi, H. (1995) *The Knowledge-Creating Company*, New York: Oxford University Press.

6  The Institute for Research on Learning (IRL) has produced quite a literature on this field. Some ideas are outlined by the editor of *Training and Development* in Galagan, P.A. (1993) 'The search for the poetry of work', *Training and Development* (October), 33–7. One of the best summaries of IRL's early work is Brown, J.S. and Duguid, P. (1991) 'Organizational learning and communities-of-practice: toward a unified view of working, learning and innovation', *Organization Science*, **2**, 1 (February), 40–57. This paper also reviews Orr's research and the important writings of Lave and Wenger. A UK analysis of this work is in Fox, S. (1997) 'From management education and development to the study of management learning', in Burgoyne, J. and Reynolds, M. (1997) (eds) *Management Learning: Integrating Perspectives in Theory and Practice*, London: Sage.

7  Porter, M. (1990) *The Competitive Advantage of Nations*, London: Macmillan.

8  The Motorola University in Asia is an example of a company seeing its role as developing suppliers. In Singapore I met a trainer whose *sole* job for Motorola was to go into suppliers, mainly in Malaysia, and develop their staff.

9  Handy, C. (1993) 'Make your business a monastery', *The Director* (October), 25.

10  Profile: Sir Duncan Nichol (1993) *Management Today* (October), 66.

11  Quotes here come from the *Rover Learning Business, Business Report 1992* (published by the Rover Group) and from Vallely, I. (1992) 'How Rover drives its learning message home', *Works Management* (August).

12  Sathe, V. (1985) *Culture and Related Corporate Realities*, Homewood, IL: Irwin.

13  I am using 'environment' to mean the world around an organization – its markets, suppliers, customers, and so on – rather than 'environment' as ecologists and green activists use it.

14  Ideas expressed here can be pursued with more rigour in the works of Prigogine on dissipative structures, and Bateson on the importance of 'news of difference'. The reference to Bateson is in note 2 above. Prigogine's ideas

are most accessibly presented (for the organizational world) in Wheatley, M.J. (1992) *Leadership and the New Science*, San Francisco: Bennett.

15 See March, J.G. and Olsen, J. (1976) *Ambiguity and Choice in Organizations*, Bergen: Universitetsforlaget.

16 Peters, T. (1989) *Thriving on Chaos*, London: Pan.

17 Pirsig, R.M. (1991) *Lila: An Inquiry into Morals*, London: Bantam.

18 The Birkbeck model was developed by Alec Rodger and colleagues at Birkbeck College, London University, mainly in the 1960s. My use of it modifies considerably Alec Rodger's terminology, but the ideas are similar.

19 Current research by my colleagues Ben Bennett, Caroline Cunningham and Graham Dawes on this subject is yet to be published. An already published article which does address this issue is: Kelleher, D., Finestone, P. and Lowy, A. (1986) 'Managerial learning: first notes from an unstudied frontier', *Group and Organization Studies*, **11**, 3 (September), 169–201.

20 A good summary of 'learning organization' ideas is in Beard, D. (1993) 'Learning to change organisations', *Personnel Management* (January), 32–5. He discusses some popular writers, including Peter Senge, Ed Schein, John Burgoyne and Bob Garratt.

# PART THREE   Good learning

---

This part follows from the last and acts as a bridge to Part Four. I shall continue the link between a learning business and personal learning and, at the end of Chapter 5, indicate a rationale for self managed learning as the optimal process for achieving 'good learning'. These two chapters will then focus on *what* is to be learned before switching in Part Four to *how* it is to be learned.

I have emphasized the organizational context in Chapter 3. This can also be taken to the level of specific relationships in organizations as a factor in learning, which will be dealt with more fully in Chapter 11. Here I want to take up a concern expressed by Bateson[1] when criticizing 'man's habit of changing his environment rather than changing himself'. While it is important to create good learning environments, it is not of much benefit without good learners.

Indeed, there is evidence to suggest that good learners can learn from and within almost any context. Some Jewish concentration camp survivors (such as Bruno Bettelheim) reported that they treated their situation as a research project – something to be learned from – and this was a major factor in their psychological as well as their physical survival. Yet a concentration camp could be viewed as the worst possible environment that any human being could inhabit.

In psychotherapy there is evidence to suggest that good patients/clients (that is, good learners) will benefit from almost any brand of psychotherapy (given a not totally incompetent therapist). This line of enquiry may be more fruitful in improving the benefits of psychotherapy (that is, identifying why some individuals benefit more than others) than in a search for the 'best' psychotherapy.

Creating 'good learners' becomes, then, a more important factor than the subject-matter of learning or the improvement of teaching/training. This also seems to be justified by research in universities, which suggests that students who learn how to play the academic game do better (in terms of marks/grades) than those who do not (irrespective of intelligence or other measures of ability). One behaviour to enhance results is 'cue seeking'.[2] This is where students look out for evidence of what their professors/lecturers regard as important, and respond to it. 'Cue deaf' students do not seem to spot the cues provided, sometimes subtly and sometimes blatantly, about how to get good grades.

It is clear that in organizations some people pick up quite quickly what they need to learn in order to progress, and others do not. Traditional IQ and other related measures do not accurately predict these differences, and I shall explore some of these factors using a variety of concepts. In some cases I shall continue ideas already outlined – for instance, the difference between first-order and second-order learning. I shall return to the 'good learner' theme in Chapter 11.

## Notes

1 Bateson, G. (1973) *Steps to an Ecology of Mind*, London: Paladin, p. 420.
2 Miller, C.M.L. and Parlett, M.R. (1974) *Up to the Mark: a Study of the Examination Game*, London: SRHE.

# 4 Capability and wisdom

## Introduction

George Bernard Shaw once said that 'success comes from taking the path of maximum advantage instead of the path of least resistance'. The following section will mention some of the 'maximum advantage' paths that seem apparent in good learning businesses; but, as Shaw implies, they're not easy. In later sections I shall indicate some reasons why only a minority of people and organizations demonstrate these qualities, and some clues as to the kind of orientation needed to get 'good learning' in organizations.

In the following section I shall indicate some examples showing evidence of a learning orientation (or lack of it). The examples are just that: not comprehensive but rather examples of issues.

## Learning from all possible sources

Clients, customers, colleagues and competitors are among examples of sources of learning. The problem is that many organizations waste the information they gather. Companies do attitude surveys or benchmarking comparisons with other organizations but often do not know what to do with the data. I have been present at boards that have looked at attitude survey data. They may say 'Oh, that's interesting. We're 2 per cent up on this category this year and 3 per cent down on that. I wonder why?' Others may also wonder, then move to the next item on the agenda. These data-gathering exercises become empty rituals without a learning focus as a starting point. Also, companies tend to invest too much in complex data gathering instead of having a strategic focus on learning needs which can lead to quick, focused data gathering of a much less sophisticated (and more cost-effective) nature.

Let us take some positive examples. Ian MacLaurin (now Lord MacLaurin) was one of those responsible for turning round retailers Tesco from a decaying business into a highly successful one. He demonstrated a clear learning focus. The sequence seems to have been:

1 Identified problems (diminishing market share, reduced profits)
2 Learned why – including the company's commitment to downmarket practices (such as Green Shield Stamps)
3 Studied alternatives (he visited three companies in the USA that had issued stamps, but stopped)
4 Took the best ideas and translated them into his own company's situation.

MacLaurin had to fight to get in a position to make these changes. He had an old guard with what he describes as 'selective deafness' – they did not want to learn about the need for change. He also unashamedly looked at the leaders in the retail field, Marks and Spencer and Sainsbury's, and learned from them. Finally, he kept up his learning, for example by spending up to half his time in stores listening to staff and customers. While his competitors used store visits to crack the whip, he used them to walk the floor or to sit in the staff canteen and listen to the staff.

This was an example of learning from good practice. Richard Branson, who founded Virgin Atlantic Airways at the age of 33, learned from others' mistakes. He studied the reasons why small independent airlines failed (the majority had, up to that time). He realized that competing on price alone would not work (Laker and People Express were notable failures on this score). He learned that service, customer care, uniqueness and specialness would be key criteria for success, and, as a result, the airline, against all the odds, now has a series of 'best airline' awards, and is successful.

Branson's success is all the more remarkable given that he had no experience of the airline industry and was entering an industry where even the large experienced companies were in trouble. He could only do it because he is an excellent learner. But his learning was not a lot of random facts and figures about the airline business. He focused his attention on what was needed. He connected between his needs and what was to be learned, and after the airline was launched he continued to learn and to apply his learning by making changes in the airline's operations.

## Learning and change

Figure 4.1 shows the traditional model for getting change to occur. This is the standard process used by traditional management consultancies and, generally, it is a poor model. It is fine if you want interesting reports to read, but action/implementation is often limited.

Figure 4.2 shows a learning-based model. Instead of a linear, sequential, one-dimensional process of 'study to

Study problem/situation

Recommendations
(in report usually)

Action
(possibly)

***Figure 4.1*** *Traditional change model*

Problem/situation
studied

Analysis of change/
learning capability

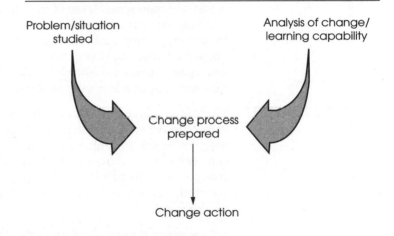

Change process
prepared

Change action

***Figure 4.2*** *New change model*

recommendations to action', this model suggests that 'learnability' is part of the starting point for planning change. There are *two* beginnings, not one. The process has to work as a pincer movement where the problem to be addressed is analysed alongside the analysis for learning and change. An example of studying change from the beginning is to use Revans's model of 'Who knows?, Who can?, Who cares?'[1]

The difficulty is that most managers are educated – in school, business school, and so on – according to the first model. Case studies in a classic MBA suggest that analysis and recommendations are all that are required. Because students on an MBA do not have to implement the recommendations they make on a case study, they begin to believe that this linear process will work. They have learned how to learn in a limited and limiting way, and tend to blame others if their linear thinking does not work. (Argyris[2] is an excellent critic of this problem.) Consultants who work in this way tend to blame resistant or inept clients rather than their own limited methodology.

IT specialists constitute another problem. A paper company decided to computerize its warehouse. Paper was to be stored in fixed points and logged on the computer. Retrieval of paper to send to purchasers could then be done automatically. They had studied the problem, recommended a solution and then acted. The problem was that no one had considered the learning needs of the warehouse staff. They carried on in their old ways, dumping paper from fork-lift trucks in any convenient place. As the computer was unaware of this, errors in shipping were enormous. At one level you can say that this is just common sense. If the IT people had had some common sense they would not have done what they did. However, putting a label on the problem does not solve it, and exhortations to IT staff 'to have more common sense next time' will not necessarily work. They have to *learn* a different way of addressing problems.

## Who learns?

There is a danger that more senior people think that others (more junior) are the main focus of learning. However, you may not be able to control someone else's learning, but you can control your own. It is probable that, faced with a change issue, the first person you ought to think of is yourself. Given that you want something different, how can you change?

Let me give the example of a secretary with whom I worked many years ago. She did not like to have more than one or two tasks at any one time. She could not sequence tasks. She panicked, became stressed, felt overloaded if I gave her more than two things at once – even though I would emphasize that they needed to be done in sequence. Task one, then task two, then task three. She somehow wanted to hold all three tasks in her head at once and, given that she could only work on one, the other two swirled around in her head, worrying her because they were not being done.

## Solutions

(a) *No learning solutions*. These could include dismissing the person. Or leaving the situation as a mess.
(b) *Her learning*. I could have decided that she needed to change. I have no idea how this would have been achieved, but it was a feasible option.
(c) *My learning*. I took the view that I had to learn. I had to change my behaviour and not give her multiple tasks. I

had to create a sequencing for myself and feed work to her from that sequence.

Many managers choose (a) or (b). They only see those two options. They are, of course, genuine options, and I would not argue against them. I am only positing the view that there are at least three, not two, options.

**Collaboration and sharing**

In a learning business, people share ideas and information. If someone sees something in a newspaper or magazine that might interest someone else, they cut it out for them. If someone goes to a conference, that person is keen to share with others any ideas learned.

This, again, requires a particular mind set; it does not just happen automatically. In some cases, people's experience at school has been not to share learning. In schools that are highly competitive, and where students are ranked in order of performance, it is not in a person's interest to help others. Indeed, collaborating in learning, for example over an essay, is called cheating and is punished. This contrasts dramatically with the Japanese school where students see it as their duty to help those who are struggling. I have spoken to a number of British and American teachers who have taught in Japanese schools and they comment on how much easier it was there than in their own countries. Because children are in a culture where they are expected to care for their colleagues, the teacher's job is helped enormously.

Ohmae[3] shows how the 'group harmony' in Japan's educational system contributes to educating Japanese managers in a collaborative style of working. Walzer[4] suggests that the 'democratic' style of learning in Japanese schools develops 'camaraderie and mutuality' and that, unlike some stereotypes, Japanese people become used to a flexible, autonomous way of working. This helps employees in companies to become capable of sophisticated decision making in collaboration with others.

This specific example, from one culture, provides a general challenge to a popular dichotomy. The distinction between individualism and collectivism is used by politicians (especially where individualism is seen as a corollary of right-wing capitalism, and collectivism a correlate of left-wing socialism). Also, cross-cultural researchers such as Hofstede[5] have popularized a spectrum of national cultures on an individualism/collectivism dimension.

I believe that Eastern cultures in general (not just Japan) challenge this dichotomy. Merton,[6] in his commentary on

Chuang Tzu's writings, suggests that 'personalism' is an apt term for Taoist ideals. As he said:

> Personalism and individualism must not be confused. Personalism gives priority to the *person* and not the individual self. To give priority to the person means respecting the unique and inalienable value of the *other* person, as well as one's own. (p. 7)

He suggests that ego-driven selfish individualism ends up as a self defeating anti-personalistic position.

There is an important distinction between 'individuality' and 'individualism'. It can be argued that *individuality* is sacrificed in highly *individualistic* modes of acting. If, for instance, a manager is to pursue his[7] own individual, selfish career needs to progress up the organization, it may be that the need to conform and play the game causes him to lose his *individuality*. Here I'm using 'individuality' in the three ways that Squires[8] describes, namely:

● individuality as *uniqueness* – the antithesis of mass standardization
● individuality as *holism* – the antithesis of a partial, usually narrowly cognitive, view of the person
● individuality as *autonomy* – the antithesis of over-dependence on others and excessive conformity to others' views.

The highly individualistic manager may have to disavow uniqueness, pretend that he does not have feelings and values and conform to organizational norms in order to progress selfishly. In this sense, then, I am with Freire[9] in his view that individuality (or, as he put it, 'full humanity') cannot be achieved through individualism but 'only in fellowship' (p. 58).

Personalism also challenges bureaucratic, centralist socialism (for example, as practised until recently in Central and Eastern Europe). It has been suggested that these seemingly collectivist cultures actually promoted selfish individualism.[10] Under communism natural communities broke down and people had to take more responsibility for themselves. Also, where there was covert secret police surveillance of individuals, people could not trust colleagues (for example, at work) and, hence, individuals were thrust into a more closed self centred mode of being. Also, many individuals joined the Communist Party, not out of ideological belief, but for the sake of their careers and their material well-being.

Individualism and collectivism seem, then, to fold into one another and in their extremes create dehumanized life styles and dehumanized organizations. Neither position is 'personalistic'.

## Key concepts

'Personalism' is a key concept. It says something about the person (of their desire to learn with and from others, their desire to support others' learning as well as their own) and about the learning business, which needs to support a personalistic approach.

In the remainder of this part of the book I want to elaborate some other key concepts and suggest that they go together in saying something about good (desirable) learning. The three main concepts are:

1 Capability
2 Wisdom
3 Holism.

This chapter covers capability and wisdom, as they balance each other. Chapter 5 covers holism and some relevant sub-categories of holism.

I shall also revisit some concepts already introduced, including:

● first- and second-order learning
● pattern change
● Dynamic and Systematic.

Before discussing these concepts, I would like to indicate another method of elaborating good learning, namely via metaphor.

### Metaphor

Metaphor was once considered an interesting poetic speech form of no relevance to practical matters such as business. Lakoff and Johnson[11] were the most influential analysts who changed that view, and Morgan[12] has been a popularizer of the use of metaphor in making sense of organizational life.

We now see that much of our thinking, as well as communicating, is through metaphor. Metaphor provides a way of understanding or interpreting relatively abstract ideas through linkage to familiar concrete objects or modes of behaving. I want here to indicate some metaphors that are used to explicate ideas about learning and, alongside these, to show how the metaphors are applied practically in learning activity. Many of the metaphors used seem to me to restrict and constrain our thinking about learning – and even the good metaphors have their limitations.

### Building

Classically much of education has been conceived of as *building up* the person, and 'units of learning' have been seen as building blocks. This has been translated into competency approaches which tend to talk of each competence as a building block towards making a competent manager. This is a reductionist view which assumes that each brick in the building can be neatly mortared to those beneath and produce a nice static building (person) at the end of the process. The concomitant of this is that if all the bricks are not in place, the person is not of much value, since a building without all its walls (and roof) is incomplete and uninhabitable. This metaphor then contributes to 'gap' models of learning, that is, that learning is to add bricks or fill in holes, and is remedial. Thus we find that competency approaches are almost never applied to top managers (who obviously cannot be incomplete persons!).

*Bucket*  The bucket metaphor is common. It assumes that the learner is an empty bucket and is filled up with knowledge and skills. Once again it is a deficiency model, though more fluid than the building metaphor. Also, as buckets tend to be leaky, there have to be top-up courses to keep the bucket filled to the brim. The bucket metaphor justifies much of traditional educational activity, especially in schools.

*Engineering*  The concept of 'human resources' in its strong (economic) sense (people as resources interchangeable with other resources such as machines) is linked to an engineering metaphor. Thus, we have reports on 'making managers'[13] and managers having 'tool kits' of skills. This links to mechanistic human resource development systems and to training courses which assume, at worst, that the person is only a walking tool kit. Resources and tools tend to get worn out and used up, so this metaphor can justify throwing used-up resources (people) 'on to the scrap heap'.

*Agricultural*  People can be seen as organizational seed corn, or as tender shoots needing fertilizing and care. In the Young Professionals Programme at British Airways the symbol for the programme was an acorn – based on the idea that 'mighty oaks grow from little acorns'. This metaphor has many appealing features, but it can also justify 'removing dead wood', 'weeding people out', 'pruning' (sacking) to justify organizational survival or growth. And this may or may not be valid.

*Human body*  The analogy here is with the physical growth of a human being. We know that growing maturity and ability are linked to physical growth (up to adulthood). So developing 'intellectual muscle' and such-like has to be a good thing. Also, the idea of people being 'fit' and 'in shape' is appealing. The 'personal growth movement' took on board much of this thinking, and personal growth approaches to training have been popular in some organizations. Like the agricultural metaphor, the challenge here is explicitly to bucket/engineering-type metaphors. The assumption is that people have the capability within them – and do not need to be stuffed with facts and theories. Rather, they need to be nurtured and supported.

*Zoology* This is, at one level, a relative of the above metaphor. However, ideas of 'breeding good staff' link more to the way we see animals than humans. Also, the idea that people are categorizable (for example, in biblical terms, as sheep and goats) can justify stratification which denies learning. This is especially so in ideas that managers are 'born, not made' – and that encouraging learning is a waste of time.

*Craft* The idea of a manager as a craftsperson (and managing as a craft) is common, though usually implicit. However, young managers are often seen as 'apprentices' learning their craft through watching their 'elders and betters'. The idea of a craft, in its best sense, also encompasses learning the values and ethos of the craft. The true craftsperson finishes the underside of the chair as well as the visible parts, because that is the proper thing to do and they care about the 'total quality' of their work (hence, also, the link to Total Quality Management).

*Artist* Vaill[14] talks of 'managing as a performing art'. The notion of 'manager as artist' adds an aesthetic and a creative dimension to managerial activity. It also balances the idea of 'manager as scientist' – and the need for some business schools to want to justify management as a legitimate academic subject through the excessive teaching and study of quantitative and statistical methods.

*Medicine* 'Diagnostic' activity is justified by a medical metaphor. Diagnosis of ills, weaknesses, and so on justifies action to solve them, and is often at the back of 'training needs analysis'. Also, the unpleasantness of some training activities can be alleviated by managers feeling that they have to 'take their medicine' (and an unpleasant taste often correlates with 'good medicine').

*War/military* Strategies, tactics and missions come from a military metaphor. They can support aggressive competitive 'fights' with the competition, or with other departments in the organization. The action learning notion of 'comrades in adversity' learning best when their 'backs are against the wall' can have excessively macho overtones for some, which is a pity, as action learning has so many good features (see Chapter 6).

The military metaphor can support macho leadership

development (especially where military leaders are used as role models, and 'beating the enemy' is used as the *raison d'être* for learning). It can also support the aggressive 'strategic advantage' school of development. Of course, if you are under attack as an organization (for example, in a takeover bid) learning to fight off the enemy can be extremely valid. But continual focus on enemies (real or imaginary) can lead to a paranoid distortion of the organization's activities, and fundamental learning can be missed.

Another example of different perspectives comes from Eastern writings on warfare. Especially interesting to me are ideas of strategic approaches which avoid battles and bloodshed – that is, that war does not have to involve fighting. Also, most martial art forms from the East have evolved as defensive methods and there is much we can learn in the West from the ways of thinking that underpin Aikido, Tai Ji Chuan, Karate and Judo.

*Naval/ships*    Some aspects of naval metaphors link to war, but others come from the merchant navy. Being 'welcomed aboard' and then 'keeping an even keel' while they get their work 'under way' is common advice to new managers. Of course, they have to make certain they 'don't make waves' or 'go overboard' and then everything will be 'smooth sailing'. They will have to look out for 'fair weather friends', those who 'sail too close to the wind' and those who 'swing the lead'. Learning in this context can be about culture (the organization as a ship, as indicated above) and methods for 'keeping the ship afloat' and not letting projects 'run aground'.

The exploration side of this metaphor can lead to notions of a learning programme as a 'voyage of discovery'. The voyage/journey metaphor has many positive aspects, and is one that is heavily used in self managed learning. (I shall return to this metaphor in Chapter 6.)

*Games/sport*    Game metaphors are sometimes close to warfare – as games can be ritualized war. There is also a heavy use of the 'team' metaphor in management with overt reference often to sport. This underpins ideas of 'team-building'. Here we have two metaphors that overlap – and in the process cause confusion. 'Building' has a static base in the building metaphor. The notion is of a team as a static entity which is 'built' and then needs regular 'maintenance' (for example, the annual off-site meeting). This loses the sense of a team as a fluid group where people come and go and where ways of working need to evolve to suit a changing world. I personally prefer notions of 'team development' as these seem more learning oriented.

Game/team/sport metaphors are used in the idea of 'coaching' in organizations, and there is frequently an overt translation of sports coaching methods into organizations. Gallwey's Inner Game[15] approach to coaching is one that I particularly like.

*Family* When working in social services organizations I found that the family metaphor was the one most used in relation to work groups. People wanted to be in happy, supportive family groups. In other organizations, ideas of family are more hidden, but in some cases the concept of mentoring is linked to a paternalistic or avuncular model of the older, wiser, family member helping the young learner.

*Other metaphors* The list of metaphors could be much longer. My purpose here is to make the point that metaphorical thinking about learning and about organizational life is crucial to understanding different perspectives on 'good learning'. 'Goodness' comes to be defined by the metaphor. So, for instance, competency approaches can be judged, as to goodness, if the building bricks are 'fit for purpose' and can be stacked up over time to make a good manager. In the next section I shall raise some other points about this approach.

As an aside, you might like to consider the metaphors *you* use to think about learning. Have you written anything that you could study to see if your metaphors support the kind of learning you want?

# Capability

It is difficult to argue against the case that managing is a *process* that needs, as an outcome, action on live issues. There is, however, no need to postulate a subject or a thing called 'management', and indeed, outside the English-speaking world it is difficult to find cultures with a noun that exactly correlates with how 'management' is used in English. Solely analytical learning of a supposed subject called 'management' must, then, be questionable, especially if learning to make things happen is neglected.

Weyrich[16] suggests that MBA programmes typically focus 70–90 per cent on analysis and 10–30 per cent on making things happen. The manager's job is 10–30 per cent analysis and 70–90 per cent making things happen. Research studies on MBAs suggest that indeed there is a major problem here. For instance, Boyatzis and Renio's research[17] suggests that on the traditional MBA, students 'do learn a range of skills' such as planning, quantitative data analysis, and so on. However, the MBA had *no* impact 'on abilities that involve interaction with people', including 'leadership skills,

relational skills, helping/delegating skills,
setting/managing to goals skills, learning skills'.

The concept of 'capability' can encompass these abilities
and is, therefore, of great value in considering what kind of
learning is needed in a learning business. The Royal Society
for the Encouragement of Arts, Manufactures and
Commerce (RSA) has, for some years, promoted this
concept through its 'Education for Capability' initiative.
They suggest that 'Capability is an all-round human quality,
an integration of skills, knowledge and personal qualities
used appropriately and effectively in a variety of familiar
and unfamiliar situations.'[18]

The 'Education for Capability' proponents have suggested
that, while capability is a 'whole person' concept, it can be
recognized in action and in people through the following:

- openness to learning
- self awareness
- problem solving
- self starting
- sense of purpose and will
- courage
- creativity

and so on.

Given the RSA's mission statement of 1754, which included
the aims 'to embolden enterprise', these qualities are
perhaps unsurprising. They do not reject the detached
analysis and scholarships of the traditional educational
world but subsume them in this wider framework.

The challenge is how to learn this, given criticisms of
traditional education and training activity. That will be
covered in Part Four. Here, however, we need to side-step
to consider the subject of competence, competences,
competency and competencies. This field has become
complex and confusing, including the problem of which of
the four labels to use. However, most people seem to talk of
'competences' and produce lists of these. The RSA response
has been to say that capability is a broader and more holistic
concept that would include (or transcend) competence lists.

I shall briefly review some issues about competences, and
suggest that the concept can be unhelpful and unnecessary.
'Capability' has its disadvantages as a concept, but is
generally more usable and more useful for learning
businesses.

**Competences**    The claims are made that ideal (competent) managerial
performance can be identified, codified and taught. Also, it

is claimed that competences so identified are of universal validity (for the level of management identified). The problem for these claims is that they do not stack up.[19] There is no solid research evidence to support the contention that developing managerial competences of itself improves organizational performance.

*Options for use of competences*

There seem to be three areas of choice available, each with two options:

1 *Level of detail*

   (a)  Detailed lists of tightly defined competences using lengthy performance criteria lists. (This is favoured at the national level in the UK.)
   (b)  General lists usually of around five to ten competences fairly loosely defined without performance criteria. (This is favoured by many organizations.)

2 *Generic or specific*

   (a)  Generic list of core competences that apply to all managers at a particular level in the organization.
   (b)  Specific lists linked to precise professional areas. (This latter option seems rare. The attraction for many organizations seems to be the standardized generic list.)

3 *Task/role or person*

   (a)  Task-/role-based lists come from a functional analysis of the supposed needs of a particular job. (This is the favoured mode in the UK at the national level.)
   (b)  Person-based lists define competences for *managers* (not managerial roles). (This is the dominant mode in the USA and in many organizations in the UK.)

*Problems with competences*

I shall take the 'generic by level' mode as an exemplar. The claim here would be that first-level managers, middle managers and senior managers would have, at each level, defined competence needs. The dominant metaphor is the building block.

A summary of specific concerns is outlined below with some reference to the preferred option of using 'capability' instead.

## 1. Past oriented

Competence lists are *always* about what has been done in the past. Much of this *may* be valid in the future, but there is usually no basis to decide what. Even in the short time of some organizations using competence lists, they have found the approach undermined by TQM changes in work practices, empowerment policies devolving decision making and de-layering of organizations radically changing managerial roles. The UK Management Charter Initiative (MCI) national 'Guidelines' stated (in 1989) that 'first-level management' (for *all* managers *irrespective* of size of organization, location, organization culture, technology, and so on) was about 'the direction and control of the activities of other people'. Self managing work teams wiped that out in some organizations. Others had long since moved away from a 'direction and control' view of management.

Capability is about response to changing circumstances. It cannot be defined in terms of the precise tasks of a manager. The capable person needs to be capable of responsiveness to changing needs.

## 2. Narrowly ethnocentric

Competence lists are usually developed in one country, and are generally inapplicable elsewhere. The idea that a list of competences for middle managers in the UK would have relevance in France or Germany, let alone Nigeria, Japan or Argentina, is untenable. Hofstede, Trompenaars[20] and others have shown quite conclusively that we transfer managerial practices directly from one culture to another at our peril.

Capability, on the other hand, needs to be concerned with capability to work anywhere; not to be perfect, but to be able to learn and to respond to needs in varying cultures.

## 3. Reductionist/fragmentary

The assumption of competence lists is that people can learn each competence in isolation without reference to other competences, and then unproblematically integrate them. The metaphor here is the notion that one could take an old-fashioned clock apart, take out its wheels and springs, throw the pieces into a box, and assume that it will still work.

Capability is an inherently holistic concept. The facets of capability overlap each other, and cannot be separately identified.

## 4. Complex, bureaucratic lists

In an effort to develop precision and specificity such that competences are relatively unambiguously defined, lists become long, complex and unusable by managers.

Capability can be kept as a relatively simple, unified concept.

## 5. Spirit and form

Gil Evans, the great jazz arranger, once said 'Every form, even though it becomes traditional and finally becomes academic, originally came from someone's spirit who created the form. Then it was picked up and taught in schools. But all forms originated from spirit.'[21]

Competences focus on form: capability on spirit and form.

## 6. Organization culture

Competence lists assume a particular kind of culture, generally that associated with traditional bureaucracies where levels and jobs are tightly defined. The MCI Guidelines for first-level managers say 'Such a management task is performed within a fairly tight group of constraints and the individual has limited freedom of action.'[22] So much for empowerment and devolved responsibility!

## 7. Individualistic

The focus in competence lists is on the isolated individual. It ignores the context within which the person works. Even more fundamentally, it assumes that competences exist in a detached, abstract state. As Wittgenstein[23] said: 'A smiling mouth smiles only in a human face.' The idea that managers can learn, say, 'communication skills' separated from the context in which they communicate is out of keeping with ideas about developing learning businesses.

Day,[24] an advocate of generic competence lists, chose to exemplify the approach by reference to 'oral communication'. His first example of an 'element of competence' was 'communicating clearly to others (groups)'. The assumption here is that we can test a person in this competence and that the test will demonstrate a universal competence applicable to groups of managers or shop-floor workers (or anyone) in *any* organization *anywhere* in the world. He quotes three 'performance criteria' for this element, one of which is 'Delivers the communications continuously, with no major hesitation'.

The first problem with this is that many successful CEOs that I have studied would fail this test. They can be brilliant one to one or in writing, but tend to ramble or lack coherence in groups. They certainly make 'hesitations'. Yet they are great communicators in the context in which they operate. They use elegant symbolism and rich metaphors in focusing on the strategic needs of their businesses. One example would be Sir Colin Marshall, chairman of British Airways.

One suggestion about great leaders is that (a) they emerge in relation to the needs of the time (like Winston Churchill, who was a failure in peacetime but a success in war) and (b) they play their strengths to the full while being incompetent at a whole range of managerial activities (Eisner at Walt Disney fits this characteristic, as do many other CEOs). Often leaders work in pairs (for example, Bill Hewlett and Dave Packard or, in football management, Alex Ferguson and Brian Kidd at Manchester United). Each brings their own contribution to the organization.

## 8. Not owned

Lists produced by national bodies or by headquarters' HR people are usually not owned by managers down the line/out in the field. The more complex the lists, the less likely are managers to understand them or to accept them.

At one conference a speaker asked the audience how many people had rented or hired a car. Most hands went up. Then he asked how many had washed such a car. One hand went up (out of an audience of hundreds). As he said: 'What's the reason for the difference? Ownership. If you don't own it, why take care of it?' I will focus, in Chapter 6, on ways of helping managers to *own* their learning.

## 9. Professional/functional differences

Generic, standardized lists of competences do not recognize differences that many managers feel are important. While it is easy to agree that breaking down departmental and functional barriers is important, enforced generalized competence lists are usually not the best way to do it. In a learning business you start where the learner is: you recognize professional values and skills in the engineer and the accountant and help them to broaden these skills to develop the capability to work in the wider interests of the organization. This encourages ownership of learning, and develops learning agendas in the language of the people involved. Imposed centralized lists are usually in the language of bureaucracy and do not generate enthusiasm in professionals.

## 10. Diversity

Organizations are becoming more diverse. In some cases equal opportunity legislation is forcing businesses to allow women and black people into the ranks of management. In other cases enlightened top managements are seeing the need to broaden recruitment and promotion strategies. It is clearly inappropriate to assume that these new managers have to fit the requirements to be like white, able-bodied, heterosexual, middle-class males. But competence lists tend, implicitly or explicitly, to reflect the assumptions and norms of this previously privileged group both in style (white, male, bureaucratic language) and content.

Capability is about people being themselves and being 'capable' in terms of their roots as black people, disabled people, and so on. A learning business needs to welcome this diversity as providing increased opportunities for people to learn from each other – white from black and black from white; men from women and women from men.

## 11. Systems thinking/Chaos Theory

Senge, from a systemic perspective, and Stacey, from a Chaos Theory perspective, show that addressing individual competences is unhelpful.[25] A systemic view shows that organizational performance is best understood by recognizing a mass of interacting factors, none of which can be viewed on its own as an isolatable reason why an organization is as it is. Therefore, to suggest that the development of more competent managers will *automatically* improve business performance is a fallacious assertion. A capability focus needs to be located in context. A person's development needs to respond to systemic features.

## 12. Epitaph

My local newspaper has features every week on famous people. They are asked a series of questions and the answers are published. The last question they are asked is what they would want as an epitaph. I have seen no one suggest that 'He or she was competent' would be desirable. And when I have tested this epitaph idea at conferences or in groups, I have found no one who wants to be labelled 'competent' as a farewell image. When asked why they would not want it they say:

- it smacks of mediocrity
- it sounds as though you're barely acceptable
- it's boring.

Capability on its own also does not turn people on: so in the remainder of this part of the book I shall indicate some concepts that do get people's attention, starting with 'Wisdom'.

## Wisdom

I was once consulting with a public sector organization and I happened to hear of an incident that had just occurred. The director of one of the departments in which I was consulting received a complaint from an old lady living on her own. The previous Friday, a group of workmen from this organization had been working nearby and had become a bit frisky at the end of the week. The old lady had an apple tree at the front of her house, and the men had decided to climb it and steal some of her apples. She wrote to complain not just about the apples, but, as a lonely old lady, she had felt disturbed at these boisterous men invading her property. It had upset her.

The director called the men into his office and showed them the letter. They realized that what they had done was not sensible and expected disciplinary action. The director suggested instead that if they tried to put matters right he would not formally discipline them. They agreed. He suggested that they buy the old lady a box of chocolates, take it to her and apologize – which they did. The following week the director received a glowing letter from the old lady saying how kind the men had been, and that she now realized that their high spirits had got out of hand. The men also thanked the director, saying that they had now formed a friendship with the old lady and would call on her when they were in her neighbourhood.

Clearly the director had done a good job. But it goes beyond 'capability'. He had to be *capable* of understanding the problem and communicating with the men. But that alone would not necessarily lead to the *wise* course of action he chose. Capability provides a basis for action – it is 'doing' oriented. Wisdom is more 'being' oriented and is associated with knowing what to do via a reflective/introspective process. Capability without wisdom can lead to unwise action. There is a Taoist saying that

> if one is smart and swift without wisdom, one is as though riding on a fast mount but not knowing which way to go. Even if one has talent and ability, if one uses them improperly and handles them inappropriately, they can only assist falsehood and dress up error. In that case it is better to have few technical skills than many.[26]

Claxton comments that:

> People are fond of quoting these days the prayer 'Lord give me the courage to change that which can be changed, the serenity to accept that which cannot be changed, and the wisdom to tell the difference'. Our dominant mythology of feelings has a place for courage, for banging one's head against a brick wall, even, but not much to say about the other two.[27]

The problem with that 'prayer' is that wisdom comes at the end of the sentence and is absorbed as the last of the three qualities. I would argue that wisdom needs to be a priority.

However, wisdom without capability can lead to inaction. It is not quite as neat as that, though, as the two concepts overlap, but when put together they can enrich understanding of what constitutes good learning.

One way of conceiving of learning is that capability may come before the wise use of capability. Keeney[28] quotes the example of the Samurai swordsman who spends an enormous amount of time and energy learning skills and techniques. 'After much rigorous training, the pupil is instructed to go meditate on the mountains. When he forgets all that he has learned, he can return and *be* the sword.' Now I do not actually think that 'forgets' should be interpreted in a Western mode. We might more usually say that the skills are internalized so that the person acts unconsciously. This is a point that Bateson[29] makes. As he says, the problem in understanding exceptional artists is that the more brilliant (capable plus wise) the artists become, the *less* conscious they are about how they produce great art. So also in management. The exceptional CEOs who seem to be able to cope with overloads of information and activity and yet make wise strategic decisions cannot usually say how they do it. Of course, if asked by a researcher they will say something about what they do and how they do it, but it is probable that these answers would not tell a novice manager how to do it.

This is why a scientific attitude is necessary. Not science purely as measurement, calculation and laboratory experiments, but science as understanding and codifying. A scientific approach to management requires the wise balancing of theory and practice: the understanding of managerial practice in depth so that we can develop good theories. (In Chapter 6 I shall suggest that the process of learning wisdom needs this scientific attitude.)

If we just assume that wisdom is inborn or learned through esoteric Zen-like practices, we will not progress. We have to map out the territory to assist other explorers.

## Beyond knowledge

Not to know is bad: not to wish to know is worse. (African proverb)

The slenderest knowledge that may be obtained of the highest things is more desirable than the most certain knowledge obtained of lesser things. (St Thomas Aquinas)

Books are there to keep the knowledge in while we use our heads for something better. (Szent-Györgi)[30]

These three quotes permit us to put 'knowledge' in context. They disabuse us of the notion that the wise person is the one who knows the most. We need to backtrack on what constitutes knowledge and wisdom.

Cleveland's[31] hierarchy of

Data   →   Information   →   Knowledge   →   Wisdom

is helpful. Data is unconnected facts – for example, financial data in a book-keeper's records. Data can be analysed to produce information – for example, the accountant's financial analysis of the book-keeper's records. However, if this information is just stored somewhere and not used, it remains as information, not knowledge. Knowledge is information in use – often through the grouping of pieces of information into models. So the board that integrates financial information with marketing information, HR information, and so on will eventually *know* better what is going on in the business.

However, wisdom is related to the way we use this knowledge. Does the board make wise decisions based on this knowledge? These wise decisions must include value judgements, beliefs about the available knowledge and assumptions about aspects of the organization and/or of the world of which they have little or no knowledge. Often this activity is called 'strategic thinking', but because of this label it is assumed to be a purely cognitive, mental activity. However, wisdom includes beliefs, values and feelings as well as thoughts. Deciding what to do also demands moral choices. If we know that closing a factory in an area of high unemployment is going to create a great deal of human misery, but if we do not do it the whole organization may be put at risk (and hence create even greater misery), we have to grapple with this not just as a rational problem but as a non-rational, moral problem. We must also have the *wisdom* to recognize that the judgements we make have these dimensions.

Schumacher[32] suggests that there are four useful knowledge-gaining activities:

(a) Finding out about ourselves
(b) Finding out about others (people, animals, things, and so on)
(c) Finding out about others' views of us
(d) Finding out about our views of others.

Activity (b) tends to be the only one in our society given the label 'knowledge'. However, the wise manager needs to develop all four. In the self managed learning work to be discussed in Part Four, we have always taken the development of all four areas seriously. However, we have found academics claiming that only (b) has any status. And, worse, they have assumed that if we pay attention to self knowledge (category (a)) then we must, by definition, be paying little attention to (b). This either/or thinking has always made little sense to me – and I shall return to this issue in Chapter 5.

**Wisdom and age**  T.S. Eliot, in the *Four Quartets*, criticizes the 'wisdom of age' as a wisdom of 'dead secrets'.[33] In its place he praises the 'wisdom of humility'. Margaret Mead would have agreed. In some of her last writings she argued that in past time the young would learn from the old as the culture and its technology hardly changed from generation to generation. In the modern world this is not so. The world in which young people are growing up is vastly different from that of previous generations. It is not just that new technology makes life more complex; it requires a whole new way of thinking. Mead argued that in this kind of world adults have to learn from their children. This requires a 'wisdom of humility' – a recognition that the young IT specialist will have something to teach the middle-aged manager – and not just about hardware but about different ways of thinking. As Mead said:

> Until recently, the elders could say: 'You know, I have been young and *you* have never been old.' But today's young people can reply: 'You never have been young in the world I am young in and you never can be.'[34]

This has a whole range of implications for learning, but it especially challenges educational assumptions about passing on knowledge to the next generation. The status of this knowledge is called into question.

**Summary**  This chapter has emphasized the personalistic approach to learning, and discussed the concepts of capability and wisdom. It has also explored the use of metaphor in learning activity and has critiqued the use of competences. The next chapter considers aspects of integration.

Notes

1  See Chapter 2.

2  Chris Argyris has produced much penetrating stuff on this issue. His book with Donald Schön is a major text: Argyris, C. and Schön, D. (1974) *Theory in Practice*, San Francisco: Jossey-Bass. His 1991 paper 'Teaching smart people to learn', *Harvard Business Review* (May/June), 99–109 is also useful.

3  Ohmae, K. (1982) *The Mind of the Strategist*, London: Penguin.

4  Walzer, M. (1983) *Spheres of Justice*, Oxford: Blackwell.

5  Hofstede, G. (1980) *Cultures Consequences*, London: Sage.

6  Merton, T. (1965) *The Way of Chuang Tzu*, Boston, MA: Shambhala.

7  I deliberately use the masculine gender here: it is possible that individualism is more a male trap.

8  Squires, G. (1980) 'Individuality in higher education', *Studies in Higher Education*, **5** (2), 217–26.

9  Freire, P. (1972) *The Pedagogy of the Oppressed*, London: Penguin.

10 Hankiss, E. (1990) *East European Alternatives*, Oxford: Clarendon Press.

11 Lakoff, G. and Johnson, M. (1980) *Metaphors We Live By*, Chicago: University Press.

12 Morgan, G.M. (1980) 'Paradigms, metaphors and puzzle-solving in organization theory', *Administrative Science Quarterly*, **25**, 605–22.

13 Handy, C. (1987) *The Making of Managers*, London: NEDC/BIM/MSC.

14 Vaill, P.B. (1990) *Managing as a Performing Art*, San Francisco: Jossey-Bass.

15 Gallwey, W.T. (1974) *The Inner Game of Tennis*, New York: Random House.

16 Weyrich, K.D. (1993) 'Key issues for business schools and executive development centres: a business viewpoint', Oslo: Paper to EFMD Deans and Directors Meeting. Consider also the following quote from *The Independent on Sunday*, 6 June 1993, p. 14, in an article by Roger Trapp:

> There is plenty of scepticism among senior business people and MBA graduates over the value of what an MBA course teaches. 'I have always found that thinking about a problem is the easy bit. Implementing the strategy is the hard part,' said Alan Bowkett, head of Berisford International. 'But it was the implementation that my MBA did not teach.'
>
> A conspicuous success (he was a millionaire before he was 40), Mr Bowkett took his business degree

from the LBS in the mid-1970s but remains sceptical of the benefits. 'It gives you a terrific bag of analytical tools; it stretches you and teaches you to work under pressure. But it doesn't tell you how to handle those difficult people called colleagues and employees, and that is the most essential skill in business.'

Because it ignored the human side of business, Mr Bowkett said, the MBA tended to make graduates arrogant – as if they need not dirty their hands with the nitty-gritty of personal relationships.

17  Boyatzis, R.E. and Renio, A. (1989) 'The impact of an MBA programme on managerial abilities', *Journal of Management Development*, **8** (5), 66–77.
18  The quote is from a spin-off from the RSA – the 'Higher Education for Capability' initiative – in *Capability News*, **11** (February 1993), 1.
19  There is a huge (and growing) literature on competences. Much of it is repetitive, unanalytical or based on unevaluated cases. Some of the best sources of discussion on competences include the following: Myer, C. and Davids, K. (1992) 'Knowing and doing: tacit skill at work', *Personnel Management* (February), 45–7; Iles, P. (1992) 'Centres of excellence? Assessment and development centres, managerial competence and human resource strategies', *British Journal of Management*, **3**, 79–90; Stewart, J. and Hamlin, B. (1992) 'Competence based qualifications: the case against change', *Journal of European Industrial Training*, **16** (7), 21–32; Burgoyne, J. (1990) 'Doubts about competency', in Devine, M. (ed.) *The Photofit Manager*, London: Unwin Hyman; Holmes, L. (1990) 'Trainer competences: turning back the clock?', *Training and Development* (April), 17–20. I have also discussed these issues elsewhere: see, for example, Cunningham, I. (1987) 'Management training: patterns for the future', *Banking and Financial Training* (Autumn), 26–30.
20  Hofstede, G. (1980) *Cultures Consequences*, London: Sage; and Trompenaars, F. (1993) *Riding the Waves of Culture*, London: Economist Books.
21  Quote from Carr, I. (1984) *Miles Davis*, London: Paladin.
22  *MCI Guidelines – Certificate Level*, National Forum for Management Education and Development, London.
23  Wittgenstein, L. (1953) *Philosophical Investigations*, translated by G.E.M. Anscombe, p. 583, Oxford: Oxford University Press.
24  Day, M. (1988) 'Managerial competences and the charter initiative', *Personnel Management* (August), 30–34.
25  Senge, P.M. (1990) *The Fifth Discipline*, London: Random

House; and Stacey, R.D. (1992) *Managing Chaos*, London: Kogan Page.

26 Cleary, T. (1992) *The Book of Leadership and Strategy*, London: Shambhala, p. 73.

27 Claxton, G. (1994) *Noises from the Darkroom*, London: Aquarian, p. 194.

28 Keeney, B.P. (1979) 'Ecosystemic epistemology: an alternative paradigm for diagnosis', *Family Process*, **18** (June), 117–29.

29 Bateson, G. (1973) *Steps to an Ecology of Mind*, London: Paladin.

30 Szent-Györgi, A. (1964) 'Teaching and the expanding knowledge', *Science* (4 December), 1278.

31 Cleveland, H. (1989) *The Knowledge Executive*, New York: Dutton.

32 Schumacher, E.F. (1977) *A Guide for the Perplexed*, London: Jonathan Cape.

33 Eliot, T.S. (1944) *The Four Quartets*, London: Faber & Faber.

34 Mead, M. (1978) *Culture and Commitment*, New York: Columbia University Press, p. 63.

# 5 Holism

**Introduction**

In discussing wisdom and capability there is a tendency for many people to see these concepts as implying a largely mental/cognitive activity. I also see them as involving:

- feelings and emotions
- physical aspects
- issues of values, morals and spirituality
- social factors to do with relationships with others.

This perspective has been labelled 'holistic' and I shall try to give my view of how this concept can be applied to good learning.

As well as basing comments in this chapter on practical experience and on authors quoted, I have also drawn on research conducted on CEOs and other top managers. This research was carried out in the USA and the UK with a view to developing fundamental, cross-culturally usable concepts and models. I shall not continue to make tedious reference to the research, but there are some published papers emanating from it to which you can refer if necessary.[1]

**Feelings and emotions**

Let me first comment on 'emotional learning'. Mike Dixon, a columnist on the *Financial Times*, once commented to me that, in management, 'thinking is embedded in feeling'. This phrase struck a chord. Managers think out of an internal context of feelings and emotions: thoughts are not produced from other thoughts. We think what it is possible for us to think as a result of the other dimensions of ourselves (as mentioned above – the emotional, the physical, the spiritual and the social).

Keutzer,[2] drawing on the work of Paul MacLean and others, suggests that neurophysiological evidence supports the view that evolution of the neocortex has produced a split between the archaic (emotional) structures of the brain and the 'thinking cap' that governs rational thought. Emotion is the older partner – and, it is suggested, the more powerful.

Thus, given the inevitable conflicts between reason and emotion, the reasoning part is 'compelled to provide spurious rationalizations for the senior partner's urges and whims' (Keutzer, p. 79).[2]

Bramley,[3] from her experience as a student counsellor, argues that many students cover up emotional problems in unbalanced intellectual development. However, if we take Keutzer's hypothesis seriously, we can see that this is misguided. As Bramley comments

> When and if a student realises, on attainment of a good degree, that his intellectual ability cannot give him love and security for which he yearns, he may become very ill indeed, and certainly several suicidal young people whom I have known come into this category.

All this was, of course, well known in ancient wisdom, and in many cultures. To take one example from the Middle East:

> Your reason and your passion are the rudder and the sails of your seafaring soul. If either your sails or your rudder be broken, you can but toss and drift, or else be held at a standstill in mid-seas. (Gibran)[4]

But the lessons have not been learned in the managerial world – or they have been forgotten or driven out in the learning environments of business schools. I shall quote just one example. The *Boston Globe* of 13 October 1986 wrote up the 25-year class reunion of the Harvard Business School 1961 MBAs. While it noted that there were positive comments about Harvard's role in making participants successful, significant concerns were raised. Edwin Stanley (chairman of Stanley Investment and Management Inc.) said that 'Business School did us a disservice with a compass locked on true north.' His criticism was of a narrowly focused driving ambition for success. Amos Hostetter (chairman of Continental Cablevision) went further when he claimed that his personal life had been 'subliminated' to business success. 'I was being a coward and afraid of intimacy,' he commented. One of the wives present criticized those who were raising these concerns. She said, 'I feel sorry for you guys. You shouldn't expect Harvard to teach you how to be human in your professional lives.'

That response was undoubtedly unfair. Business schools claim to equip people for managerial roles and if they pretend that personal feelings and values have no place, or if they force the sublimination of these in a pseudo-rational analytical atmosphere, then they do deserve to be criticized.

La Bier's clinical research on young managers[5] produced clear evidence of this problem. He found that there were managers who superficially were climbing the corporate ladder with apparently consummate skill and who behaved in ways that were totally 'normal'. However, from an in-depth clinical study he found that they were, to use his words, 'quite sick'. He described them as 'dominated by irrational passions of power lust, conquest, grandiosity and destructiveness or, conversely, by cravings for subjugation and humiliation'.

On the other hand, he found another group who seemed to display some neurotic symptoms but were psychologically normal. These he saw as growing up through learning about and struggling with the difficulties of corporate life. This could be painful, and they sometimes showed it (for example, through anxiety feelings or sleepless nights). The problem – to which William Temple alluded earlier this century – is that we are taught to think together and feel separately, whereas we need to think separately and feel together. That is the mark of good collaborative practice, such as teamwork.

Evans and Bartolomé[6] discuss these issues, drawing on writers such as Vaillant and Schein. They agree with the latter that 'the distinguishing characteristic of a top level executive is not his skill or ability but his emotional competence'. They show how, for instance, a successful manager may have to do an unpleasant task such as firing someone. They may feel bad about it, but will nevertheless confront it and do it. In other words, they experience negative feelings, but they deal with them appropriately.

**Metafeeling** The term I use to elucidate this emotional sophistication is *metafeeling*; that is, the emotionally mature person may feel bad but will feel OK about feeling bad. He or she knows that life has its ups and downs, and accepts it. The mature person experiences crises, but works them through.

Metafeeling, then, is about how we feel about how we feel. People go to sad films, cry a lot and say how much they enjoyed it. They feel good about feeling sad. However, a person could experience some difficulty in life (for example, loss of job), feel sad about it (reasonably), then feel bad about feeling sad. This can lead to a downward spiral of depression.

Some Buddhist monks have a routine each morning of thinking of all the problems they and others have or could have, then laughing out loud about them. They recognize problems and the negative feelings around them. They are not covered up or pretended away, but are put into perspective. (If you have to address a problem, try the Buddhist technique. If you are driving to a tricky meeting and worrying about it, recognize the worries, then laugh out loud about them. You might be pleasantly surprised at the result!)

Bio-rhythm evidence suggests that we go through cycles with ups and downs. It is suggested that we inevitably have emotional highs and lows, irrespective of what is going on in the world around us. While I am unsure of the wilder claims about bio-rhythms, it seems undeniable that people do experience patterns of internal change, for example hormonal, which have an effect on our emotional states. If we accept this, then we can metafeel OK – we can know that we will not be on top form every day of our lives and that these variations are not to be blamed on anyone – least of all ourselves.

## Connected-ness

One of the important aspects of good learning seems to relate to *connecting*. This includes *internal connecting* which integrates

- thinking
- feeling
- physical (body)
- believing/valuing (including spiritual beliefs).

These internal processes need to come together. Holistic learning is not about developing each aspect sequentially. When we learn, in the best sense, we have *feelings* about what we *think* and we integrate these in our *value/belief* systems. A useful concept in explaining this connection is *centredness*. We also engage in *external connecting* – that is, we interact with the world around us. *Grounding* is the concept I shall use to explore this (see Table 5.1).

*Table 5.1   Connecting*

| Process | Internal connecting | External connecting |
| --- | --- | --- |
| Links/integrates | Mind<br>Body<br>Feelings<br>Values/beliefs | Self to world and world to self |
| Way to achieve it | Centre | Ground |

I'll take the two concepts of centring and grounding in turn. They both came from Eastern thinking and are most visibly used in martial arts training, but are best seen as 'learning for life' in its broadest sense.

## Centring

In some approaches to learning developed in China and Japan (such as Tai Ji and Aikido), the concept of the Centre is important. It can be viewed as the centre of a single person, as the centre of gravity around which the body revolves (not literally!). It can also be seen that a person's Centre is the centre of the universe from that individual's point of view. It is the place from which to connect to others (people, things, animals, and so on); therefore it has an ecological sense. The Centre is the harmonizing focus of energy fields and patterns of relationships.

This can all sound pretty flaky, esoteric stuff if the language and way of thinking is new. But it is highly practical. There is a demonstrable difference between centred and uncentred people. Let me elaborate some features of centredness.

## Harmony

'Harmony is an attunement of opposites, a unification of many, a reconciliation of dissentients' said Theon of Smyrna. Harmony is not, in music, unison. It is the aesthetic 'centring' of difference (different voices, different instruments). We each have these differences within us. Some psychologists and psychotherapists refer to our different parts as 'subpersonalities'. Berne,[7] in developing Transactional Analysis, used the idea of 'ego states' which he labelled 'Parent', 'Adult' and 'Child'. Irrespective of their theoretical base, there is much agreement among psychotherapists that they are in the business of helping a person integrate or harmonize or come to terms with these differences.

In terms of developing a holistic sense, the harmonizing required here is of head, heart and guts. Particularly as applied to centred managers, we are thinking of the person who

- demonstrates harmonized energy;
- shows congruence and coherence in integrating theory and practice (in doing this, the person would bring together 'theory-in-use' and 'espoused theory', as Argyris and Schön[8] suggest);
- is able to work with difference and ambiguity, and has the self awareness to do this;
- 'listens to the inner voice' – which is a term Bennis[9] uses about highly effective leaders (the influence on Bennis is from Ralph Waldo Emerson's essay 'Self Reliance'); the

inner voice, if it is to be heard and believed, comes from
the Centre;

● is able to be inside and outside at the same time –
(Postman and Weingartner[10] call this 'the anthropological
perspective', meaning someone who can understand the
rituals, norms and culture of the group or organization –
the insider perspective – and is able to stand outside,
examine them and operate out of the inner voice);

● has personal theories and meanings which may not
conform to the textbook (see McLean et al.[11]).

**Balance**   Centred managers may not always feel 'in balance', but they
are aware of the value of balance. They recognize polarities
and dualities and address them as such. However, we can
get inappropriate balance as in the suggestion that the
balanced middle manager has a chip on both shoulders!
Without a centred way of operating, and attention to some
of the factors above, balance on its own is insufficient.

I shall spin through some polarities that are relevant here,
but they are not exhaustive of all the possibilities.[12]

### DOING – BEING

Centred managers are aware of what they *do* and who they
*are*. The verb 'to be' is often used in their language (for
example, 'I am . . .').[13] This balance is a mirror of the
capability/wisdom balance since the former is associated
with doing, the latter with being. (Like most of the issues in
this part, I shall show in the next how a self managed
learning approach can develop this balance.)

A related polarity is

### PROACTIVE – REACTIVE

Proactivity is usually lauded as being better than reactivity,
but it is clear from my research that this criticism is of the
wrong kind of reactivity. Wise reactivity is at the heart of
the best customer care practices – flexible, thoughtful,
caring response to customer requests and demands.
Proactive organizations, which push their technology on to
the market with little reactive wisdom in their responses to
the market, tend to suffer the consequences eventually.

Another related balance is

### EXTROVERT – INTROVERT

This factor focuses on the individual personality. The
common assumption is of a linear one-dimensional scale as
in Figure 5.1(a).

(a) One-dimensional spectrum

|———————————————————————————————————|
Extrovert                                                          Introvert

The usual psychometric tests place a person at a point on this scale

(b) Two-dimensional

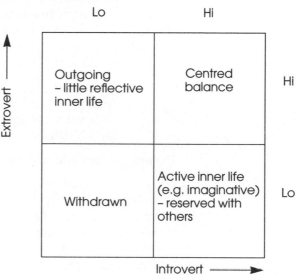

*Figure 5.1   Extrovert–introvert mapping*

However, as shown in Figure 5.1(b), there is an alternative two-dimensional mapping. While such a mapping helps to challenge unidimensionality, it is not a truth. The harmonizing of extrovert and introvert aspects of the person is complex. Another mapping might be a double helix (comparable to DNA) with introvert and extrovert characteristics interweaving in three dimensions.

Taoists use instead the polarity

YIN – YANG

which is often translated as yin (feminine) and yang (masculine), but the concepts are looser and more sophisticated.[12] They can, for instance, be seen as subsuming proactivity (in yang) and reactivity (in yin). Taoists emphasize the complementarity and interpenetration of these apparent opposites. The Taoist principle of mutuality suggests that it is not possible to have one pole without the other. The analogies are that there is no night without day, no light without dark and no valley without hills.

**Learning process**

In the above I have outlined some outcomes of 'good learning'. Learning to be centred provides a basis for effective managing *and* effective learning. It is therefore also part of the *process* of learning. Fiol and Lebas[14] suggest that there is a range of balanced outcomes necessary from a learning programme and that the *process* of the programme is the significant factor in bringing about change. They researched a senior management programme in a French bank, studying participants before, during and after the programme. They interviewed in depth all participants before the programme to identify each person's profile on a series of polarities. These included:

| | |
|---|---|
| Short term | – Long term |
| Abstract | – Concrete |
| Backward looking | – Forward looking |
| Individualistic | – Collectivist |

The process they adopted was:

1 Connect with the person's strong area. Thus an auditor might typically be strong on backward looking (as his or her job role focused on past records) but weak on forward looking. Or a strategic planner would be strong on forward looking (as his or her job role focused on the future) but weak on backward looking. This connection to the person provided a base for the next stage.
2 Help the person to balance; create opportunities to redress their weaker side.
3 Help the person to develop both sides synchronously.

Fiol and Lebas focused on the *process* of the learning programme as a way of developing this balanced progress. Individuals were not taught the weak side, for instance. They undertook activities which encouraged this development. I shall indicate some of these activities in Chapter 6.

The Fiol and Lebas approach makes a link back to some earlier themes, for example the balance of Dynamic and Systematic. Figure 5.2 shows how this can be translated into a map of learning approaches. The suggestion is that competence-based learning is too narrowly Systematic whereas approaches which emphasize only self/personal development may be too overbalanced towards Dynamic. In Chapter 6 I shall suggest that self managed learning provides an optimum balance.

**Theory/practice**

This is a classic polarity which often surfaces in discussions about management. Business schools justify an overweening interest in theory by quoting aphorisms such as 'There's nothing so practical as a good theory.' In their

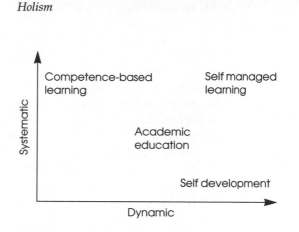

***Figure 5.2***   *Learning approaches*

turn managers attack academics. Two 'question and answer' pieces indicate this.

1  *Question:* If you push the Professor of Marketing and the Professor of Finance off the roof of the University, which one hits the ground first?
   *Answer:* Who cares?
2  *Question:* Why are academics buried 30 feet under the ground?
   *Answer:* Because deep down they're OK.

One cause of these divides is indicated in Table 5.2.

***Table 5.2***   *Theory and practice*

| Theory | Practice |
| --- | --- |
| Generalization | Experience, wisdom |
| Classroom | Job |
| Solution | Problem |
| ● Specialization | ● Person |
| ● Subject | ● Pattern |
| ● System | ● Process |

The dichotomy in Table 5.2 postulates two 'worlds'. The first is a world of theory which tends to be concerned with teaching generalizations about management in a classroom. Such teaching gives managers *solutions* to apply to their problems. They tend to be taught *specializations* (HR, marketing), *subjects* (economics, sociology) and *systems* (IT, OR). This 'S' world can also include precise *skills*, and often particular *structures*.

The second world is one of practice, where managers learn most of what they need to learn (research suggests 80–90 per cent of the abilities of successful managers have come from this world).[15] Managers learn by experience and from received wisdom (bosses, mentors, and so on). The learning is job based and is often a response to live *problems*. For example, if a new IT system is installed, managers have a problem if they do not know how to use it. So they learn. Such learning is very *people* oriented; it is often about changing *patterns* of work and learning new *processes*. The 'P' world is readily recognizable by managers.

There are two difficulties with these two worlds. First, there is the 'S to P' issue. This is where managers are taught solutions and then have to find appropriate problems or people to use them on. Or, even worse, they distort the problems to fit the available solutions.

As an example, I was trained initially as a chemist. At one time I was offered a job as a research chemist in a pharmaceutical company. If I had taken that post, I might have been presented with the problem of alleviating or even curing a particular mental illness (say, depression). The solution I was trained to provide was a chemical one. Presented with such a problem the *only* solution I would conceive would be a new drug. My training had convinced me to look for chemical solutions to such problems. Some years after leaving the world of research chemistry I became involved in the field of psychotherapy. Here, presented with problems of mental illness, the therapist will commonly talk to the patient/client. They will look for solutions to the problem within the confines of the particular theoretical framework in which they have been trained. What the therapist will not usually do is search for a chemical solution to the problem, just as the average chemist would not think of refusing to search for a new drug and suggesting psychotherapy instead. Mental illness presents major problems in Western countries. It is arguable that developing apt solutions to these problems is hampered by the inability of the various professions involved to talk to each other (and this problem seems to worsen as the subject boundaries are strengthened through increasing specialization).

This issue affects the managerial world quite broadly, and in training leads to difficulties such as 'the transfer of training' problem (a trainer euphemism for 'we taught them things that are no use in their work and therefore they don't apply them').

A different issue from the 'S to P' syndrome is 'P' only. This is where managers say 'I've learned all I need from experience. I don't need to explore new ideas being promoted by a bunch of ivory tower academics.' The difficulty with this approach is that experience is all about the past. If, as we assume, the future is not going to be like the past, this makes experience-only learning very limited.

As Fiedler[16] has shown in his research, highly experienced managers/leaders function well in situations that require little or no learning. These especially include high-job-stress situations such as fire-fighting. Someone leading a group of fire-fighters will draw on experience very heavily. They will not, while fighting a fire, stop to think about learning issues. They work to well-rehearsed grooves, and stopping to think could be a dangerous activity. On the other hand, Fiedler's (and others') evidence suggests that in the low-job-stress world of the average corporation, intellectual and creative ability is more likely to predict good leadership performance than experience. Note that I say that the average corporation has low 'job stress', not necessarily low 'interpersonal stress' – that is, managers may not get on with each other (hence producing interpersonal stress) but their jobs are not inherently stressful (for example dangerous, as in fire-fighting).

The two dangers I have identified, namely 'S to P' and 'P' only, need addressing. The answer seems to be 'P to S', that is, going from *problems* to *solutions*, or from *people* to *systems*, and so on. The point is that experience cannot be the only teacher. New ways of doing things are needed. There is a value in the expert, the professional, the academic. But each should be more in a role of responsiveness to the needs of people, problems, patterns and processes than is often in evidence. This example shows the need for balance to be driven more from one direction. That, however, is not to deny the need for balance. And sometimes the back-room boffin will offer a solution to a problem that no one knew existed (or which was downplayed).

## Grounding

I have emphasized so far the idea of centring, and I have suggested the importance of internal balance and harmony. However, this is not enough. For instance, I quoted Bennis on 'listening to the inner voice'. But suppose the inner voice is coming from some disconnected, crazy place? At worst it could be a schizophrenic delusion.

Also, centred managers can be lively, creative entrepreneurs, but without connection to the wider society they may go off at tangents. The managers who are centred *and* grounded have a sense of these wider connections. They are the people who take environmental and ecological issues seriously. They do not just see their roles as complying with the law or avoiding bad publicity if they pollute rivers. They see themselves as integrally involved in the planet and all life upon it.

Grounding can be grounding in

- *spiritual and religious beliefs* which provide a well-worked-out faith
- *professional values* – a sense of belonging to something bigger than the organization. (As one civil engineer in a public organization said to me: 'If my employers were to ask me to build something I thought might be unsafe or unwise, I'd refuse because my professional values override my loyalty to my employer.')
- *family and community* – a feeling of belonging and of intimate connection to others.

Grounding connects the inner to the outer worlds (and vice versa). It provides a solid base from which the manager can operate. Grounded managers are not pushovers. This is literally true. I often demonstrate this in groups by using Ki Aikido techniques to show how if people physically ground themselves they literally cannot be pushed over. If, on the other hand, they are not physically grounded, they can be knocked sideways with a moderate push on the shoulders. People in organizations often intuitively recognize these differences. They recognize who's a lightweight and therefore easy to roll over in a conflict – and they recognize who not to take on in a fight.

Centring and grounding need to be brought together. Grounding without centring can lead to inertia and lack of change: centring without grounding can lead to burn-out.

## Morality and ethics

Rushworth Kidder[17] was the first Western journalist to visit the Chernobyl nuclear power plant after the accident there. He discovered that the accident had occurred because two engineers conducted an unauthorized experiment on reactor number four. In order to do this they had to override *six* separate computer-driven alarm systems. Now these engineers were highly competent, highly able men. The accident did not occur because of human error, in the sense of someone making an unknown mistake.

As Kidder commented, the accident was 'not a question of technology. It's a matter of ethics.' By this he meant that he saw the engineers' actions as requiring 'an ethical override'.

The question I have from this is: what was missing in their development and learning that left out ethics (or at least this kind of ethical issue)? Another incident points to this same problem. Richard Grabowski was, by all accounts, a brilliant aerospace engineering student. He was offered jobs with two prestigious companies, both of which would have involved designing weapons systems. On 16 October 1985, while considering these job offers, he committed suicide. His suicide note read:

> If I were to live out my potential, I would only destroy life ... I have such unbounded respect for the practical application of physical ideas that I would go so far as to murder humans ... I am incapable of love. I am incapable of compassion. I can only respect rational, physical ideas. It is for this reason that I must die. If I were to continue living, I would only prolong my death. I cannot 'live' by any sense of my imagination producing weapons. (Quoted in Skolimowski[18])

That is pretty terrifying stuff. What, again, was there in this person's learning and development that created this awful end for him? We can guess that examination of morality and ethics – and the struggles we need to make with moral and ethical choices – was missing. But in an era where old certainties no longer exist, where post-modern views of knowledge encourage a nihilistic relativism, new bases for action are necessary. This points to a moral basis for managerial activity – and therefore the need to learn to make moral choices.

I do not want to preach a particular moral position. That discussion, to do it full justice, belongs in another book. My point is about learning. It is possible to argue that rather than seeing ethics as an interesting option in the business school curriculum, we need to *start* managerial learning on a base of examining issues of morality, ethics, values and social responsibility. The decision of what is right and good for a manager to learn must start from rightness and goodness being treated as moral questions.

There is much debate at present about what a good company is, or should be. Many, myself included, would say that the 'bottom line' is insufficient justification for the existence of a company or for measuring its success (goodness). Struggles with moral dilemmas, such as the interplay between the need for profit, the needs of employees, and the needs of the planet, are at the heart of the strategic learning that is needed in business. And moral development is

(a) a learning issue, and
(b) learnable.

Indeed, in Iris Murdoch's statement that 'learning is moral progress'[19] we have a clue to how to proceed. She points out that good learning develops wisdom and subtler visions, and diminishes crass egoism. This kind of learning does not come from didactic preaching; it comes from individuals working openly with colleagues in exploration of moral dilemmas. Haste[20] suggests that moral development comes from two factors:

> First, a caring community of which the individual feels a valued member, where mutual respect and justice are enacted, not just preached. Second, an environment which continually encourages reflection on the wider implications – including personal responsibility – of everyone's actions.

We come back, then, to the needs of a learning business, and we see the emphasis on the autonomy of learners. This will be the starting point for Chapter 6 in Part Four.

## Summary

These two chapters have explored facets of 'good learning', largely through the discussion of key concepts. While it has overlapped with the wider field of what makes a good manager, I have tried to keep the analysis within bounds. Hence there is much more that could be said about issues only alluded to here.

## Notes

1  My colleague Graham Dawes contributed to the research in the USA. One short paper which provided a background piece is: Cunningham, I. (1988) 'Patterns of managing for the future', *Industrial Management and Data Systems* (Jan./Feb.), 18–22.

2  Keutzer, C.S. (1982) 'Physics and consciousness', *Journal of Humanistic Psychology*, **22**, 3 (Spring), 74–90 (esp. p. 79). The popularity of Daniel Goleman's summary of research in this field is evidence of a growing awareness of these issues. He makes a similar case to Keutzer, for example when he says that 'The emotional faculty guides our moment-to-moment decisions' (p. 28 in Goleman, D. (1995) *Emotional Intelligence*, New York: Bantam).

3  Bramley, W. (1977) *Personal Tutoring in Higher Education*, Guildford, Surrey: Society for Research into Higher Education, p. 16.

4  Gibran, K. (1972) *The Prophet*, London: Heinemann.

5  La Bier, D. (1986) 'Madness stalks the ladder climbers', *Fortune* (1 September), 61, 64.

6  Evans, P. and Bartolomé, F. (1980) *Must Success Cost So Much?*, London: Grant McIntyre, p. 155. See also: Schein, E.H. (1978) *Career Dynamics*, Reading, MA: Addison-

Wesley; and Vaillant, G.E. (1977) *Adaptation to Life*, Boston: Little, Brown.

7 Eric Berne wrote a number of books. The most interesting in this context are probably: *Games People Play*, London: Penguin (1964); and *What Do You Say After You Say Hello?*, London: André Deutsch (1974).

8 Argyris, C. and Schön, D. (1974) *Theory in Practice*, San Francisco: Jossey-Bass.

9 Bennis, W.G. (1989) *On Becoming a Leader*, Reading, MA: Addison-Wesley, p. 34.

10 Postman, N. and Weingartner, C. (1969) *Teaching as a Subversive Activity*, London: Penguin, p. 17.

11 McLean, A.J., Sims, D.B.P., Mangham, I.L. and Tuffield, D. (1982) *Organization Development in Transition*, Chichester: Wiley.

12 I went into some detail on these issues in Cunningham, I. (1984) *Teaching Styles in Learner Centred Management Development Programmes*, PhD Thesis, University of Lancaster.

13 I have analysed language issues in Cunningham, I. (1992) 'The impact of who leaders are and what they do', in Clark, K.E., Clark, M.B. and Campbell, D.P. (eds) *Impact of Leadership*, Greensboro, NC: CCL. This chapter also analyses 'doing/being' matters.

14 Fiol, M. and Lebas, M. (1992) 'A conceptual model of management leading to the development of a professional management learning tool', Paper to EFMD workshop *How Managers Learn*, Tampere, Finland (October/November).

15 Our own research confirms this. A good analysis of this issue, with references to research, is Burgoyne, J. and Reynolds, M. (1997) *Management Learning: Integrating Perspectives in Theory and Practice*, London: Sage.

16 Fiedler, F.E. (1992) 'The role and meaning of leadership experience', in Clark, K.E., Clark, M.B. and Campbell, D.P. (eds) *Impact of Leadership*, Greensboro, NC: CCL.

17 Kidder, R.M. (1992) 'Ethics: a matter of survival', *The Futurist* (March/April), 10–12.

18 Skolimowski, H. (1986) 'Destruction through education', *The Scientific and Medical Network Newsletter*, **31**, 1.

19 Murdoch, I. (1992) *Metaphysics as a Guide to Morals*, London: Chatto & Windus.

20 Haste, H. (1993) 'Guilt and the struggle to teach right from wrong', *Guardian Education* (March), 2–3.

# PART FOUR  Self managed learning

This part of the book moves from the general issues discussed so far into more specific ideas and approaches for learning. Self managed learning was outlined in Chapter 1 through two examples of programmes. The three chapters in this part elaborate SML principles, strategies and tactics.

There has been a considerable amount of research on self managed learning. Rather than break up the flow of these chapters with continual reference to research evidence, I have added an Appendix (Appendix I) which outlines the sources of research papers and so on.

# 6 Principles

## Introduction

This chapter builds on the previous ones. It shows how a self managed learning approach is strategic for organizations and individuals (hence exemplifying a strategic learning perspective). SML is a key part of developing learning businesses as the approach synchronizes managing and learning, so that they are not artificially separated (as in bureaucratic educational and training approaches). SML is a *process* by which people engage in 'good learning', hence showing practically how ideas covered in Part Three can be achieved. In Chapter 7 I shall show more specifically how SML designs work out, and I shall elaborate on ideas discussed in this chapter.

Much of what has been raised in the earlier chapters is lauded by other writers. Organizations are exhorted to do better by a wide range of commentators. Here, I want to suggest that we have to move beyond exhortation into practical, usable methods that achieve the ideals many espouse.

## Comments on SML programmes

Before getting into the ideas, let me give a range of quotes from people who have been on SML programmes. The quotes allude to some of the issues I shall discuss, as well as mentioning ideas from earlier chapters.

> The really important knowledge that managers need is constantly changing. So the results of knowledge-based courses – even so-called leading edge programmes – are quickly obsolete. The key thing for me is learning how to learn – and learning a way of thinking that enables me to take on and manage new knowledge as it develops.
>
> *(Philip Smart, Channel Tunnel Project Manager, Railfreight Distribution)*

> Everybody has their own learning style and the strength of this [SML] programme is that it allows me to express and expand my own ways of operating. This has been the key benefit for me.

All my learning during the programme proved immediately valuable and usable back at work. During the programme I moved into a new board level role. The programme had a great effect in changing the way I interact with my colleagues as well as helping me develop a new way of looking at the business.

As a result, the European team in which I work operates much more effectively. I am able to contribute at a strategic level and make contributions across different disciplinary areas.

I've learned all the knowledge and skills of a traditional MBA. But I've changed. I'm different. I have more wisdom.

*(Dick Wood, Director of Customer Services,*
*System Integrators Europe)*

The strength of self managed learning is that it encourages you to get up and take action to solve problems. Working in small groups helps by ensuring we push each other to get things done. The result is a programme that is much more rigorous than distance learning.

*(Paula Stewart, Company Secretary, Leica UK)*

The approach is flexible in the way it can be tailored to the participant's personal and company requirement, making it a truly individual programme. The learning contract requirement within the self managed learning format creates this unique approach. This is enhanced by operating in a learning set. These features encourage the manager to develop learning which can only be of great advantage in an increasingly complex business environment.

I believe good general management moves beyond the rational approach of business disciplines and recognizes broader interrelationships both inside and outside the company; takes longer term views; develops congruent visions for corporate aims and harnesses all interests in working towards common goals. Inherent in this is the individual manager's willingness to be open to learning, to increase self awareness and focus on personal development issues.

I believe my experience has improved my managerial ability, broadened my outlook and enriched me as an individual and in doing so has increased my overall worth and contribution to my company.

*(Paul Kraus, Personnel Manager, Yorkshire Water)*

I find meeting once a month provides a regular and convenient structure, without interruptions to my work schedule. The regular meetings are also a constant motivator to keep up with the work and preparation required to make progress.

Self managed learning has proved a highly efficient way of learning that integrates theoretical background with practice. Developing my own syllabus was a useful exercise and is the most appropriate way to learn in the middle of one's career.

*(Jörg R. Janke, Applications Localization Manager, Oracle, Germany)*

Self managed learning is a unique and powerful approach that is about solving problems in a more holistic way, rather than emphasizing narrow competences. The freedom to set one's own learning goals is marvellous, but that does not make self managed learning an easy option. Drawing up the learning contract is a challenging and rigorous process.

*(Terry Piper, Internal Management Consultant, British Gas)*

What has this [SML] course uniquely provided? The content is devised to suit my individual needs. It has forced me to confront issues that, given the option, I would have ignored. It has taught me skills in personal relationships that I would not have developed easily in any other way. It has taught me how to work effectively as a member of a team. Most important, I have discovered a method and style of study which is effective for me. Self managed learning has had a more profound effect on me than any other single learning experience.

*(Peter Maher, Deputy Head Teacher in East London)*

**Response to comments**

The kinds of things people say about SML programmes exemplify some of the points made in the previous chapters. They comment on being able to do more – not just in a disjointed way, but linked to their own and their organization's needs. They show developed wisdom. They rarely use the word 'wisdom', but they do show that they are able to operate more wisely. Comments also show the balanced development necessary (for example between theory and practice) and people often talk in more holistic terms. More important, probably, than participants' words are (a) their actions and (b) the response of others around them (colleagues, managers, friends, and so on).

An example of the evaluation by an organization of SML is that by the BBC. Their senior personnel staff found the following benefits from an SML programme for new personnel managers:

- 'They learned how to learn.'
- 'They ask more questions' (than previous trainee personnel managers).
- 'They are more tolerant of ambiguity.'
- 'They are able to get their *own* jobs.'
- 'They are more open and accountable.'
- 'They emerged more self assured, more enterprising.'
- 'The culture we are trying to create is that it is as important to help others succeed as it is to succeed yourself. SML helped us to put this across in a relevant way.'
- 'The SML approach enabled the BBC to reduce the length of the personnel training scheme from two years to one – while increasing its effectiveness.'

Achieving these results is not easy. Merely to tell people to shape up and take charge of their own learning is ineffective. Even when one has a sophisticated, well-designed SML programme, it is not a smooth, comfortable process assisting people's learning. And, given the objective of linking learning to organizational strategies and culture, programmes can be complex to operate.

This chapter makes the case for autonomy, personal responsibility and self control. It continues with pointers on how SML has evolved in order to meet these requirements. There is then some discussion of aspects of SML designs before moving into more concrete, specific issues. The next chapter goes into more detail on precise practical applications.

## Autonomy, responsibility, self control, choice

Although these concepts are linked, I shall first consider responsibility.

### Responsibility

Sheila Corrall,[1] director of Library and Information Services at Aston University, wrote about her experiences on two SML programmes. She included in her comments the following:

> Sceptics may say this 'DIY' approach is simply a management cop-out! I am convinced that this approach genuinely offers a realistic way forward, a means of empowering staff to achieve their full

potential. Individuals must be prepared to take responsibility for their own development; they are the people best placed to analyse and assess their past experience, and to define their own priorities and future career goals. Self-development starts with self-awareness and requires sufficient self-knowledge to diagnose what has to be developed, but once this diagnostic work has begun – and it must be seen as a continuous process – the individual will be in a much better position to identify and take advantage of development opportunities as they arise.

The key issue in Corrall's piece is that of *'responsibility for'*. The SML position is that the learners must be responsible *for* their own learning. However, others have a responsibility *to* the learner. 'Others' might include:

- *Colleagues* who may accept responsibility *to* the learner to be supportive and understanding in their struggles to learn.
- *Leaders* who may accept responsibility *to* people who report to them to allow them to learn, to coach them as needed, to facilitate access to learning resources, and so on.
- *Professionals* (HR staff, trainers, teachers, and the like) who accept their responsibility *to* learners to work with integrity, to provide access to resources, to respond to requests for help, and so on.

Hence there can emerge a collective responsibility *to* people in support of learning. But the person always retains responsibility *for* their own learning. A learning business cannot operate under any other conditions. This has important ramifications for individual learners and for the organization. Some of these will be discussed in this chapter, and later chapters cover the role of professionals and the need for good contexts for learning.

**Self control**    Under this heading I shall also consider the linked concepts

- self influence
- sel regulation
- self monitoring
- self reliance

and the overarching idea of

- self management (that is, I take self management to include all the above).

The basic argument, from much research literature, from experience and from matters of principle, supports the centrality of these issues.

Goodwin[2] reviews research which suggests that 'changes which are self attributed are maintained to a greater degree than those which are believed to be due to external causes'. He argues that improvement through successful self reliance is more easily renewable.

Manz[3] reviews an impressive array of literature as well as drawing on his own work. He counterposes assumptions of external control through performance standards, appraisals, reward systems, and so on with self control processes. He shows that individuals use their internal self control systems to self evaluate, to set personal performance standards and to self reward. As he says, 'organizations provide organizational control systems that influence people, but these systems do not access individual action directly. Rather the impact of organizational control mechanisms is determined by the way they influence . . . the self control systems within organization members' (p. 586). He does not deny that external factors influence people, but he does reach the conclusion that 'the self-influence system is the ultimate system of control' (p. 586).

This perspective on self control must be a facet of a learning business. We know, as the saying goes, that you can take a horse to water but you cannot make it drink. Individuals often need help in identifying what is needed to be learned and how to learn it. But they must control their own learning. This flies in the face of standard assumptions about education and training which erroneously assume that external controls are the main determinant of learning. Hence standardized courses assume that what is taught equals what is learned. The reliance on a predefined curriculum assumes that learners will be externally controlled and that their internal self control systems are relatively unimportant.

## Autonomy

The issue of controls links to the case for personal autonomy. The self control case rests more on practical and behavioural grounds, whereas the case for autonomy is a matter of fundamental principle. However, they come together in the self managed learning approach.

When I say that fundamental principles are involved here, I am drawing on the views of educational philosophers who suggest that autonomy is *the* underpinning value in learning, that is, learning to be autonomous is the most valued outcome of learning activity. David Aspin[4] included within personal autonomy

● critical thinking
● being a master of one's own situation

- making informed judgements
- planning courses of action for oneself.

His views were expressed in a conference group which included two other eminent professors of educational philosophy. They concurred with his formulation. As a member of this same group I suggested that if this was an outcome, the *process* of learning should mirror it, since we know that there is the need to integrate means and ends. If we want to develop autonomous people, that could not come through an authoritarian process. The other people in the group (all educationalists) could not accept this. They asserted (without giving *any* basis for this assertion) that autonomy would just come about by people learning theories and ideas from teachers and academics. I confess to being unable to understand this argument. It seemed, rather, that the individuals, like so many other professionals, wished to justify their existence by irrational assertions about the importance of their role, while ignoring the incongruence of a role that was achieving the opposite of their espoused outcome.

Young people coming out of schools and universities have often maintained a level of personal autonomy through bucking the system. Many successful business makers, such as Virgin's Richard Branson, did not go to university. Companies such as British Airways have been turned round by people who did not go to university (in their case Lord King, when chairman, Sir Colin Marshall as CEO and Gordon Dunlop, who was finance director of BA).

It is clear, then, that people do develop autonomy in varying degrees, and often through self managing their careers (and the learning that has gone with it). In my own research into successful CEOs, I found that they talked a lot about learning, but it was usually learning they had initiated, and very little came from formal educational or training activity.

The issue of autonomy has, however, a wider impact than that on the person. There is the role for a learning business in providing more autonomous working in order to foster good learning. We know that lack of autonomy increases stress and other dysfunctional characteristics (see, for example, Broadbent[5]). It also inhibits learning, and makes the 'good learning' already referred to difficult, if not impossible.

People, of course, can trap themselves. They can create low autonomy for themselves as a 'security blanket'. This links to issues of responsibility. People can deny responsibility for their actions on the grounds that they were following the rules or obeying the boss. In its extreme, individuals who wish to deny responsibility for their own lives do find SML difficult.

This, then, raises an important matter of principle. Should someone who cannot manage themselves be allowed to manage others? This is a moral question. By what right should a person take the status, power, rewards and privileges that typically go with a managerial role if they cannot manage themselves? Can they morally justify managing others in these circumstances? I don't think so. Indeed, the prime basis for considering someone for promotion to a managerial or leadership role of any kind should be the capability and the desire of the person to manage their own learning.

**Choice**    Stewart[6] has suggested a framework for looking at managers' jobs. She suggests three categories:

1  *Demands*. These are the things the manager *has* to do; what absolutely *must* be done. She excludes from this 'oughts', for example what another might think the manager *ought* to do.
2  *Constraints*. These can be external or internal. They put limits on what is allowed to be done.
3  *Choices*. These are activities the manager chooses to do.

Research suggests that less successful managers see themselves as having fewer choices than a neutral observer might identify. These managers often infer from situations that there are demands or constraints which, if tested, prove to be false. But many do not test. The successful, creative, entrepreneurial-type managers tend to be the ones who see more choices. Partly, this links to beliefs about autonomy – the person who feels more autonomous will push the boundaries of the role farther; partly, it requires that individuals have good 'maps' of the 'territory' in which they operate (and I shall cover this issue later); and partly, it requires the learning business to create a culture where people are encouraged to break out of their self imposed strait-jackets.

Self managed learning encourages managers to seek more choices for action (including for learning) through providing a level of autonomy and appropriate linkages into the wider organization. It also provides choice of *processes*. For instance, managers can choose the mode of learning that suits them. This gets over the problem that people have different learning styles and different preferred modes of learning.

**Some history**    It may help here to outline the history of the development of self managed learning. SML is the integration of various ideas and methods. Some aspects are original; others not. However, we have found that this integration is more than the sum of the parts. So although I am showing the roots of SML in other approaches and ideas, it is not merely a throwing together of these approaches and ideas. I shall start with my personal experiences and then move into more general issues.

**Early experiences**

School and university were disappointing for me from an educational point of view. However, my experiences pointed to things that I saw needed changing. These included:

- *Issues of authoritarianism* – I found I learned best when I decided what I needed to learn.
- *Subject divisions* – I was intensely frustrated by the subject divisions that were for the benefit of academics but not learners. For example, I was reprimanded by my professor of physical chemistry for asking 'what is an electron?'. I found Quantum Theory exciting and challenging but also confusing. My professor said that I was asking philosophical questions and this was not allowed. I knew I was asking philosophical questions, and I felt that they should be taken seriously.
- *Disconnection from the world* – what I was being taught seemed unconnected with real problems affecting ordinary people. I had chosen to study chemistry at university because I thought it would be practical and useful. I found that, at graduation, employing organizations were going to have to show me what it was really like to do practical research and development.

I used my time at university to engage in student union activities, ending with two years as a part-time member of the National Union of Students' Executive (1966–68), and then full-time National Secretary (1968–70). The first sit-in in Britain was in 1968, so I was around during an eventful period in the student world. The focus of much of this activity was more outwardly directed. Even inside higher education institutions the effort of students was addressed to structural and power issues: student participation, and so on.

This had its place in the changes that I saw as necessary, but apart from the art colleges, few of the militant activities were addressed to fundamental issues of the nature of education. It did not seem to me that merely getting students on to committees would change what went on in the lecture theatre, and most students had little idea of an alternative to replace what we saw as a discredited educational system.

However, a few insights were creeping in. Summerhill, A.S. Neill's so-called 'free school', attracted attention, and there were outcroppings of Summerhill copies. But almost none survived, and radical alternatives in the state system were quickly squashed. In seeing why Summerhill survived (and flourished) where others failed, it was clear that the sloppy, disorganized, pseudo-egalitarianism of late-1960s hippies was ill suited to the rigours of making a school work. Neill's success was due to his clear, tough-minded leadership, his wisdom in developing appropriate structures and his capability in relating to young people. Neill was a visionary who could also make things happen. He stood his ground when the going was sticky (and when less resolute and less able people gave up).

These lessons were all important for the development of SML.

**Training**   When I started my first training role I had a chance to apply my ideals. The move to providing learning that was practical and not subject-dependent was not difficult. The training world is not bad at that. Also, the courses I was involved in were more participative in nature than my university experiences, and a lot more fun for all of us (participants and trainers). However, I was concerned about a number of factors:

- Transfer of training to the job did not go smoothly.
- Learning seemed shallow – and people slipped back.
- Participants did not have a say in course content.
- Doing more training did not seem to have much impact on organizational performance.

**Regional management centre**   In joining a regional management centre I had a chance to design longer programmes that were problem based. In the early 1970s these seemed quite radical. We designed a Diploma in Management Studies in 1972/73 which, instead of having subjects taught in the standard way, was problem based. There were thus modules on decision making, the environment of the organization, managing change, and so on. Each of these was handled in an interdisciplinary way, often with team teaching around live cases. I find it fascinating that, all these years later, some business schools are thinking of making what, for them, are radical shifts into working in this way. I would say to them that it does not go far enough.

Teachers still wanted to teach, so participants on the programme still had little say in course content. Also, the modular nature of the course still broke up what is a holistic activity (managing). The problem-based divides were just as arbitrary as subject divisions.

**Independent study**     In 1973 I joined the team that was developing the School for Independent Study at North East London Polytechnic (now the University of East London) on an 80 per cent secondment from the regional management centre. In 1974 we launched the two-year full-time Diploma of Higher Education as an independent study course (shortly followed by a degree programme). The approach was totally new in British higher education.

There were no entrance requirements beyond motivation to study and some understanding of the course. We had some students who had been expelled from school, some who had been rejected by other institutions, and some who had never passed any exams (as well as some who had). There were no course objectives; there was no syllabus; and there were no end-of-course exams. Students entering the programme were allocated a tutor group. They used this as a base for planning their programme of study. They had a 'planning period' of six weeks in which they wrote a statement of what they would do for the remainder of their two years. They split their time between specialist study in their chosen fields and group work, where they worked on projects they chose, in order to develop competences that required such collaborative activity. At the end, assessment was based on the two parts of the programme.

The great success of the School for Independent Study was that it showed that:

- people could design their own courses and set their own learning goals;
- the success rate was similar to traditional courses – despite supposedly lower entry standards;
- people grew in self confidence and wisdom – they did not just develop competences;
- it was possible to provide a structure within which individual differences were respected – and achieve high standards.

However, while independent research confirmed the above, it also showed problems. First, some students complained of isolation – not having anyone to talk to about their work. This especially applied to students who had chosen not to attend lectures or seminars, but rather to pursue a wholly individualized programme of study (apart from their group project work).[7] This linked to the problem of students making choices – they struggled because often they did not really know what they wanted to learn.

Research also showed up the tension between what was labelled:

## Structure vs Freedom[7]

This dichotomy was an interesting example of how the interplay of language and thought about these issues produced confusion. For me, there is no necessary clash between structure and freedom. What happened on the programme was that some students wanted more *structure*, more *support* mechanisms (for example, to overcome isolation). Staff interpreted this as a need for more *direction* and *control* – and some became more authoritarian as a result. Structure and direction can be relatively independent variables. Indeed, in the programme, staff who became more directive did not, in the process, provide better structures. Isolation continued, but students were now pushed more in particular directions or controlled through the assessment process.

The solution to better structures lay in lessons from action learning, which I shall mention shortly. Also, action learning addresses another weakness of independent study, namely the tendency for students to stay within the institution for their learning (and hence not tackling problems of usefulness and practical application).

**Action learning**     Shortly after taking up responsibilities in the School for Independent Study I became involved, as a consultant and as a set adviser, in action learning programmes. These programmes were like independent study in

- having no fixed curriculum;
- responding to individual learners' needs.

They differed in being

- for managers;
- more action oriented – requiring managers to work on live issues in real time;
- problem based and open ended – addressing problems which did not have a predefined solution;
- more supportive of learners through the use of 'sets' of about five learners and a set adviser (to help the set to function and to assist individual set members in their learning).

These latter positive features give clues as to how independent study programmes needed to change to be more effective. However, I also observed problems in action learning and these were subsequently confirmed in research I conducted.[8] The problems included:

- Some nominators of participants on action learning programmes were only interested in action (problem solving) and did not support learning.

- Links into organizational needs varied – at best projects carried out by participants were integrated with strategic changes in the organization; at worst they were invented projects just to provide something for the participants to do.
- Projects were often imposed on participants and proved poor vehicles for learning.
- In the absence of any pre-planned learning objectives, learning could be random, haphazard and not meshed with organizational needs.
- Participants often did interesting analyses of problems and then presented recommendations for action to, for example, their board or their manager. As there was no implementation, proper action learning did not occur.
- The idea of a 'project' could constrain the learners – they would be hemmed in by the definition of a project and were not able to explore other avenues of learning.
- While Revans and other proponents of action learning argue that Q (questioning knowledge) needs integrating with P (programmed knowledge), these two were often separate and unintegrated. So Q would be pursued in the set and P provided as an add-on in lectures, seminars and workshops. Theory and practice became disconnected again.
- Course participants usually had little or no say in the programme design. If there were workshops and seminars, these were imposed by programme organizers.
- Constituent members of a set were not the sole repositories of wisdom on issues around the projects being tackled – but often sets 'closed in' on themselves and did not seek other perspectives.

Many of these problems were overcome in the very best examples of action learning that I saw. However, it seemed that there were potentially some structural and design possibilities that could more easily overcome the downside of action learning.

**Self directed learning/person-centred approaches**

In my research on effective management developers,[9] two names were given more than any others as influences on people's professional practice: Reg Revans and Carl Rogers. Rogers was especially influential in the 1970s through his book *Freedom to Learn*.[10] Rogers provided a passionate and well-argued case for a person-centred approach to learning which respected the individual learner and removed authoritarian controls on individuals. His argument for 'facilitators of learning' rather than didactic teachers struck a chord with many, and numerous experimental programmes were established in the wake of his influence. However, like the free schools, few survived. Rogers himself acknowledged the problems in his follow-up book *Freedom to Learn for the 80s*. Allowing for these, Rogers was able to quote credible research[11] in schools which showed the following kinds of positive results from person-centred courses:

● greater gains in learning conventional subjects
● students more adept at using higher cognitive processes such as problem solving
● more positive self concept in students
● less discipline problems
● lower absence rates.

Other writers in the 1970s espoused a learner-centred approach referring to the concept of 'self directed learning'. Many management trainers and educators were convinced, in the post-1960s euphoria, of an inevitable move in this direction. Except that it did not happen. Most programmes collapsed because:

● Staff suffered burn-out in their over-zealous desire to respond to whatever learners asked for.
● Lack of structure in courses produced too much mess for traditional universities and company training departments.
● Some learners complained about not getting their needs met in these highly open-ended learning programmes; for example, sometimes the basis for any activity was simply being able to shout the loudest or make the most aggressive demands at meetings.
● Those programmes that succeeded did so because of the staff: when staff moved on, the programmes became diluted or were closed.
● The times changed. The 1980s were more materialistic, less open to experiment: humanistic ideals were submerged in instrumentalist career management (from both managers and academics).

## Experiential learning

This 'catch-all' phrase became popular in the 1970s and 1980s. Some used the ideas of David Kolb[12] and his learning cycle model as a basis for planning learning activity which drew on managers' direct experience as a way of developing generalizations for future action. Others saw experiential learning as covering project-based approaches (which again drew on live experience). Another group equated experiential learning with T-groups, encounter groups and other intensive group-based approaches. Finally, there were those who saw 'experiences' occurring in lectures and through reading books as well as from projects or T-groups. Here the notion of 'experience' is particularly linked to non-cognitive aspects (such as emotions).

Given that most now associate experiential learning with the 'learning cycle' model, I shall discuss this specifically. The advantages of this approach include:

- direct challenge to academic theory-based learning
- use of live problems for managerial learning
- encouragement of a 'practice to theory' link, that is, not a-theoretical
- ease of use – managers understand the model and usually accept it (though Kolb's instrument linked to his model is less user-friendly).

The problems with an overbalanced enthusiasm for this approach include:

- Experiences can be unhelpful in providing a basis for learning; for example, the person who learns (from experience) to hate snakes can develop a dysfunctional phobia through generalizing from one experience.
- Not only is direct experience of work problems an experience, but also reflecting on experience is an experience, theorizing about experience is an experience, and so on. It is not possible neatly to compartmentalize 'experience'. It is also a problem to know if you have had an experience if you do not have concepts and theories (maps) to help you to identify it.
- Experience is always past – we can reflect on *memories* of that past and generalize therefrom, but there are dangers in applying such generalizations to future events; for example, the world may change.
- There are a lot of things that are best *not* learned from experience; for example, the effects of putting your hand in the path of a circular saw, the effects of AIDS, and so on. *Most* learning that is of use to us is probably *not* experientially based; we rely a great deal on the experience of others.
- People operate out of deeply grooved patterns: just reflecting on and analysing these will not necessarily lead to change.
- In management much of the feedback from our actions takes a long time.
- Strategic decisions may take many years to come to fruition and before we can reflectively analyse the pros and cons of such decisions.
- Experiential learning (of this variety) is very 'first-order' oriented: second-order learning comes from reflecting on our reflections, theorizing about our theories and experimenting with our experiments. It is a meta-level process requiring a leap out of existing learning patterns.

**Self development**    Pedler[13] suggests that 'Action learning starts with the person going out into the world, whilst self-development begins with retreat from it' (p. 56). He goes on to suggest that in reality action learning and self development can come together, and that there is no need to postulate a rigid dichotomy. Hence a programme can have the label 'action learning', but move closer to an introspective mode in sets. And 'self development' groups can dwell a great deal on action issues. In this respect 'self development', as a popular idea in the 1980s, became an overarching term to cover a range of non-curriculum-based, learner-centred approaches to management development. One benefit from self development was the emphasis on the 'self'. This promoted a holistic, balanced approach to learning. However, many people came to feel that the worst kind of self development degenerated into solipsistic navel gazing disconnected from organizational life. Hence some advocates of self development have become more associated with developing ideas about learning organizations/companies.

### Holistic education/ confluent education

These terms were popular, especially in the USA, in the 1970s. Confluent means 'flowing together' and I link it with holistic education as both labels were used to cover approaches that moved beyond the cognitive. So in schools which adopted these ideas, young people addressed emotional, spiritual and physical development. At best this assisted people to acquire the kind of qualities described in the previous chapters. At worst it produced distortions of educational activity and did nothing to redress teacher authoritarianism. To be told to meditate is not fundamentally different from being told to write essays.

### Open and distance learning

These terms became popular in management development in the 1980s. I lump them together because their advantages were similar, namely:

- the development of more user-friendly materials (audio tapes, video tapes, nicely designed packages, and so on)
- the opportunity for learners to choose the time and place of learning.

Their disadvantages are similar to standard taught courses:

- pre-fixed goals and learning methods
- if there is assessment, it is unilaterally controlled by academics
- rigidity and disconnectedness from the live problems of managers
- heavy cognitive bias to learning.

### Self managed learning

In SML my colleagues and I wanted to pull together the best practices from the above approaches. Also, we did not neglect the fact that traditional universities had within them experts who could be used, though we did go with the Civil Service notion that experts should be on *tap*, not on *top*. (The role of experts ought to be to engage in dialogue with managers and to answer questions formulated by managers, not to distort the needs of managers to fit their expertise.)

In drawing together best practice I only had a way of judging 'best' because I had a vision of what learning could be and ought to be. I glimpsed examples of incredible learning in some of the approaches mentioned, but these were isolated examples or were not sustained. Therefore, the micro designs and methods that appealed did so because they contributed to a vision of a total architecture; and, in order to complete the picture, new facets had to be added.

**One manager's comparison**

In order to exemplify this issue of drawing on examples of effective learning and how we moved SML along based on these experiences, I am reproducing here one manager's comparison of his experiences of action learning and of self managed learning. The manager, Jim Chitty, works for Arun District Council and I'll leave him to tell his story.

> As a practitioner of self managed learning, I am often asked if the process is a hybrid of action learning. I always reply that, although there are some similarities, there are also many unique differences. Indeed, a recent debate with action learning colleagues led to the challenge to define those differences and write them down.
>
> However, before I begin to outline those differences, I would like to say that I do not see this piece as action learning (AL) versus self managed learning (SML), as I believe they both have important roles to play in a learning organisation, especially when redefining why mass training needs to change and become an individual's learning strategy.
>
> I have experienced both processes and, although I practise SML, I studied for my MBA at Brighton University in an action learning set. Both AL and SML challenge many of the existing educational and training systems that are still in place today, and give people real choice about how, when, where and what they learn. When in 1992 Dr Ian Cunningham, the creator of self managed learning, introduced the concept to my organisation, I had already suffered from a formal education that rejected me as a 'no hoper' and struggled painfully in adult life through a BTec CMS, CiM and DMS as the 'talk and chalk' brigade happily handed me more and more books to read whilst asking me to copy

out notes to re-write and re-read later. Now, short-term
memory is a wonderful thing and I obviously retained
enough information to pass exams; however, little (if
any) of that information stayed with me, and I doubt if I
could have re-passed those exams three months later,
let alone now.

So, how did self managed learning help me? Firstly, it
made me understand about myself, how I learned and
what I needed to do to learn. This, I believe, is the first
major difference with action learning, where the
emphasis is on action (the task in hand or a problem to
solve) rather than on the individual's learning needs,
which in AL still remain, as with other options,
accidental or random. Self managed learning is a
planned and tailored approach to the individual's
immediate and future learning needs. At this point in
time, one of life's lucky coincidences allowed my new
thought processes to be further strengthened when I
heard Tony Buzan, of mind mapping fame, put forward
his theory that, if we really believe in the life-long
learning process, then surely we must reverse the
previous emphasis of teaching the individual, en masse,
facts about other things and first teach them facts about
themselves: how they learn, think, recall, create and
solve problems.

By now, having completed my first SML experience, I
had as part of my learning contract, another major
difference from AL, to find an organisation that would
provide me with the opportunity to study for an MBA
the way I knew I needed to learn. In my ideal world,
that would have been a self managed learning MBA.
However, reality in the form of both budgets and
distance ruled out that option. Happily though, for me,
I found an action learning alternative and it worked
extremely well. There was a task – gain my MBA; and I
was in a group of my peers who challenged and
supported me as necessary. The work programme
consisted of residential workshops; management issues
that needed resolving, put forward by my organisation;
and the whole process was backed up by day long
monthly set meetings facilitated, in this case, by an
adviser/tutor. My evaluation of that experience shows
that I retained so much knowledge that I still regularly
use the various models and theories, and remember
vividly virtually every aspect of some eighteen months'
work.

So, after such a superb AL experience, why do I
continue to advocate self managed learning in most
cases? The main answer must be the learning contract

which, I believe, should be at the very centre of any people development programme. The learning contract asks five questions of each individual in the self managed learning set, consisting of between 4 and 6 people facilitated by a set adviser.

Question one asks *'where have you been?'* and is normally illustrated by a 'lifeline', which is then individually presented to the set. Action learning quite often uses this technique as well and, while both AL and SML use it for set bonding purposes, my experience has been that SML sets use the lifeline for additional thought and reflection, looking for both patterns and trends of decision or non-decision making, mistakes and successes in our lives that enable us to learn so that we may replicate the good experiences and learn to have choice and avoid repeating the mistakes of the past.

Question two asks *'where are you now?'* It is here that the use of various diagnostic methods, competence audits and preferred learning styles is explored to create a learning strategy that is right for each individual. Once achieved, this can be used on every future learning opportunity to both deepen and accelerate the learning from those experiences. It is best described as reality, a very clear picture of where you are in terms of strengths and areas where you need to obtain future strengths. Additionally, as with any journey, it is good to know where you start from and what resources you have at your disposal.

You are now ready to answer Question three, *'where do you want to get to?'* and, once written as a learning contract, the challenge and support of the set process stops this element ending up as the usual wish list or New Year's resolution, both of which seldom, if ever, happen. This element will often dovetail with the competence audit of the 'where are you now' section and highlights the areas where improvement or more resources are required in order for you to complete your journey.

Question four, *'how will you get there?'* follows on and allows your plan of action to be formulated: what resources will you need; how much time will be required; and what are the budget and policy restraints of your current organisation, assuming they have both input into the contract and are part or fully funding the cost? An interesting situation that often occurs at this point is that, having made up your mind on a course of action, limiting factors such as lack of funding often become just other issues to resolve in doing what you want, rather than giving you a reason not to do it.

Question five, *'how will you know if you have arrived?'* is the evaluation part of the process. You will demonstrate to the set where and how you have achieved your goals. Have no doubt, this is a rigorous test of what you have done and you will have either completed your learning contract or consciously changed it, justifying those changes to the set. Indeed, this whole process instills a self-discipline that is much more powerful than that of any other approach I have experienced.

The five stage process I have just described is, I believe, uniquely different because it takes you below the superficial and general level that training often stays at and is wider than a single issue or problem to complete or solve.

Of course, there is learning in those other shared experiences: 'have you tried this?'; 'when that happened to me I did this'; and, of course, 'I know what you need to do', which takes us back to teaching others facts that they need to know – or not?

Self managed learning, I believe, gives the individual time and space to understand themselves. It breeds confidence and gives focus and clarity of direction which, in turn, gives the individual real choice to carry on as they are or change and, when they change, it is because they want to, which also means it will happen, regardless of any limiting factors.

The issues that Jim Chitty raises here will be covered more fully in later chapters. My objective in reproducing Jim's piece here was to show how one manager had made a link from one experience he valued, in action learning, to the practice of self managed learning.

## Summary

Before moving on to Chapter 7 to give an overview of the total architecture of SML, I shall summarize the main aspects of what SML draws from the approaches discussed in this chapter.

1  There is no need for a predefined syllabus to a learning programme; indeed, it is constraining and unhelpful.
2  Learning should start from the needs of the learner and the organization – individual differences need to be recognized.
3  Personal autonomy is a means and an end of good learning. Means and ends need integrating.
4  Holistic ways of working are also means and ends – learners engage head, heart, guts and more in the process of good learning and the outcome is a more integrated person.
5  Learners need to play an active role in learning; passive

reception of knowledge encourages passivity in management (an undesirable outcome).

6 Learning needs structuring and supporting; it does not just happen. Liberating people from the constraints of traditionally taught courses does not necessarily produce good learning.

7 Learning in collaboration with others is crucial – again means and ends must mesh. If we want collaboration and mutual support in the organization, the learning process must mirror this.

8 Resources need to be provided to support learning – but these may not be of the traditional kind.

9 Leadership is important: organizational leaders need to model good learning, and leaders of organized learning programmes need to accept their responsibilities *to* learners (while learners retain responsibility *for* their own learning).

10 All learners are able to draw up statements of their learning needs and negotiate these with their organizations (as 'learning contracts'). This negotiation, if done well, can ensure integration of personal learning within the wider organization.

11 Learning by individuals and within organizations needs to connect to wider issues outside the organization. A developed sense of ecology demands that we feel part of the planet and become involved in what is going on in the wider world around us.

12 The results of learning need to be assessed and evaluated, but such assessments must be initiated by learners and not imposed. However, self assessment needs checking with others – again to encourage collaboration and sharing in the organization.

13 Managing and learning must be integrated; processes of learning must match processes of managing.

14 The roles of those assisting other people's learning are crucial. Helping someone to learn is not easy, and this process also needs to be learned.

The next chapter will continue the task of putting these ideals into practice.

## Notes

1 Corrall, S. (1992) 'Self managed learning: the key to professional and personal development', in Foreman, L. (ed.) *Developing Professionals in Information Work*, Circle of State Librarians, London: HMSO, p. 13.

2 Goodwin, L.R. (1981) 'Psychological self help: a five step model', *Journal of Humanistic Psychology*, **21**, 1 (Winter), 13–28 (esp. p. 24).

3 Manz, C.C. (1986) 'Self leadership: towards an expanded theory of self-influence processes in

organizations', *Academy of Management Review*, **11** (3), 585–600.

4  Aspin, D. (1983) Contribution to 'Education Challenge' Conference, Salford University (April).

5  Broadbent, D. (1987) Quoted in *Personnel Management* (February), p. 13.

6  Stewart, P. (1982) *Choices for the Manager*, London: McGraw-Hill.

7  Percy, K. and Ramsden, P. (1980) *Independent Study: Two Examples from English Higher Education*, Guildford, Surrey: Society for Research into Higher Education.

8  Cunningham, I. (1991) 'Action learning for chief executives', in Pedler, M. (ed.) *Action Learning in Practice*, 2nd edn, Aldershot, Hants: Gower.

9  Cunningham, I. (1984) *Teaching Styles in Learner Centred Management Development Programmes*, PhD Thesis, University of Lancaster.

10  Rogers, C.R. (1969) *Freedom to Learn*, Columbus, OH: Charles Merrill.
*Note:* The later (1983) edition of this book is called '*Freedom to Learn for the Eighties*'. Other details are the same as the 1969 version.

11  Aspy, D.N. and Roebuck, F.N. (1974) 'From humane ideas to humane technology and back again many times', *Education*, **95**, 2 (Winter), 163–71.

12  Kolb, D.A. and Fry, R. (1975) 'Towards an applied theory of experiential learning', in Cooper, C.L. (ed.) *Theories of Group Processes*, London: Wiley.

13  Pedler, M. (1984) 'Action learning and self development: the knight and the monk', *Management Education and Development*, **15**, 1 (Spring), 55–8.

# 7 Strategy and designs

## Introduction

In this chapter[1] I shall pick up the threads from Chapter 6, and start with a model which expands the view of SML as part of a strategic approach to learning. I shall then elaborate some of the strategic choices available. SML can be used as an umbrella strategy which allows for considerable choice beneath it. However, there are some givens and non-negotiables within the idea of SML, especially around autonomy and responsibility, as outlined in Chapter 6.

This chapter is somewhat abstract in style as I want to put over some key ideas and models. The practical applications will emerge in later chapters. Please stick with it even if it seems heavy going in places. The material here helps to provide a firm foundation for later parts of the book.

I shall be emphasizing, as elsewhere, the use of SML for managers. However, in other programmes SML has been used with non-managers. The assumption that SML is only suitable for the more senior or the more able is not supported by research. For example, Gruber and Weitman's research[2] showed no correlation between the ability of people to take responsibility for their own learning and intellectual capacity or previous education.

## A model for SML strategy

The historical analysis in the previous chapter emphasized practical issues. I would now like to return to the more strategic dimensions and integrate these with practice. I want to reiterate that self managed learning provides a strategic approach to learning. In this context strategy is for individuals and for organizations. Strategy is organized activity over the longest time horizon that the person and/or organization wishes to project. So a person may want to think long term about their career and the organization may wish to project ahead to address its vision.

I want to distinguish strategy from tactics. Tactics are short-term activities designed to meet strategic goals. What is common to strategy and tactics is that they are organized and time bound: the main difference is the time horizon. Figure 7.1 suggests a relationship going from abstract, longer term to more concrete, shorter term.

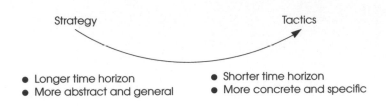

Strategy                                              Tactics

- Longer time horizon          - Shorter time horizon
- More abstract and general    - More concrete and specific

***Figure 7.1***   *Strategy and tactics*

It is important to distinguish between strategic goals and objectives, and tactical goals and objectives. We can have goals and objectives for tactics and for strategy but they will be of a different kind. For instance, an organization might have a strategic goal of putting all its managers through a self managed learning programme over a period of three years. This was so for Sainsbury's with the programme for the personnel function. Nearly 700 personnel professionals went through the programme and that strategic goal was met. However, there were other strategic goals relating to the need for the personnel function to change its role (and just to achieve the quantitative goal (700 people through a programme) without the qualitative goal (a positive change in the effectiveness of the personnel function) would have been useless).

In order to achieve the strategic goals, tactical goals had to be put in place. These included starting the programme with about 150 head office staff in the first year; budgeting for this; developing set advisers to carry it out, and so on. As you can see, the tactical goals become more specific and concrete.

The purposes of learning, discussed in Part Three, feed into strategy. Strategy is the practical working out of purposes. So purposes are more abstract than strategies. Purposes are also expressed in timeless terms and are not worked out as organized plans. The 'good learning' I have argued for (autonomy, wisdom, capability, holism, balance, centring, grounding, and so on) is elaborated in just such terms – that is, timeless, generalized, abstract. This is indicated in Figure 7.2. Thus the *strategy* of SML is the way of operationalizing 'good learning'. The strategy is more concrete, planned and specific (compared with purposes).

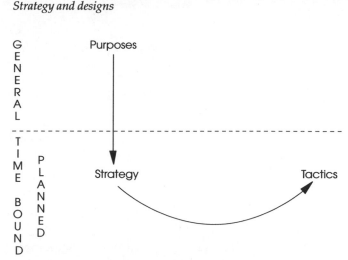

*Figure 7.2*  *Purposes, strategy and tactics*

So in the example of the Sainsbury's programme, the key purposes were related to the capability of the personnel function to deliver effectively to the line. And behind this were the commercial imperatives for the business to get its people strategies right. It was recognized that this would only happen if personnel professionals themselves learned to work in different ways. Hence a learning-based strategy emerged.

A further addition can be made to the model in Figure 7.2. Tactics lead to action, to purposive human behaviour to make things happen. The *action* level is where real live learning takes place. So Figure 7.3 represents a more fully worked-out model.

Again to refer to the Sainsbury's example, the actions needed to implement the tactics included a whole raft of things such as setting up workshops; choosing sets and getting them going; ensuring that everyone wrote a learning contract – and made it happen; providing support for sets in their work; and so on. (The specifics of making this work will be covered more fully in later chapters.)

The model in Figure 7.3 contains a number of important features.

**Flow**  The U shape indicates a flow from abstract to concrete, as shown by the arrows going anticlockwise.

**Relationships**  There are horizontal relationships. At the top, *purposes* and *action* are generalized; that is, purposes have general applicability – they are not context or time specific. Indeed, many of the ideas expressed about good learning come from the ancient China of the Taoists and from ancient Greece.

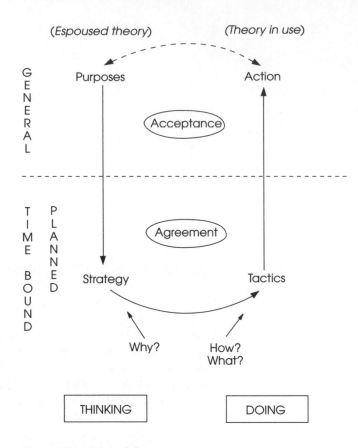

*Figure 7.3    U model*

The way we act is also not fixed by time or context. Hence, in pursuing learning the kinds of actions people can undertake (using experience, listening to lectures, reading books, meditating, and so on) can be carried out in any time frame or (almost) any organization.

At the bottom of the U, strategy and tactics are more bounded. SML is a specific response and it needs to be designed to suit the circumstances of organizations and individuals, including their time constraints.

Another distinction between top and bottom in the U is the mode of dealing with learning. At the bottom there needs to be collective *agreement* on strategy and tactics (in a learning business). Objectives need to be negotiated and the resources and design of programmes need to be agreed. However, *purposes* and *actions* need *acceptance*. There may not be collective agreement on these issues, and it may not be sought. So if organizations are serious about empowerment they will recognize and *accept* that individuals will learn in different ways. They will be more interested in whether the person learns what needs to be learned than in precise hour-by-hour behaviour.

**Coherence**    In order to move round the U and check for coherence, particular questions can be used. To go from abstract to concrete (anticlockwise) one asks *how*? or *what*? So if I say that I want to develop autonomy (purpose), I can be asked *how*? and the answer should be *strategic* (through an SML programme). If I am asked *how* the SML programme will work, the answer will be *tactical*. So I would indicate particular aspects of the design of the programme showing *how* strategy is implemented in tactics. Lastly, I could be asked *how* the tactics will work out, and I can respond with reference to precise *actions*.

An alternative is to go clockwise round the U. If you observe me doing something (for example, asking a question of someone in order to learn something), you may ask *why* I am doing that. My answer would be, to explain the tactical basis of my actions (for example, the person is my mentor and I am going to feed the responses I get into my set). If you ask *why* I am using a set and a mentor to assist my learning, I can reply strategically (for example, this is part of an SML strategy, and sets and mentors are tactical designs for implementing this strategy). If you ask *why* I use the strategy, I may reply that the programme is improving my capability (a purpose).

**Divisions**    There are vertical divisions in the U. Roughly, the left-hand side is associated with *thinking* and the right-hand side with *doing*. Also, taking the top left and top right, these encompass Argyris's distinction between espoused theory (purpose) and theory in use (action). The dotted line at the top shows that there should be congruence here. If, for instance, I am developing autonomy (purpose) and I show by my actions that I am not behaving autonomously in my learning, then there is an incongruity to address. This, then, needs second-order learning: I have to step outside the model to explore the incongruity. So the model is only a map to aid thought, analysis and integrated action. I should also 'step outside' at any time if I consider it to be necessary.

**Change**    'Ease of change' goes from top to bottom. By this I mean that changing fundamental purposes or changing action and behaviour can be more difficult than changing strategy and tactics. Individuals become wedded to purposes and patterns of action. A great deal of effort can be needed to make changes at this level – and it is often second-order (not first-order) change that is required. However, strategic and tactical plans usually need only first-order change. For instance, a tactic may be to offer a course on some topic. If it proves unpopular it can be scrapped or modified. There is some effort required to achieve this, but it is not comparable to the effort necessary to change some fundamental organizational purpose or principle. The thesis, then, is that the most abstract dimension (top left) and the most concrete (top right) are the most resistant to change and the most embedded. The middle ground of strategy and tactics is easier to work with.

## Strategic learning and SML

Figure 7.4 shows, diagrammatically, linkages from purposes through to SML as strategy. The strategic role of SML is to bridge between overall purposes, and tactics and action. I shall describe in this chapter some key strategic processes which provide the basis for this bridging.

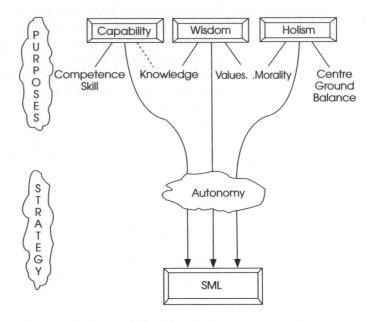

**Figure 7.4**    *Strategic learning: linking purposes and strategy*

## Processes

There are four overarching processes, namely:

● preparing
● resourcing
● collaborating
● judging.

These are all deliberately formulated as verbs. There are subprocesses under each of these four headings, and these will also be outlined. The four main processes roughly follow in sequence, although it is normally not as neat as this in practice. All four are core processes for strategic managing, and the basis of SML is the mirroring of managerial processes in learning.

**Preparing**   Preparing can be subdivided into other processes including:

- mapping
- diagnosing
- planning
- contracting.

The nature of preparing in this context is preparing to learn. Of course, this itself is a learning process. This self reference is both a strength and a difficult complexity of SML. As with all other processes discussed here, these four subprocesses provide a basis for the *content* of learning – that which usually looks like a syllabus or curriculum or timetable or set of objectives. But the *process* of learning in this way provides the basis for learners to develop this process ability – in this case the ability to prepare themselves for action – and I would argue that this process ability is of a higher value. However, it can be less easily recognized because of its verb form in the English language. We tend to make processes into nouns in order to give them status – a pretend concreteness. So managing becomes management and as such it provides a basis for 'management' to become a subject within which other subjects (formulated as nouns) are studied (economics, psychology, statistics, and so on).

SML provides a way of addressing this issue by its process focus. However, this is a weakness in that, culturally, processes (verbs) are less acceptable as a basis for learning. Our noun–verb–noun syntax predisposes us to expect sentences of the form: 'Jim (noun) learned (verb) economics (noun).' 'Jim learned preparing' does not sound quite right because of the conventions of the English language. But English grammar is only a convention – and one that, in this context, gets in the way of clear thinking and sensible action.[3]

Having made a case for this process orientation, I would now like to show the rationale for the four subprocesses under this heading. Figure 7.5 shows diagrammatically how these processes link up.

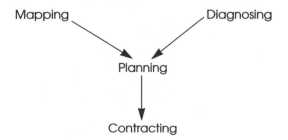

*Figure 7.5   Preparing for SML*

Essentially, mapping is the process of the learner using knowledge of 'the world out there' in order to prepare for learning. Diagnosing provides self knowledge – developing a sense of 'the world in here' (who the learners are and what they are able to do). These processes come together to provide a basis for the learners to plan their learning (including objective setting, programming, and so on). This, then, provides a basis for contracting – for agreeing with others the necessary basis for learning and for negotiating appropriate arrangements. The artificial separation of these four processes may imply greater complexity than in fact occurs. The processes flow together and occur in the same time frame. The separation here is for the purpose of analysis and exploration only. In practice it is important that they integrate.

*Mapping*  This process, like all the others described in this chapter, is a way of assisting a person to develop

- capability
- wisdom
- holism
- autonomy.

People who are better able to map their world and use the maps of others enhance their *capability* and their *wisdom*. Such mapping can facilitate *holistic* integration and balance, and can help the individuals develop *autonomy* through their increased ability to journey through more 'territory'. Rather than tediously repeat the above for each process described in this chapter, I shall leave it to you to make the necessary connections. The key question to ask yourself is whether you would contribute to developing 'good learning' through each of the processes described.

I shall devote more space in this chapter to mapping than to any other process. This is partly because of its importance, but also because I am aware that it is less well understood and less valued than some of the other processes.

### The nature of maps

When I first came to London, as a child, I believed that the maps of the London Underground system on tube trains were an accurate representation of the tube lines – that is, that they ran in straight lines and smooth curves. My naïve belief was not a hindrance as I could find my way around the system, and work out where to change trains. When I discovered that tube lines were more complex, it was an enlightening discovery, and it enhanced my capability to find my way around above ground.

I suppose this was one of the earliest experiences that made me realize that 'the map is not the territory'. A map became, to me, something I could use but it clearly did not necessarily show everything that was going on.

Schumacher made a similar point. He found, when visiting Russia (during the cold war), that churches were not shown on official maps, yet when walking around he could see them. As he said, it was not the first time in his life that a map failed to show things of importance.

> All through school and university I had been given maps of life and knowledge on which there was hardly a trace of many of the things that I most cared about and that seemed to me of greatest possible importance in the conduct of my life.[4]

He commented on how this perplexed him and that the breakthrough for him was to stop suspecting the sanity of his perceptions and instead to 'suspect the soundness of the maps'.[4]

### Mapping in practice

When we launched the first SML qualification programme in 1980, we described our stance on knowledge and mapping in the following terms:

> In management education, there has been a move away from teaching the traditional academic disciplines (for example, psychology, sociology, economics) into teaching based around perceived management functions (marketing, personnel, etc.). Some would see this as progress in that the teaching is built around supposed needs of management (as opposed to subject disciplines). However, what now seems to have happened is that these new areas have become (for teaching purposes) subjects in their own right and we have once again lost sight of the possibility of responding flexibly to managerial needs. Marketing, personnel, etc., all now have the barriers around them that the 'classic' subject disciplines have (for example, separate journals). The trouble is that management problems do not crop up solely within the boundaries of, say, 'marketing' or 'production'. These artificially defined subjects meet the needs of *teachers* but not of *learners*.
>
> Teachers can develop their subject knowledge within a field, and feel secure about their competence within the boundaries of their subject. However, managers have to tackle problems on their merits – they cannot be controlled by the limitations of teachers.

We went on to say:

> We will initially help learners to:
>
> a. identify their needs and
> b. understand and make use of existing conceptual maps of the field of management.
>
> Thus the programme of study of each individual will come out of an interactive process of comparing needs with existing conceptual maps. Each person will then be able to identify a tentative programme of action around some generally defined goals for them.
>
> We believe that the process of making explicit to students existing conceptual maps in management is important. The student needs to be aware of the existing body of knowledge in management so that they can choose from it what is relevant to their needs. We use the term 'conceptual mapping' to draw the analogy with the geographical process of mapping. We can show the learner existing models and theories of the territory of management. These models and theories are themselves built on concepts which the learner needs to be aware of.
>
> To take the example of the body of knowledge encompassed by 'organization development' the learner needs to know of the concept 'change agent', before they can make sense of theories of change which use change agents. If they know of the basic concepts of organization development (OD), they will be able to make sense of the body of knowledge encompassed by OD. Hence, if they become concerned about organizational change, they can evaluate whether OD has anything to offer them. If it might appear to do so, they can then explore the territory more effectively with the help of the conceptual map provided by OD.
>
> To take the 'map' analogy further, learners will in essence need to pick a route across the territory of management, and the map will aid them. Naturally once they have an outline route they will see where they need a more detailed map of parts of the territory. In a sense, we as staff will initially provide a broad map in outline only. We will show the main features, but not the detail. Once the learner has an idea of a route, they can then get fine detail filled in.
>
> The analogy should not be stretched too far. Our main point is that the learner needs to know (in outline) what they don't know in order for them to make choices. Without such knowledge, their choices may be based at worst on random guesses or prejudice.

*Mapping and teaching*

In the above we wanted to make a distinction between mapping and teaching. Teaching has been associated with a view that the teacher is imparting objective knowledge for the learner to absorb. Even in approaches such as the case study method, the teacher tends to suggest to learners the correct and incorrect ways of doing things. Also in business school courses, the assessment and examination process provides a control on what is legitimized knowledge.

Mapping is about showing people maps, and helping them to become cartographers. Experienced managers will always come to a course with existing mental maps. These mental maps give them a basis from which to find their way around. Faced with, say, a selection interview to carry out, they will have a mental map of what to do (for example, prepare for interview, send job description, read person's application form, set aside one hour for the interview, and so on). These internal instructions are vital to our everyday activity. If we did not have mental maps to guide us we would go crazy trying to create procedures for everything that came our way.

However, people's maps are always limited, and the mapping process at the start of an SML programme assists people to

● see other people's maps
● evaluate their own maps
● create new maps.

Presenting other people's maps to learners must be done as an *offering*, not as an *imposition*. In organizationally based programmes, middle managers need to know the public maps of top management. They need to know maps that are articulated as corporate objectives, corporate culture and strategic directions. Newcomers to organizations are especially in need of maps. These are often offered in the form of organization charts, company policies and information on markets, technology and products. In offering mapping devices to newcomers, I have never come across an organization that does this in order to produce clones of existing staff. It is recognized that newcomers need to know how things are done around the organization, but that each person will have a level of uniqueness in his or her style of doing things. Hence the maps help the person to make choices, but do not dictate every element of the person's behaviour.

*Limits to maps*

Barber and Broad[5] suggest

> Maps are one of the greatest illusions known to man and yet we instinctively put our faith in them.

I do not see this as necessarily instinctive, though mapping (in the literal sense) is common to all major cultures. However, I do agree that the faith we put in maps can be problematic. Here I shall outline a range of limitations to maps, and use the example of the organization chart to exemplify this. Figure 7.6 shows a typical example.

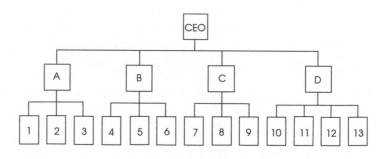

**Figure 7.6**   *Organizational mapping: the organization chart*

The limits to maps are as follows:

1 Maps *generalize*. The organization chart shows a generalized view of the organization, but it does not show specifics.
2 The organization chart is a *distortion* of how people actually relate to each other. Each line does not represent the same process. Manager A may relate to their direct reports in quite a different way to manager B.
3 The chart *leaves out* a lot. It does not show who is friendly with whom; nor does it show the politics of the business.
4 Information can be *suppressed* by the map maker. The chart is unlikely to show who is more vulnerable to being fired or who is expected to get the next promotion.
5 Whoever draws the maps is *not neutral* in organizational processes. Organization charts can be created for political purposes. They are also based on assumptions, beliefs and cultural norms. The chart shown in Figure 7.6 shows a classic pyramid with the highest status person at the top (the CEO). This is a cultural norm ('up' is of a higher status than 'down'). If we invert the pyramid this challenges cultural norms – and some organizations have done this precisely to try to show a new cultural development (for example, where customer care

initiatives suggest that front line staff should be at the top as they deal with customers, and the CEO is at the bottom because that job is to support them).

6  We can only put on to a map what are *representations*. In the case of Figure 7.6 this is a two-dimensional map, and it can therefore only show relationships in two dimensions. This problem has bedevilled proponents of complex matrix structures because if you go to four dimensions it becomes impossible to show it on a page, or a computer screen (three dimensions are possible, but not as neat as two).

7  The *metaphors* we use in mapping limit us. I have mentioned the pyramid metaphor. Some talk of 'organizational trees' and apply that metaphor to the organization chart. Whatever is used creates certain meanings and excludes others.

8  In modern fast-moving businesses maps such as organization charts and phone directories rapidly become *outdated*. People move upwards, sideways or out, and the map becomes inaccurate.

9  Figure 7. 7 shows a *strip map*[6] for a person's reporting relationship.

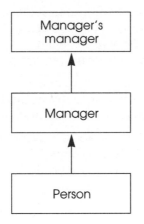

*Figure 7.7  Strip map*

A strip map shows just the main route. Motoring organizations often provide these to show how to go from one town to the next. They may not even be shown visually but rather give verbal directions. Furthermore, if you ask someone for directions, that person will tend to give you a strip map – for example, 'go down this road until you reach the traffic lights, turn right then take the second left ...' A strip map provides choice points, and

marks a route. It has the advantage of simplicity and
clarity, and it leaves out confusing detail. However, strip
maps also leave out detail that might be useful. In Figure
7.6 this *context map* might help a newcomer who fits into
box 4 to know that there are others at the same level in the
hierarchy, and there are other senior people in addition to
their own manager. Context maps fill in more detail and
can help the person have more choices.

To return to road maps, it can be useful to know not just
the main route from A to B, but also side roads to use in
case of a road blockage. Hence, context maps are more
empowering and give the user more opportunity to make
a better judgement about action.

### Choices in mapping

Learning to recognize the limits of maps is a starting point
to moving into doing one's own mapping. In SML a key
phase in learning is making this move. Learning about
others' maps is first-order learning. It is valuable, but has its
limits. Creating one's own maps needs second-order
learning. It needs the ability to step out of the maps of others
and make one's own choices.

The first aspect of choosing is choosing purpose. We need to
be clear about our purposes in order to make choices. Why
do we want the map and what will we use it for? In
management some of the reasons include developing

● wisdom – being able to make wise choices of action
● capability – having more choices through enriched maps
   (for example, *context* in addition to *strip* maps).

A key role of developers is to assist learners to make these
second-order learning shifts. (This will be explored more
fully in later chapters, especially Chapter 9.)

### Maps in SML

As individuals develop richer, personally owned maps,
they become more *centred* and more *grounded*, as described
in Chapter 5. This allows them to dispense with guides. If
we do not have a map of a territory, we may be reliant on a
guide who does. In an organization this can be a leader, a
trainer or an expert of some kind. Hence enriched maps for
individuals can be a threat to the insecure (uncentred,
ungrounded) person who is in the leader/trainer/expert
role. That person can find it difficult to move from being a
guide, in control, to being a companion walking alongside
the other person. (This is one reason why SML approaches
may not be implemented in organizations.)

*Diagnosing*  Another part of 'preparing' is the process of 'diagnosing', which matches 'mapping' and usually in SML programmes occurs within the same time frame. Diagnosing is more internally focused than mapping. While it has associations with a medical model (for example, diagnosing illness) it tends to be a commonly used verb in the development field. There is not a verb 'self awarenessing', though 'self knowing' might do. All I mean by the term 'diagnosing' is finding out sufficient about yourself to provide a basis for learning.

Much of the methodology and technology is well known – as is the value of the process – so this section will be shorter than the last. However, there are a few facets of the process which need to be emphasized in an SML context.

First, there is the issue of balance. If we are to project into the future in planning a learning programme, then this needs balancing with a past orientation (as shown in Figure 7.8).

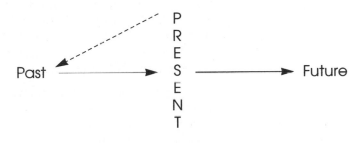

*Figure 7.8*   *Balancing past and future*

An aspect of my research on effective CEOs is relevant here. Mostly I found that they talked about time and in specific ways. If they faced a current problem they tended to progress in the manner shown in Figure 7.8; that is, they looped back to past experience from present issues. They might, for instance, check their own experience to see if they had faced a similar problem in the past. They would then project that past experience back through the filter of current circumstances in order to plan future action. This seemed to provide an excellent preparational base for action.

The value of this is important. Many managers want to leap straight into planning, goal setting, and so on, without exploring their own history. Yet when we have urged people to explore previous ways of doing things they have often identified patterns in their behaviour which they were about to repeat; they were wanting to base objectives on deeply ingrained mental patterns that emerged from the past. So exploring the past is not self indulgent time wasting but, if focused on needs for the future, is essential to effective planning.

The process encourages learners to think about the way they think (have thought) and hence promotes second-order learning. Diagnostic activity can raise issues of personal strengths and weaknesses, but if the learner merely produces a pedestrian list without critically examining it, then learning can be superficial (though not valueless). Also, there is an initial tendency for managers to take a 'doing' focus in diagnosis. They may say 'I can do X, but I can't do Y' and focus then on learning to do Y. A balance to this is a 'being' position. As well as asking the person to say what they can and cannot do, it is important to ask them who they *are*. Answers to this question are different from the 'what they do' domain, but both are important. 'Doing' answers give more of the basis for capability development; 'being' answers assist the person to see ways of increasing wisdom. I have implied, though, in the above that there needs to be the outside question-asker. As the Chinese saying goes: 'The eye cannot see its own lashes.' In SML the role of others in assisting diagnosis is crucial, and will be explored more fully under the heading 'collaborating'.

Finally, while much of the standard technology of assessment centres, psychometric tests and appraisal interviews provides certain kinds of data, it usually needs to be elaborated, modified or even toned down or rejected. A problem with this standard technology is that the process is 'outside in' – that is, judgement is provided from someone else's perspective. In SML the focus is on the learner driving the process.

*Planning*     The five-questions approach mentioned in earlier chapters is a valuable planning tool. Figures 7.9 and 7.10 show the basis of this. However, it is only a tool. There are other ways of planning. The issue is for learners to engage in a planning process. Specifically it engages people in a holistic look at themselves and the contexts in which they operate. It is not meant to be a hurried, mechanistic process. For instance, in addressing Question 3, individuals have to consider their own values and ideals, and in the process they may need to re-evaluate these: deeply held career goals may need re-examining. Those who set their minds on becoming CEO by 40, or making their first million by 30, might have to re-assess the realism and validity of such goals.

As with 'diagnosing', this planning process is best carried out with others. Individuals need to engage with fellow

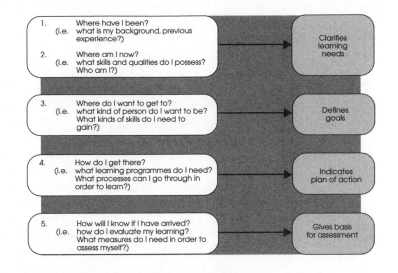

**Figure 7.9** *Planning learning in SML*

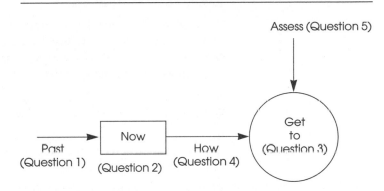

**Figure 7.10** *Problem solving and learning: five questions*

travellers through life who also have to grapple with their values and ideals. The collaboration is, however, not for people to copy each other, but to learn to improve their own processes.

I have indicated above the use of the metaphor 'life is a journey'. This is a common metaphor in our culture[7] and provides a readily understandable basis for planning. From this metaphor we assume that:

● people are travellers
● purposes are destinations
● means for achieving purposes are routes
● difficulties are impediments to travel
● staff on programmes are guides
● progress is measured by distance travelled or destination achieved

- landmarks gauge progress
- choices are crossroads.

Like all metaphors, however, the journey metaphor enriches meaning and at the same time constrains and closes in. Life is not a journey: it is just life. But we feel we need ways of making sense of our lives and in Western cultures we want to be more in control. We may look down on, say, the Hindu as too fatalistic. But perhaps our metaphors become too entrapping. In planning we need to balance attempts at control with serendipity and a recognition of non-controllable events. In learning it is good to plan and also good to welcome and recognize unplanned learning. In SML programmes people say that they benefited from setting objectives and trying to achieve them. They also say that they learned much more that was not in their plan.

Often the learning that comes in the unplanned category is at the 'being' level. People say that they *are* different, not just that they *do* different things.

This balance issue is reflected in the way the five questions can be tackled. I have already mentioned the balance of past (Question 1) with future (Question 3). Also, in addressing these questions learners can balance

- concrete and abstract (in Question 5)
- rigour and creativity (in Questions 3 and 4)

and so on. This balance also leads to the need to link individuals to their contexts and reflects the value of contracting.

*Contracting*    Planned learning can be encapsulated in a 'development plan', but such a plan can so easily abstract the person from the context. In SML we suggest people develop a learning contract as a basis for creating their learning within a wide context. Hence the contract needs to be negotiated and agreed with others (a plan may not be). Such agreeing will typically be with fellow learners and with those in authority in the organization. Those in authority may be those authorized to provide resources (especially money) or to allow the person to use time to attend set meetings, for example. There may be a third party to the contract if an outside organization is involved (for example, in providing set advisers).

The negotiating of a contract is another aspect of the rigour of SML and its integration into the life of a business. If contracting works well it weaves together relevant threads to enhance the benefits of learning for all involved. However, it is often not quite so smooth. Organizations that are not moving in the direction of being a learning business still see learning as detached from core business issues. So we find that a manager may authorize a person to go on a course, with fees paid, but take little or no interest in what the person is learning.

This is one of the major challenges for the development of SML. We know that people can go on SML programmes and develop enormously, but in too many situations we have found the newly developed capabilities being under-used because significant authority figures have not taken an interest in the person's development.

The other main challenge in contracting is to make the learning contract live. It must not become a dead document to be followed mechanistically. It must be possible to renegotiate it, and especially to improve it as time goes by. The contract can act as an umbrella document in showing how tactical learning elements are encompassed in an SML strategy. And it can enhance coherence and realism.

The learning contract will need to spell out the resource implications of a person's proposed learning, and this is discussed in the next section.

**Resourcing**    The previous section covered issues of mapping, diagnosing, planning and contracting. This *preparation* has to be matched with resource considerations.

There is not a great deal that needs to be said under this heading. Resourcing issues are part of managing – and are mostly to do with getting resources (money, materials, and so on) and working with limited resources. (With unlimited resources, lots of managerial problems disappear.) A major difference of SML from traditional education and training is in the control of resources. Participants are usually given significant control over resource decisions such as budgets. A typical programme will provide for individuals or sets to have a budget for learning purposes, and the learning contract is used to justify resource use. If a person wishes to buy a book or attend a workshop, then that person may be able to spend money from his or her budget (subject to its being in the learning contract).

Chapter 8 will show some more concrete (tactical) activities under this and other headings in this chapter. It is important to emphasize here, though, the high priority a learning business needs to give to strategic decisions about resources for learning.

**Collaborating**    I have already indicated in the preceding sections of this chapter the importance of collaboration in learning. Also, in an earlier chapter I referred to a personalistic stance which transcends individualism and collectivism. In SML, allowing people to be themselves and legitimizing their right to speak solely for themselves encourages a personalistic collaboration. People hear each other – in depth and on fundamental issues. As a result they are more able to see their connection to others. In sharing joys and fears, needs and desires, values and beliefs, people come to see each other's humanness in situations where they may previously have felt disconnected and isolated.

A problem is, though, that connection to others is sometimes seen as creating uniformity and insipid compromises. Mutual support is characterized as being counter to individual freedom and individuality: it is seen as creating sameness and not allowing difference. In SML, collaborative modes such as the set are important as vehicles to encourage *oneness* and *difference*. Each individual is pursuing a personal programme, but other members of the set learn to care about the goals of others and their struggles towards those goals. So a collective entity exists where each person is encouraged to manifest his or her own uniqueness, while at the same time being at one with others. There is equality *without* conformity.

People often find this confusing at the start. Some want to copy others – for example, one person talks of their own interests and others may want (inappropriately) to copy that, as a means of security (rather than develop their own thinking). This results from the pressure for conformity and sameness that institutions such as schools promote.

A crucial problem for people in a set occurs where assessment is involved. Some find it difficult to cope with the idea that their assessment is unique: they want comparators; they want to measure themselves against others rather than against specific goals. This is an example of the compete/conform polarity emerging: either we compete to beat others or we conform. We need to dispense with the polarity altogether. It is not about choosing to compete or to conform: it is about each person choosing his or her own route and yet supporting others in their own chosen paths. Not competing *or* conforming – *neither* is useful. We may learn from others – listening to ideas that others offer – but a slavish conformity means that the ideas are only introjected without being absorbed. They do not become *part of us*, but a bit tacked on at the side. There is a difference between refining and enlarging one's own cognitive maps and swallowing an undigested part of a map belonging to someone else.

The two can be compared as in Figure 7.11.

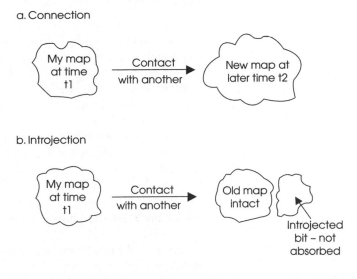

**Figure 7.11** *Connection vs introjection*

Thus in the set, each person has to learn how to learn from others, and at the same time how not to impose on others. The set adviser must assist in this at times, especially in halting any attempts to force ideas on to a person by someone else.

The set is not the only collaborative forum in SML programmes. The wider community of learners is also important, as is networking with other parts of the organization. Mentors can play a significant role in making these links, and they often assist in taking the learning from SML beyond a defined programme. This latter aspect is important as a structured SML programme is best seen as the *start* of a person's continued development, not as a separate, distinct event. In evaluation of SML programmes ex-participants often comment that they have applied more of their learning after the programme than during it.

**Judging** This is the fourth of the major strategic processes in SML. Like the others, it is an aspect of effective managing. Managers have to judge courses of action and make decisions on the basis of judgement. It is rare to have all the information one needs such that a decision makes itself. Mostly decisions are made in the absence of full information and therefore rely on good judgement.

In SML the judging process can be subdivided into

● assessing, and
● evaluating.

Judging occurs at various stages:

1  Before an organization decides to use SML it has to *assess* if it will be of use and perhaps *evaluate* previous experiences of development activity (for example, has management training been of value in the past?).
2  If an organization decides to go ahead on the basis of a well-considered judgement, individuals need to *assess* if SML will help them.
3  On joining a programme, the diagnostic activity at the start requires judgement. Participants have to *assess* their previous learning and make judgements about their current abilities (and hence about learning needs).
4  During a programme, participants need to judge if they are on track. Are they meeting the objectives they have set?
5  At the end of a programme participants need to *assess* their learning.
6  After the programme there is a need for *evaluation*. Did the programme work? Was it cost-effective? Is it worth continuing with?

In all of these processes collaboration with others is crucial. Prior to a programme there is a need for dialogue between relevant parties, and for collective decision making. In examples mentioned earlier, such as Allied Domecq and Sainsbury's, it was essential to have discussions in top management, with staff providing the programme so that a fair evaluation could be made of the validity of the approach. Part of the evaluation could come from information. We could, for instance, provide examples of previous programmes, but the judgement to go ahead or not involves other non-rational elements (such as *feelings* about this kind of learning approach).

This process of judging at the start is repeated through the programme. There is always an intertwining of information/facts and response to the information. SML makes this more open than is often the case in managerial decision making, and in the process helps improve strategic decision making in organizations.

The end point assessment is also unusual in organizational programmes. Many organizations now engage in judging *prior* to a programme – for example, through the appraisal process or through the use of assessment centres – but then do not encourage assessment down the line. Individuals may leave an assessment centre with development plans to focus on learning things that have been identified as weaknesses. They are then left to solve their problems, often without proper support and without any process at some future date to assess their improvement, if any. When this happens it seems that assessment centres (even if called 'development centres') are low on cost-effectiveness.

Another crucial difference between SML and traditional assessment processes is that the learner drives the assessment. The learner makes self assessments which are tested on peers, managers, programme staff or any other relevant person. Eventually this produces a consensus which, by virtue of such collective agreement, has greater power and effectiveness. If all relevant parties reach a consensus (and this is normal in 99 per cent of cases), then the base for future action is extremely solid. Many appraisal schemes are now moving in this direction, especially with the emphasis not just on self assessment but on getting the views of others through 360 degree appraisal.

In judging activity and learning, this has to be placed alongside processes of feedback. In earlier chapters I emphasized two kinds of feedback:

● primary – sensory based, direct
● secondary – verbal judgements, not direct.

Secondary feedback, in some respects, comes between primary feedback and judgement. Primary feedback is unadorned data; for example, a salesperson has sold $X$ amount of a product. Secondary feedback might be a manager's response to this – for example, 'I'm not happy with this.' The judgement process then may follow, for example assessing the implications of the situation and making a judgement about future action.

A danger in some SML sets is where participants want to stay at the level of comfortable, low-judgement feedback. This might include such comments as: 'That report had $X$ and $Y$ good features, but it needed a bit more work on section $Z$.' Eventually such generalized feedback needs shaping up. Learners need to move from asking for such feedback to a situation where they can say: 'I set $A, B, C$ goals in my learning contract. This report is meant to demonstrate these. I feel I surpassed these goals for $X, Y, Z$ reasons. Do you agree?' Responses can then be sharpened into 'Yes, I agree and these are my reasons' or 'No, I don't agree. You met goals $X$ and $Y$ in my judgement, but not $Z$. And these are my reasons for saying this.'

Judging is a central process in management. It is a continual process in the life of a manager – and hence can be missed. Self judgement is also part of judging. Managers have to judge whether they are up to a particular job or not, what career moves to make, and so on. All this requires the ability to assess and evaluate oneself. Hence a strategic learning approach needs to develop this capability through the *process* of learning. Sitting people in classrooms and putting them through exams encourages them to leave judgement issues to others. This can be a problem in SML, particularly with young new graduates from university who have been successful in the traditional education process. If they come from a prestigious university with a so-called 'good degree' they naturally tend to feel that judgements by others are OK. The downside of this reliance on others is that they often make poor self judgements, especially about career decisions.

Those who do full-time MBAs in their 20s also suffer from this; hence the criticisms from employers about the unrealistic expectation of young MBA holders. Also, seemingly successful MBA holders may suddenly face an existential crisis in their 40s when they realize that they have unthinkingly followed an inappropriate career path. Their self judgements in early career have proved to be poor.

In SML, therefore, this emphasis on self judgement can initially be uncomfortable. Learners want external validation, but time and again in evaluation of SML programmes people say that the final assessment was a high point of the programme. Rather than submit themselves to the judgement of others, they had to struggle with developing a realistic sense of themselves and their capabilities. And they had to engage in open judgement of colleagues. All this benefits their later ability to select people, make career choices, and work effectively in groups with others.

I would never wish to place people in positions of responsibility unless they were prepared to judge themselves. This is not to say that they have to do it perfectly; that is not possible. Just to do it is the issue. And if we realize that we often do it inadequately, we should be very humble about our judgements of others.

## Summary

This chapter has outlined SML strategy. The U model provides a basis for linking purposes, strategy, tactics and action. I then discussed four strategic processes:

- preparing
- resourcing
- collaborating
- judging.

These intertwine with each other. Also, learning through these processes assists effective managing by using them so explicitly. It is like DNA – a spiral interweaving of some complex processes. It provides a model of the life of managing and learning and, like DNA, allows for replication and growth.

**Notes**

1 This chapter draws on the work of Bateson and his followers, specifically Bandler and Grinder (see Bandler, R. and Grinder, J. (1975) *The Structure of Magic*, Vols I and II, Palo Alto, CA: Science and Behavior Books).

2 Gruber, H.E. and Weitman, M. (1962) *Self-Directed Study: Experiments in Higher Education*, Boulder, CO: University of Colorado Press.

3 Gregory Bateson was the best writer on this issue (see Bateson, G. (1973) *Steps to an Ecology of Mind*, London: Paladin). He points to the split in Greek thinking at the time of Pythagoras, and how the latter had a more process-oriented view of the world which was lost in the dominant thinking of other philosophers after Pythagoras. Noun/thing thinking also dominates other Western (occidental) languages, hence providing a powerful force to maintain these conventions.

4 Schumacher, E.F. (1977) *A Guide for the Perplexed*, London: Jonathan Cape, p. 9.

5 Barber, P. and Broad, C. (1993) *Tales from the Map Room*, London: BBC Books, p. 8.

6 Fiol, C.M. and Huff, A.S. (1992) 'Maps for managers: where are we? Where do we go from here?', *Journal of Management Studies*, **29**, 3 (May), 267–85. These authors review a range of literature and provide an excellent exposition of the importance of maps. The whole issue of the *Journal of Management Studies* (**29**, 3, May 1992) is a valuable collection on mapping for managers.

7 See Lakoff, G. and Johnson, M. (1980) *Metaphors We Live By*, Chicago: University Press.

# 8 Tactics and practice

In this chapter I shall show some ways in which the
purposes, principles and strategic processes of SML can be
implemented. I shall not go into great detail on precise
methods and techniques as these matters will be covered in
a separate book; however, I shall quote from participants
about aspects of SML programmes so that there is some
concrete information about practice.

A particular emphasis in this chapter will be on structures
used in a wide range of SML programmes. However,
although I shall point up these programmes, SML and its
place in strategic learning is broader than this. Figure 8.1
indicates how programmes fit strategically.

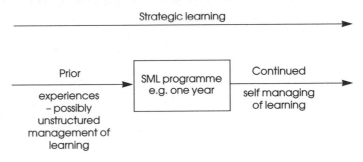

**Figure 8.1**    *SML programmes in context*

People will have already managed their learning to some
extent prior to getting involved in SML. What SML does is
to sharpen, focus, organize, and perhaps reframe, the
existing management of learning. Also, after a structured
programme, people continue to manage their own learning
for the rest of their lives.

Programmes, by definition, introduce structure and precise
processes into learning. Hence, while there is in SML the
highest possible flexibility in terms of content of learning,
structures limit flexibility in process, but such limits are

necessary to provide boundaries within which to exercise freedom and choice. The analogy (taken from Taoist ideas) is the glass. It is a rigid, unbending transparent structure into which the user is free to put any desired liquid in any desired amount (subject to the size of the glass). Taoists[1] point out that use comes from space that is bounded. But it must be tightly bounded in places. A floppy glass would be no use. A wheel needs to be solid and rigid but it is useless without a hole at the centre to put the axle in. Although the structures of SML seem initially unusual, people can rapidly integrate them into their overall patterns of working and learning. Let me give two quotes from people on a two-year post-graduate diploma programme.

> How has it worked for me? I initially accepted at a cognitive level the theory of self-determination of learning objectives and methods. I had had some short experiences of unstructured courses which I had found very exciting in learning terms. It seemed to make perfect sense to me that if managers were being asked and paid to determine their own work needs and routines and those of others, then they were equally capable of determining their own learning needs and routines. I was also strongly committed to the necessity of management learning to be as relevant as possible to individuals' situations. Busy managers have enough to worry them in their working lives without being overloaded with unnecessary information either at a cognitive or affective level. I was therefore quite shocked at my own reaction to the realization in the second term that I was apparently losing sight of where 'work' ended and 'course' began. So deeply ingrained in me was the conditioning that formal education should be something extra, academically removed from reality, that I began to worry that I was not doing something which was, in my perception, on a different plane from my work. I took the problem to my set who eventually helped me,
>
> 1  to understand what I was saying and therefore to reconcile my acceptance of the theory of self-managed learning with the practice, and
> 2  to see that what was in fact happening was that I was working at a more advanced level. I was actively seeking and taking on work from which I would hitherto have shied away. (Liz Atkins,[2] p. 8)

A normal management course would have taught me a lot of things I don't really need in my career. On the other hand, the self managed learning diploma allowed me to concentrate on just what I needed to learn. It was very useful working with other people in a group, because they helped me see what my weaknesses were. It was the first time I'd been able to sit down with a peer group of people prepared to listen to my personal development problems. Indeed, the group members found it so useful that they still meet regularly every six weeks, even though their course finished more than six months ago. They still find they can help each other tackle current job problems. (Rob Holmes, quoted in Clutterbuck[3])

Both managers found that learning and working merged, and that the learning approach carried on beyond the programme. And structures such as sets and learning contracts continue to be of value. However, one of the problems with the possibility of using SML structures quite widely is that they can be used in a way which is not self managed learning. Programme organizers can say 'We're using sets and learning contracts, so it's the same as SML' or 'Within our course we give participants freedom to choose a project – and therefore it's SML.' It is not. Figure 8.2 shows two distinctions.

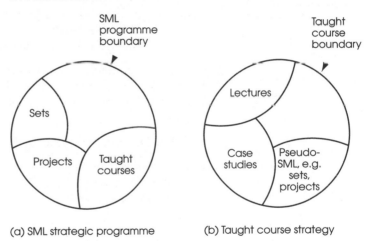

*Figure 8.2* *SML as strategy, not tactics*

Figure 8.2 suggests that SML provides a strategic frame within which individuals may, because of the needs of their learning contract, attend a standard short course. This latter is then a *tactical* means towards achieving *strategic* ends. SML allows for almost any choice of tactics. The example of pseudo-SML is where within, say, an MBA, participants do some self development or undertake a project. But assessment stays controlled by professors, and the general curriculum is determined by the faculty. This kind of programme has nothing to do with self managed learning.

I have found myself criticized by others who see my stance as too rigid. They suggest I am being too purist and that compromises are necessary. The issue of purity is interesting. The opposite of pure is impure, and in this respect I do not support impurity. Compromises on quality are just that – they reduce quality and produce second-rate learning. I am not suggesting that SML is a Utopian strategy. But if I knew of anything better, I would do it.

## SML programmes

At this point I shall outline a basic design approach for SML and later I shall discuss some of the elements of SML programmes. Some of these have already been introduced in earlier chapters, and here some of the earlier themes will be pulled together.

### Designing

Chapter 9 indicates the role of designing in SML programmes. The key to successful design is to get a good basic macro design, so that micro elements can evolve to suit learners and their organizations. I remember one CEO criticizing his trainers for over-elaborating designs. They had done a good basic job for him, and then wanted to gold-plate it. As a result it lost contact with his needs.

In any design there will be aspects which are non-negotiable. These need to be made as clear and as explicit as possible. Typical non-negotiables might include:

● resources available, such as budget
● time – length of programme and off-job time possible
● use of certain structures such as learning contracts and sets.

In SML the negotiables typically include:

● location of set meetings
● content of learning contracts
● criteria for assessment.

### *Robust design: the idea*

Allowing for these variances in negotiables and non-negotiables, there is a good basic robust design for SML programmes. The idea of a robust design is an analogy with, say, the design of the Boeing 747. This aeroplane has been enormously successful because it has a basic robust design. Robustness comes from the ability to modify the basic design to respond to a wide range of customer needs. Airlines have been able to specify to Boeing a wide variety of needs within the basic framework of the 747. Table 8.1 compares some features of the Boeing 747 and a robust SML design.

**Table 8.1**  *Robust design*

| Boeing 747 | SML robust design |
|---|---|
| Possible to stretch or contract length of aircraft (within limits) | Possible to stretch or contract length of programme (within limits) |
| Possible to furnish interior differently | Possible to have different content to programme |
| Possible to vary seating arrangements | Possible to vary arrangement of elements |
| Possible to vary power supplied by means of engines | Possible to vary resources supplied |

Such analogies should not be pushed too far. A programme is not a physical structure like an aircraft, and cannot be treated in the same way.

*A robust design*
*for SML*
Figure 8.3 shows diagrammatically a robust design for SML programmes. It shows the processes discussed in Chapter 7, and specific activities along the bottom of the diagram. The essence of the design is a first phase which uses a start-up event and set meetings to assist the learner to produce an agreed learning contract. The learner will also be doing individual work such as writing the contract.

In phase two the contract is put into practice using live work experience and regular set meetings. This leads to an end

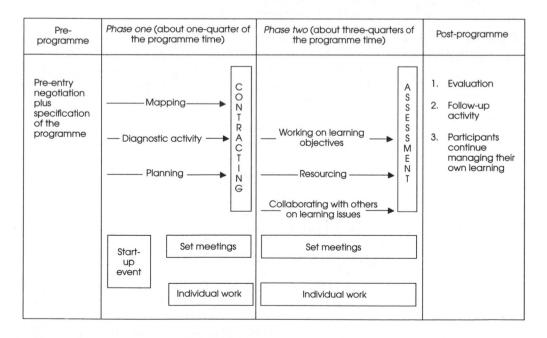

*Figure 8.3*  *SML robust design*

point assessment. The diagram also alludes to the importance of pre- and post-programme activity.

This design is not intended to represent all the possibilities for SML programmes. Rather it shows one design that can be modified to suit a wide range of possibilities. For instance, in Shell the ten-month programme leading to a Certificate in Management Studies (CMS) had the following features from Figure 8.3:

- a start-up event of two days
- set meetings over ten months (one day per month)
- learning contracts developed and agreed in the early set meetings (phase one)
- final assessment for the CMS
- individual work on learning objectives
- collaboration with others in the set and in the company
- resources allocated to sets to meet learning needs and workshops to support learning.

Additional features not in Figure 8.3 include:

- mentors for programme participants (these were arranged during the start-up event)
- group and individual projects during phase two
- a handbook for participants to provide basic data, guidance notes on resources and an explanation of the programme
- access to a 'learning community', that is, when sets came together on common issues.

**Elements of SML programmes**

Figure 8.4 shows how the strategic processes in Chapter 7 are delivered as tactical elements of programmes. On the left are the processes and on the right examples of tactical elements. An asterisk marks elements that have already been identified as part of a robust design.

*Start-up event*

In a typical programme within an organization one or two days might be allocated to a start-up event. Activities within this can include:

- explaining SML
- explaining the programme
- locating the programme in the organization's strategies
- introductions – participants to each other, participants to staff
- agreeing ground rules for working.

Much of this would be expected in any significant management development programme. The key difference is the need to get people into the SML process. Also, typically in a start-up event there is the need to form learning sets of around five or six persons each.

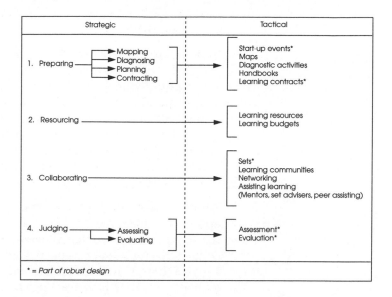

**Figure 8.4** *Strategic processes to tactical elements*

*Maps*  Chapter 7 discussed the value and importance of mapping. In translating this into practice some issues stand out. First, in an organizational programme there needs to be an organizational map. This might include:

- strategic directions, mission and vision statements, and so on
- competence lists, if the organization uses them
- organization charts
- HR/personnel policies
- technology, products, markets, and so on.

Many organizations are now using competence lists for selection and appraisal. If this is so, it is likely that these will 'map' the views of HR or top management on development issues. I have already indicated the severe limitations of competence maps, but if they are being used, then people have to respond to them. Managers might be joining an SML programme following an assessment/development centre and come with a competence map given to them as a result of feedback from the centre. They often need help in making sense of the map and of the diagnostic information accompanying it.

Competence lists imply that they cover the territory of management. However, it can be useful to expose managers to other maps to help them to make choices about learning. A typical map is the standard curriculum of an MBA. This can then be broken down into subjects (HR, strategy, finance, and so on).

Instead of presenting maps, it can be valuable to pursue two alternative methods:

1  Help learners to map their existing knowledge and hence see what concepts and theories they currently work with.
2  Use a questionnaire to ask learners about their knowledge of standard methods and techniques in management. Table 8.2 shows part of a strategic management questionnaire. This questionnaire (or rather the full version of it) can be given, in advance of a workshop, to participants; it can then be collected, analysed and used as a basis for a workshop session.

An alternative to using standard maps is to show a different approach to mapping. I prefer to use process maps (rather than content maps) so that managers can insert their own content. Examples such as the triangle model (linking Why?, What?, How? and Who?) and the U model shown earlier in this book have been used on SML programmes to develop strategic leadership.

I also like to 'nest' models and maps inside each other. The analogy here is with, say, a map of the world which can be broken down into maps of a country, regions in the country, towns and districts. A district map is 'nested' inside a town map, inside a regional map, and so on. An advantage of nesting is that it improves ease of use. This is especially so if one applies Miller's theory[4] of short-term memory. Crudely, Miller suggests that we can hold in short-term memory $7\pm2$ chunks of information ('chunks' may be concepts, words, variables, and the like). If we take the lower limit of short-term memory (5 chunks) then 1 'chunk' is used to process and link other concepts. Hence, it is desirable to restrict models to four variables if they are to be remembered (and hence usable). You will note that in this book I have

*Table 8.2   Extract from questionnaire on basic strategic management ideas*

| Issues/methods | Know and use | Know well but do not use | Know a little | Don't know |
|---|---|---|---|---|
| Boston Consulting Group approach | | | | |
| Contingency planning | | | | |
| Environment scanning | | | | |
| Forecasting, e.g. Delphi | | | | |
| Mission statements | | | | |
| Porter's model | | | | |
| Scenario methods | | | | |
| SWOT analysis | | | | |
| Visioning | | | | |

generally followed that theory; for example, in Chapter 7 I discussed four basic processes and then subdivided these (nesting subprocesses where needed). The U model and the triangle model also have four basic variables (chunks) in each.

*Diagnostic activity* To balance the mapping processes learners need to acquire information about themselves, their strengths and weaknesses, values, interests, and so on. Often there is considerable data available, but it may be in a poor state of analysis. Managers can often draw on:

- appraisal data about themselves
- day-to-day feedback
- assessment centre feedback
- psychometric tests and instruments
- colleagues' views
- subordinates' views
- data from family and friends
- data from career counsellors, and so on
- 360 degree feedback.

The trouble is that data may conflict, may be missing key dimensions, may be poorly presented, and so on. Sets can be of enormous help to individuals in assisting them to sift and sort data. This is especially so in low-trust cultures where it is not possible for the person to test data in the organization.

*Handbooks* Over time we have found it valuable to produce handbooks for significant SML programmes. These have varied from guidance notes about the programme, contact points in the organization, and the like to more lengthy documents which include diagnostic instruments, handouts (to assist in mapping), and so on.

I mention this detail here to exemplify the need for good structuring devices in SML. These devices look different from those used in traditional programmes, and hence often need thinking through carefully.

*Learning contracts* The first point to emphasize is that by a learning contract I mean a document written by an individual specifying that person's learning proposals. Some writers use the term 'learning contract' to mean a set of ground rules agreed in a group.

For example, Lee comments:

> The first session was introductory, getting the students to talk about themselves and their expectations, trying to establish rapport and build up a *learning contract*. The basic messages were:

- this is a low threat environment in which we can learn together;
- you will have control over both content and process, I will be here to help;
- we are all responsible for this course, it will be what we make it;
- I do not consider myself in charge. (Lee,[5] p. 33)

I would accept that this has an element of contracting to it, but it is better characterized as a 'process contract', not a 'learning contract'.

In order to indicate how learning contracts are used in SML I shall quote from three programme participants. First, Michael Skilton, a housing manager:

> The contract requires an honest self analysis of one's present position and identifies how that position was reached. The contract also requires identification of the progress the writer wishes to make, an analysis of what must be achieved to obtain that progress and a checklist of anticipated indicators that one has arrived at one's objectives. The other fundamental aspect of the contract is that although it is negotiated and written at an early stage of the course it need not be a rigid document and can at any time be renegotiated. My contract identified eight projects needing to be achieved. For instance, I have been looking at how computerisation can help the working of the department, at internal training and at problems identified in involving tenants in management.
>     Now, at the start of my second year, I am renegotiating my contract. My work in the first forced me to take a close and critical look at the way I applied myself to some of the problems I was currently experiencing. I became aware that, although my knowledge of housing was reasonably good, my understanding of some basic concepts was lacking. Further, it is now clear that when I started the course I had not been able to identify properly my requirements in relation to what I was trying to achieve. A major difference between this course and more conventional courses is that part of the process of learning is to reach an understanding of why you are learning, which helps you to identify what you should be learning. This is not available in traditional courses, for once you have embarked on them you are committed to either completing or abandoning the process of learning. (Skilton,[6] p. 4)

Nigel Boldero, a policy analyst, commented as follows:

The first term (out of a total of six) was spent in small groups (or 'sets') considering the content of members' contracts – these documents set out the areas to be studied, skills and experience to be acquired and methods for so doing. The development of these statements of an individual's needs were supported by a series of 'taster' sessions on the range of disciplines and approaches which form the core of the term 'management'. The contract also included arrangements for assessment (the contract and these arrangements are negotiated and agreed within each set and with the external assessors).

I found this period useful in enabling me to look fundamentally at my career pattern to date. As a result I had a clearer idea of my future intentions and the *skills* and *experiences*, as well as the *knowledge* I would need to acquire to achieve these.

With the help of fellow set members (which included a set adviser), I identified four main areas of work:

- management accountancy;
- organizational behaviour and development;
- operations management (including operations research);
- a range of communication and other interpersonal skills. (Boldero,[7] p. 292)

Peter Maher, a deputy head teacher, commented on the value of working with others:

I learnt a lot from discussing other set members' contracts as they are interested in topics beyond my own experience. The process of negotiating the contracts was just as edifying. (Maher,[8] p. 8)

The positive comments above are in keeping with the research evidence in Malcolm Knowles's book on learning contracts.[9] Research that he and others have analysed suggests the following benefits:

- more effective integration of theory and practice
- greater sense of ownership of own learning
- increased ability to define and set measurable goals
- enhanced self concept
- greater self motivation to learn, participate and achieve more realistic attitudes towards work and career
- enlarged awareness of individual strengths and weaknesses.

Steiner[10] makes a point of comparing contracts with legalistic contracts. As he points out, they need to meet at least three criteria:

- Mutual consent – there has to be explicit, clear agreement on all sides that the arrangements are voluntarily accepted. Also there is the understanding that there will be mutual effort to meet the contract.
- Consideration – meaning that, for instance, a learner may pay an educational institution for a course and expect 'education' in return.
- Lawful – a contract must not violate any laws.

In SML there are extra features of a contract, especially given the involvement of a range of parties (for example, the learner, set colleagues, the learner's manager, and so on). Figure 8.5 shows the range of influences on a learning contract.

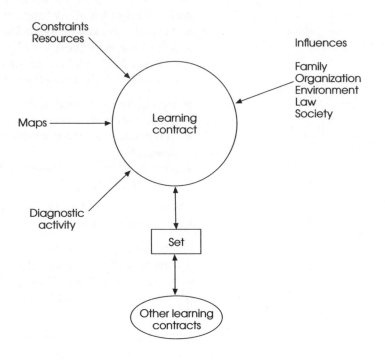

**Figure 8.5**   *Learning contracts*

*Learning resources*   Access to a range of learning resources is crucial in SML. However, an advantage of the SML approach lies in liberating learners from the constraints of traditional learning modes, and in encouraging learners to be creative in their choice of methods. Here is another quote from Nigel Boldero:

> There are a range of mechanisms available for managing the contract. My programme has drawn upon:

- a specialist seminar group on finance, including a tutor and financial managers from both the public and private sectors;
- library and video resources available in the Management Centre (computing facilities are also available);
- specialist tutorial assistance from a work colleague on certain management accountancy techniques (my contract includes an emphasis on projects which are centred upon 'live' work activities);
- training sessions/workshops on particular skills – so far there have been three residential weekends aimed at developing a variety of 'interpersonal skills';
- a 'learning set' – the same set which helped develop the contracts is now taking on the role of monitoring progress on them, resolving particular learning problems, considering approaches to projects, supporting and confronting individuals' work and a forum in which developing skills can be 'tried out' and discussed. (Boldero,[7] p. 292)

The following is a list of some of the learning modes used on SML programmes:

- Work experience – work itself
  - culture
  - boss
  - colleagues
  - other employees
  - projects
  - secondments
  - mentor/coach
- Outside organization
  - travel
  - courses – employer sponsored
           – adult education
  - therapy/counselling
  - reading
  - TV/radio/cassettes
  - family/friends
  - retreats
  - museums
  - libraries
  - art galleries
- Internal courses
- Team development/organization development.

*Learning budgets*   In SML it is important that participants are able fully to realize their responsibility for learning. This ideally includes some control over budgets for financing the kind of learning activities mentioned above. In some programmes, individuals have been allocated a personal budget to meet the requirements of their learning contract. Thus the person writes into the contract where financial assistance will be required for particular activities. The organization, in agreeing to the contract, agrees to the financial and other resource needs.

In some programmes the budget is allocated to the set, and they have to justify, collectively, to those in authority how they wish to spend their budget. This responsibility passed to participants not only ensures ownership of the learning, but also adds the dimension of the concomitant duty to the organization to be working within resource constraints.

Participants usually show great care in handling budgets, and the process does not throw up any issues not already present in budgetary systems in organizations.

Providing individuals with the budget helps them to realize the costs involved in activities, and to develop a real sense of cost-effectiveness. For instance, where participants collectively agree that they want to learn something, they may decide to hire an eminent professor. When they discover what the professor will charge to do a one-day workshop, and compare it with the cost of the professor's book, they may elect to buy the book instead! They may not, of course. They may want the interaction with some famous guru, and decide it is worth it. Hence, they may economize on other activities.

I have also found that when participants on a programme are given budgetary responsibility they become quite frugal in their use of resources. They will negotiate with speakers to keep fees down; they will invite company people to provide sessions (so that they do not have to pay for them); they will see the value of less expensive resources such as audio tapes and print material.

All this contrasts with traditional training approaches where managers often feel happy to apply for expensive courses, without a thought about cost-effectiveness, because it is out of someone else's budget. Many HR development people would like managers to appreciate that training courses form only one learning mode among many. However, if they insist on holding the training budgets, and do not encourage people to take responsibility for their own learning, then they will continue to be unsuccessful in changing attitudes.

*Learning sets*     Learning sets are central to SML operation. However, because in SML they are used in unique and particular ways, it is often difficult to describe their value and their function. I shall begin with a lengthy quote from a piece written by a woman who was a member of a set with whom I worked in the 1970s. Out of the many examples I could have chosen, I felt hers was interesting because it shows her own growing strategic sense. It is also an example of someone – who was not a manager – struggling to establish independent self employed status (which she achieved). I have only lightly edited her comments in order to keep it to what she wanted to say, and in her own style.

> When I went to the set I had not heard of the theories of self managed learning and for some weeks I had no clear idea of what was going on. I heard the explanation of how the group was expected to plan their course but it was like listening to a foreign language which I had learnt but before my ear had got attuned to the sound of the words spoken by a native of the country. I was confused and unclear about what each person wanted to achieve and only gradually saw that other members of the group were also confused. It then became clearer that the group discussions were the process of clarification being worked through together. What was new to me was the idea that I could design a programme to meet my own personal needs and it took me a long time to grasp this and experience that idea in a way that I could feel it belonged to me. And that this groping towards solutions together was a learning process in itself which we were each experiencing for ourselves as well as observing it in each other. The idea that I could focus on my own personal needs and requirements for training and education; that I could decide for myself what these were; that I could plan how to get them and not fit into someone else's programme was so new and alien it took a long time to recognize what this meant as an experience. My degree had seemed to be a task and a programme of work set by someone else and I had then squeezed myself into a shape that would fit their requirements and expectations like an Ugly Sister distorting herself to fit into Cinderella's shoe. Now I was free to create my own programme and I didn't know that I was free. I had always had that freedom, but I had not been able to use it because I didn't recognize that I had it. The moment of realizing this was full of excitement for me and I felt warm and loving and grateful to each person in the group for the way in which our working together had produced this feeling as an experience of release. It wasn't something which happened suddenly and easily however but was the product of many hours thrashing

out problems together. The essential change for me was the transformation from knowing something with my head to experiencing what I knew with my emotions.

The way we worked in the set was that we were each responsible for asking for the time that we wanted and for deciding for ourselves what the area was on which we wanted to work. At first I considered only practical questions but as I became more confident in the group I began to bring up personal questions because that was what was the most important focus for me at that moment. In the past I would not have considered that appropriate to bring into a study group, and, as at college, I would have thought only academic problems were legitimate questions to bring up. Neither would I have thought of approaching a tutor to discuss an emotional problem. I made the assumption that he was only concerned with my academic progress. It gradually became clear that our academic progress was linked with our personal development and that personal issues often stood in the way of making academic progress. And these were what needed working through first. At the end of each meeting we set ourselves goals to be reached within a time limit, often before the next meeting.

These goals were not always reached and that focused our attention on how we were not keeping our agreements with ourselves. We challenged each other's justifications or rationalizations for failure to keep a contract and the work in the set was often centred on the areas in which we were blocking ourselves. I saw that, as we got to know each other, a caring and supportive relationship built up between us where I could be open about my own feelings and frank in my response to others. I came to feel accepted and supported no matter how challenging the set response was to me. The challenge was not presented in terms of advice or help but more in terms of questioning what was going on in my life and then of us sharing with each other our own experiences. The tutor and members occasionally gave specific information and suggested directions in which to move, but mainly the aim was to assist us in reaching our own decisions to suit our own needs.

This meant being clear about what these needs were. In my case I wanted to plan my life and my means of earning money in a way which satisfied me. I didn't know clearly how I wanted to do this and the set became a place where I learnt to explore that question more effectively as well as to learn to know myself better. These two aspects were closely linked.

My position at this time was that I had worked in public relations and had qualified as a teacher before bringing up three children who were then aged 4, 9 and 11. To return to teaching seemed an obvious solution. I would be earning money and it had been a job that I'd found challenging and interesting. However, I wanted to work where I felt fully committed and invested in what I was doing and I did not want to do a job only because it was convenient through lack of making a clear choice on the matter. I wanted to make a conscious decision to do whatever I did because it was what I wanted – and convenience might be the deciding factor – but I didn't want to slip into a convenient situation without choosing to commit myself to it. The manner of working in the set, encouraging each other to become more autonomous and self directed, increased this feeling and also gave me the confidence to act and plan a freer life, which was what became clear was my preference. So eventually I chose to work freelance in several different areas. I could equally have chosen freely to work full time in an establishment, but decided that it suited me better not to do that.

When I first went to the set, apart from caring for a household of five people, I was coaching in English part time, interviewing and writing articles for a careers magazine and attending a variety of growth groups as part of my wish to further my own personal development and also in order to gain experience to train as a group facilitator. My motivation was to earn money to supplement the costs of the family and the household and to re-establish myself as an individual with an identity outside the family. However, it was rather a chicken or the egg situation. I needed to develop skills and gain experience in order to develop the confidence that comes from doing something and at the same time I needed more personal development in order to go and do what I wanted. The set was a place where both these things could happen.

My sense of personal identity seemed to me to depend mainly on my roles as a wife and mother and both were defined relative to and dependent on very special relationships. After 10 years in these roles I didn't have a strong sense of personal identity.

I went to a wide range of groups through which I began to know myself better and to extend and challenge myself. The set provided a long-term situation where I could go and discuss and make sense of this variety of experiences with members who also had experience of group work and who could provide an environment where I could digest and assimilate a fairly rich diet. The quality of the environment provided by the set varied for me. At first I was pleased to meet with friends who were open and welcoming and interested in my activities, as I was in theirs, but as time went on the very real sense of caring which we shared was very important as well as the feeling that I could turn to any person in that group at any time if I wanted a friend. And this was based on me as an individual and in no way was connected with my previous roles or dependent on them. The set became perhaps a different sort of family and one where it was alright to make mistakes and that was a great release to not have to be perfect all the time.

I realized just how much I was waiting for life to be interesting so that I could commit myself, and I switched to seeing that it was my responsibility to make it interesting for myself and only I could put in my energy and investment and not to wait for the activity itself to come up and grab me and in some way make it all magically work. This applied equally in personal relationships. I had always thought that it was my responsibility to make things work. I became much more aware of this as a personal experience and more able to put the idea into practice with an awareness of what I was doing, which I found strengthening. I was less fumbling along with a well-meaning idea and more accepting my responsibility for making life work for myself and at the same time accepting that I was not responsible for making anyone else's life work. I then felt less guilty towards the family when I went out to meetings, and with my change in attitude I found that they became less resentful of my outside activities. What seemed to happen was that I accepted their anger and hostility as theirs and with accepting it the anger seemed to evaporate.

The set also focused my ability to give and to receive; that it was alright to give whatever I wanted to a group member and I discovered my ability to receive too so that when someone told me that through working with me they had found their own self confidence I could accept that and receive it and feel good. In the past one way I had reduced my self esteem was to disbelieve any positive feedback. Now I didn't need to believe it. I could just receive it and choose to either make myself feel good with that or undermine it by disbelief and feel I was being conned. Once I was aware of this I was less likely to cheat myself of something good and so reduce the quality of my experience.

The quality of Ian as the set adviser was most important to me. My experience of schools and of university had been of very hierarchical organizations where students were told or advised what to do and where on the whole the atmosphere encouraged the student to feel that authority knew best, and perhaps it is necessary for me to say that my own education had been very authoritarian. My experience of teachers and tutors had been that there was an absence of empathy and a large measure of criticism and judgement. I never felt criticized or judged at any time in the set by Ian or by anyone else, and I think that this atmosphere of detachment was a quality which came from Ian. There was also a caring and an understanding. This detachment was in no way a cold quality, and I felt I could expand and grow in this atmosphere that he encouraged. I also felt that I was free to make mistakes for the first time in my life – and again I didn't feel judged for this. The result of this for me was that I felt freer to be myself in the set than anywhere I'd ever felt before. I felt free to give and to take and to expose myself and be open emotionally in a way that I hadn't permitted myself to be before. He created a containing space where I could look at my abilities as well as my weaknesses. He showed no impatience, but waited for when the time seemed right, for each member, to challenge them when he saw that they were stuck and needed to do something in a particular area in order to move on. I never saw him push anyone and my own experience was that when he challenged me it was very clarifying to have to confront myself at that point. I didn't feel reaction or resistance being stirred up and I think that this assisted my own developing and learning in the set.

All of these experiences seemed to apply to other members and from the first it was clear that the relationship between Ian and the student was person to person – which I now take for granted but which surprised me originally. There was no sense in which Ian suggested that he knew better than the students. Any information was given in the sense of sharing of his own experience or knowledge and he listened with attention and without ever dismissing or discounting a reply. He gave unstintingly of time and hospitality as well as of his own personal possessions, e.g. books and car. I found that to be given to so freely in this way was a tremendous form of being affirmed as a person and to be given to without any strings attached gave me a lot of pleasure and energy and a feeling of self esteem. This seems to be part of his personality. He gives totally of himself in terms of investing himself during a meeting. I always feel him as totally present and interested. He never encouraged us to make the set the only place where we could enjoy these experiences and it was from the set that we all moved out taking and using the results of our work with us.

I think that I have gradually changed from either resisting or submitting to life to more often creating what I want. I have moved from avoiding to confronting situations more readily. Confrontation is something I'm only just moving towards and see as my next step forward before the next and the next. None of which I know right now but which I look forward to with excitement.

## Nature of learning sets

What I hope the piece shows is that a set is quite *unlike*

- a team
- a business meeting
- a syndicate or group discussion
- a therapy group
- a T-group
- a support group (sets do more than just support)
- an action learning set (where the focus is more on projects)
- a seminar
- a group tutorial.

Table 8.3 compares a less-than-ideal seminar and a good learning set.

I shall also quote here from the views of a student who had taken a degree by independent study, where she used tutorials as her main focus of interaction with others.

I have been involved as a participant in a set for a period of approximately one year. Prior to this, I received my 'tuition' in a one to one tutorial situation. Thus, what I want to do here is compare my experience of the use of a set and the use of a tutorial as methods of exploring intellectual and personal problems.

*The tutorial*

My first experience was of the one to one tutorial. I was able here to test out ideas and clarify areas of confusion. However, the ideas were being tested on one person only – an 'expert' opinion on matters. This immediately puts the student into a Child state and the tutor into a

*Table 8.3* Sets are not seminars

| Seminar | Learning set |
| --- | --- |
| Ideas discussed are 'out there', i.e. they are someone else's *and* someone else's choice for discussion (usually the tutor's) | Ideas discussed originate from individuals. These are not separate from the concerns of the person. The person raises issues because they *mean* something |
| People often try to 'win' in debates, e.g. by knocking down others' ideas | People are not trying to win by debating. Respect is shown for others' ideas |
| • by pushing in to the discussion to create space for themselves | There is no need to push in as each person has his or her own space |
| • by seeking approval, e.g. from tutor | Everyone assesses final work so tutor's approval is less crucial |
| • by trying to *look* smart (irrespective of whether they are being true to their own views) | People try (usually) to be true to their own beliefs |
| People are often thinking up the next bright thing to say, so they do not listen well to others | People are given space to struggle with ideas, so listening to others comes naturally |
| People are sometimes put on the spot in a Socratic manner. They then feel the need to defend ideas to the last, even though they may not care about such ideas (or even believe in them) | People are helped with their ideas. Questions are asked for the benefit of the person, not in order to put someone on the defensive. People's feelings are taken into consideration. Arguing is avoided as this usually serves to entrench ideas, not change or improve them |

Parent state (in Transactional Analysis terms). I found that my way of coping with this was to try to 'wangle' my way out of doing things! More importantly, I think, was that I felt that I was producing work to please my tutor – not for myself. In other words, I was not taking responsibility for my own learning.

*The set*

The set was formed comprising myself and four other students. I found distinct advantages in this method of operating, for several reasons.

1 There is a more equal distribution of power. Every member of the set both gives and receives help thus setting up an Adult to Adult relationship.
2 I think as a direct result of the above, the responsibility for learning lies in the hands of the learner.
3 The *set members* have a responsibility to others as well as *themselves*. Therefore, I think, *they* are more likely to attend meetings.

4 The set members are answerable to other members of the set as well as the tutor and are thus less able to wriggle out of doing work. (It is embarrassing to admit to others that you have not done something you agreed to do!)

5 The students can test their ideas out on more than one person and therefore get more than one perspective on them.

6 Questions are posed to the student by other members of the set as well as the tutor. The questions asked by the other set members may have been overlooked by the tutor.

7 The members of the set are 'all in the same boat' and are perhaps in a better position to understand each other's problems.

I think that I need here to mention how I perceive the role of the set adviser or tutor. Whereas in a tutorial I think the tutor's main function is to help the student by giving 'expert' advice, I think in the set his main function is to facilitate learning. More specifically, I think this includes asking pertinent questions, moving the set member(s) to explore problems at a deeper level, refraining from advice giving and directing communication to maximise benefit for the student(s) (eg bringing people in, shutting people up). In addition, he is also another member of the set who has a body of expert knowledge which can be 'tapped' by the students. To sum up, the one to one tutorial and the set are two methods of helping a student with their learning. The features of each situation as I see them are summarised below.

| Tutorial | Set |
| --- | --- |
| Unequal power (Parent–Child relationship) | More equal power (Adult–Adult relationship) |
| Student gains opinion of expert | Student gains opinion of expert and laypersons |
| Student answerable to tutor | Student answerable to tutor and set members |
| Tutor as 'expert' | Tutor as 'facilitator'[11] |

**Factors in set organization**

Some of the factors that impinge on the organization of learning sets include the following.

*Size*

Five is the ideal number (plus set adviser). This, in a one-day meeting, allows everyone to get at least an hour's time if they need it. Also, the organization of meetings is easier than with a larger number (finding time in people's busy schedules can be a problem). With only four in a set there is a problem if someone is absent. A set of three reduces the level and quality of interaction and can put more pressure on the set adviser to take part. Six works reasonably well – it just puts a bit more pressure on the set to be well organized and pay attention to time. Seven becomes a strain (I have worked with a set of seven, but I was relieved when one person dropped out). Eight is impossible: people have too little time to explore issues in depth, and the process becomes too superficial.

*Heterogeneity/ homogeneity*

Learning sets work best when there is sufficient commonality between set members to bond the set yet sufficient difference to produce creative tensions. Usually the latter factor is there without prompting. So in helping sets to form I tend to encourage people not to consider personality factors and other aspects of potential difference. In sets of managers it can be useful to ensure that, in an in-house programme, people are not at highly disparate levels in the hierarchy. It is not possible to have the CEO and a junior manager in the same set.

Some other interesting differences include age, gender, nationality and colour, which are discussed in a later chapter on diversity and difference. The token woman or token black person may initially experience difficulty in some sets. The set adviser must be able to raise these issues of difference, and get the set to recognize their impact (if they do not already).

*Set formation*

I prefer to have an open discussion in a start-up event about set formation. I encourage people to consider initially only two factors – time and location; that is, a set may form around people who can meet on certain days only, or in certain geographically defined locations. Usually most people have some flexibility on these issues, and therefore sets can group around these common factors.

*Location*

Sets can meet anywhere. I have held meetings in training centres, offices, board rooms, people's homes, hotels and, in good weather, out of doors.

*Scheduling*

An ideal is for sets to meet about once a month for a whole day over a period of at least six months. However, in Cable and Wireless a set of secretaries met every week for one hour, in their lunch break. It was not ideal, but they could not get time off work. The set still provided enormous value to these women and they made it work. If sets meet infrequently (for example, at more than six-weekly intervals) there can be too much catching up to do – unless set members have known each other for some time, when two-monthly intervals can work.

Sets often continue to meet after formal programmes. I know of one that is continuing 13 years after it was formed.

**Learning set processes**

To function well, a set needs:

- a reasonable level of openness so that set members will discuss genuine issues
- sufficient trust so that people will feel able, for instance, to share confidential information
- good listening from everyone
- set members to 'own' what they say, usually by using 'I' statements (for example, I believe this, I am concerned about that, and so on)
- a preparedness for people to act non-defensively – to hear ideas without premature negative judgements
- space for people to reflect on what comes up – not pressure to rush on from item to item
- limited advice giving – too much is intrusive
- questions and comment made between participants designed to help people learn (not to play clever).

The qualities described here are consonant with the notion of a set as an environment for dialogue. Dialogue has become a fashionable idea, especially among some learning organization devotees. Often, though, there is little knowledge of how to create dialogic groups. A set could be seen as an exemplar of the dialogic mode of interaction. It is different from discussion where what is addressed is a topic that no one owns. The key idea in a set is that if something is worked on it has to be owned by someone. The ideal is that nothing is considered and talked about in the set unless someone owns it as an issue or problem. If an item is on the agenda it is because someone has a burning desire to work on it and is prepared to take action , if needed.

*Guidelines for set meetings*

A way of assisting a set to develop its processes of working is to have explicit ground rules agreed at the start. These ground rules provide a basis for agreed modes of operating. Even if they are violated, which they usually are at times, their explicit nature allows for the set rapidly to get back on track (by referring to the rules). The following is a list of ground rules that I have used in some sets.

1 Accept responsibility for your own learning – no one else is responsible for it. If you need help, ask for it. Other people are not mind readers.
2 Collaborate with others in their learning, but do not try to take it over for them.
3 Listen actively to everyone. If you find it difficult to follow someone – tell them.

4 Do not try to make people be like you – accept them as they are.

5 The detail of what happens in the set is confidential. However, general decisions taken will need to be communicated outside.

6 Try to be as honest and as open as possible, while being sensitive to the needs of others.

7 Everyone has the right to a reasonable part of the set's time for his or her own problems and concerns.

8 Do not pretend that things are not the way they are: try to present honest concerns.

9 Speak for yourself and avoid generalizing. Use 'I' rather than 'we', 'you', 'they', or 'one'.

10 Everyone has the right not to answer a question if that seems appropriate.

11 Set advisers are bound by the same rules – and they have trouble following them too!

12 The set adviser in a set is another *person* – he or she is not here to prop up the set or to take decisions for it.

13 Decisions that need to be taken are made collectively, by consensus.

In order to short-circuit needless discussion, I have tended to offer a list like the above for the set to consider. It is not imposed; it is merely a mapping device to help the set. The set can reject it, modify it or accept it as it is.

## Structuring of set meetings

A typical structure might be as follows.

### 1. Checking in

Set members each say a few sentences on anything that has happened since the set last met, or anything that might be an obstacle to their participation at this meeting. This process lasts perhaps ten minutes, but can be a valuable reconnecting device.

### 2. Agenda setting

The members, in turn, might suggest what they want to raise at this meeting, and how much time each might need. Also, there may need to be time available to discuss general set issues, for example dates and venues of future meetings.

### 3. Working through the agenda

Usually people need more time than they estimate. They might say that they need 30 minutes to raise an issue, but their colleagues may question them on it to a greater extent than they predicted. The agenda, therefore, has to contain some flexibility, but a problem can occur if insufficient time remains to discuss the last person's items. Hence the set needs to develop time awareness so that this problem is minimized or eliminated.

There may also need to be a space between items so that

individuals can record agreements, commitments and decisions, before continuing.

**4. Checking out**    A round of responses to the day can be of great value. People can express how they feel about how the set is going, or clear down unfinished items. This is usually a ten-minute process.

**Comments on sets**    I shall end this section with two more comments on sets, from participants on the two-year post-graduate diploma.

> SML is different from other courses: first was 'the set', a group of five fellow novices, a second year 'adviser' and a tutor also acting in an advisory capacity. This 'set' of disparate personalities has helped plan my study programme and monitor my progress through the course. Initially they seemed to have nothing to offer me but within a short space of time my attitude had changed. While they had no right of veto over my work plan (or 'contract'), they put me through some hoops trying to justify it. Issues of my own personal and professional development were brought together to construct a learning contract that has become important to me. (Maher,[8] p. 1)

> The most important element of the course for me has been the set. Without that vehicle, the problems I had would possibly never have been raised let alone so thoroughly and effectively worked on. The set becomes different things to different people, but, for me, some of those things are – a sounding board for ideas; a confessional for a variety of problems, many of which could not be discussed as fully at work for reasons of both vested interest and time; sometimes an uncomfortable put-on-the-spot experience where I have really had to face up to my own responsibility for my actions; and an invaluable support group. The other members of my set would have other perspectives, but we are all agreed that that experience has been the most powerful throughout the whole course.
>     The process is also about taking risks. The ethos is about change and change can only happen if you are prepared to take risks. The set helps you to take risks as indeed does the whole 'Community', i.e. the other members of all the other sets in both the first and second years. (Atkins,[2] p. 18)

**Learning community**    The last sentence in the quote from Liz Atkins above leads us from sets into the idea of a learning community. Peter Maher comments:

> The community – staff and students – exercises control over the way that the course develops. This forum, which now numbers fifty souls, is the arena for debate about any issue relating to groups or individuals. It also provides a resource for learning and allows participants with common interests or goals to learn together or share experiences. (Maher,[8] p. 1)

The example above is from a programme in a higher education setting. But in-organization programmes also develop as a learning community, for example Shell, BBC and British Airways. In all these organizational programmes participants did not just draw on their set for support, learning, risk taking and stimulation; they also used the wider community of all the sets in the programme. The use of this wider community is not essential to SML, but there is no doubt that it not only assists individual learning, but also supports the development of a learning business. As people see that they can draw on these wider resources for learning they start to reach out to others in the organization.

Hence the notion of a learning community in SML ideally broadens to encompass the whole organization (though this is not easy to achieve). I want to emphasize that the learning community idea fostered in SML is not like a closed clique. It is to do with broader development. However, I have drawn on the ideas of others in developing the use of the learning community in SML. Pedler's review of the field is particularly valuable. His definition of a learning community is helpful. He says it 'involves bringing together a group of people as peers to meet personal learning needs primarily through a sharing of resources and skills offered by those present'[12] (p. 68). His paper elaborates the points in this definition and he shows how five activities are required, namely:

1 *Building the climate:* establishing openness, interdependence and mutuality.
2 *Sharing needs:* of all the persons present and the legitimacy of these individual needs.
3 *Providing resources:* both without but particularly within the persons present.
4 *Community planning:* to establish a 'programme' to meet needs, share resources, to learn and develop.
5 *Evaluation:* identifying criteria for success; looking at where we've come from, where to go next; resolving conflicts. (Pedler,[12] p. 69)

In SML, in addition to the focus on personal needs, there is the linkage to organizational needs. Through the use of learning contracts and other mechanisms SML makes it easier for a learning community to work effectively. For instance, people work out their needs in a set such that their interactions with colleagues in the wider community outside their sets are more focused and clear.

**Networking**    The learning community can facilitate networking. Networking may be

- within the learning community
- outside it.

In either case SML encourages people to explore wider resources, and link with a range of people. Sets can be especially helpful in encouraging people to develop new contacts, and to use others to assist their learning.

As Stella Jackson, Head of Management Development in the London Borough of Lewisham, comments:

> The value and power of networking has been a particularly strong feature [of SML] with regard to changing the organisation culture. Many senior managers now choose to meet and discuss situations informally, with a view to resolving problems in a mutually agreed way ... This is creating greater flexibility, and speed of response, and reducing unnecessary blocks and misunderstandings – a significant contribution to the devolution of power and accountability which the authority is trying to encourage.

**Assisting learning**    Part of the collaborative activity in SML is assisting others to learn. Sets and learning communities only work really well when participants see that they can

- assist colleagues in their learning
- ask for assistance for themselves.

Interestingly, in many organizational cultures asking is more difficult than giving. People can feel inhibited to ask for assistance if it implies a weakness. This is especially a factor in macho power cultures: you are a wimp if you do not demonstrate total self reliance.

But SML is not about such individualistic modes of operating. A learning business cannot develop without asking and giving. Another imbalance is in social services, education and other 'helping professions'. So-called 'helping professionals' can exhibit a pathological desire to help others – to give unstintingly of themselves so that they smother other people. They can need as much assistance as the macho manager in recognizing the value of asking.

In order to get this balance (and to do many other things)

SML programmes delineate the role of staff as 'learning assistants'. In sets the role is usually described as 'set adviser'. In one-to-one work the assister may be called a mentor or a coach, and I shall discuss these roles more fully in Part Five. However, I would like to re-emphasize here the role of 'peer assisting'. In some programmes we have encouraged people to assume the role of 'co-set adviser'. In the post-graduate diploma already mentioned, second-year course members would volunteer to work with a member of staff in co-set advising a first-year set.

Liz Atkins indicates the value of this:

> There is opportunity also within the programme for course members to take the role of set adviser. I became a set adviser to a first year set in my second year as part of my contract was about improving my set advising skills. This was an invaluable experience which has helped me at both the technical level of acquiring skills and at the personal development level of getting feedback from both the set and the set adviser on the way I function. I am continuing to act as set adviser for that set although I have finished the course and am continuing to grow and develop through it. (Atkins,[2] p. 18)

What Liz Atkins does not mention is the value to those in their first year. They have indicated, in evaluations, how helpful it can be to have someone present who can model being a self managing learner, and who can show how peer assisting can work. It is also important in the programme to show how the authority role of staff can be de-emphasized by trusting second-year participants to work with staff in this way. However, to make this process work requires the development of co-set advisers. On the post-graduate diploma programme we held a two-day workshop every year for co-set advisers, we developed a pack of materials for their use, we held regular meetings of all set advisers throughout the year to review progress, and co-set advising pairs (staff plus second year) met after each set meeting to review their own working. Set advising does not just come naturally, and Part Five emphasizes the importance in SML of getting this activity right. Chapter 10 shows some concrete examples of set adviser development.

## Assessment

Assessment in this context is about assessing learning. Specifically, in SML it is important for learners to assess if they have achieved the objectives identified in the learning contract. However, as indicated in the last chapter, individuals almost always learn more than is in their contract. This also may need recognizing. So at the end of an organized programme the learner, in conducting a self assessment, may raise wider issues than those in the learning contract. Also, a set may agree some common 'framing' goals, such as that all members of the set need to be conscious of their own learning and be able to make self assessments. These framing goals are, as implied, a way of providing a frame or a series of parameters for assessment. They indicate what the assessment is about and in what context it is undertaken. A particular 'given' in SML is the expectation of collaborative assessment. This means that the person's self assessment is checked with

- peers (usually the set)
- a set adviser
- those external to the set (for example, mentor, manager).

Also, in a programme for an educational qualification, such as a diploma or Master's degree, the role of external examiner/assessor/validator must be accommodated.

The basic issues of collaborative assessment are explored elsewhere,[13] and will not be repeated here. Rather, I shall refer to a few specific factors that affect SML practice as described in this book. First, however, I shall present two quotes to set the scene.

> Finally the style of assessment. The parallel has been drawn between the set and jury trial. The jury, unusually, includes the defendant, who not only has an opportunity to frame opinion, but also has a vote! The assessment is no less rigorous for this. Past experience has shown that the harshest critic is often the very set member whose work is being assessed. (Maher,[8] p. 1)

> Now, after two years of this learning experience I have accepted Self Managed Learning at an affective level. I have felt the process and lived with it and through it, and it is now becoming a way of life. I cannot accept that the final assessment is in any way final. It is to me merely a statement of where I have got to by that particular moment. I feel no more 'qualified' now than I was when I started. The programme has simply begun the process of opening up paths of learning and has helped me choose for two years the path to follow. It has also given me an internal mechanism to help me choose paths for the future by providing me with insight into how I learn and, therefore, how I should tackle my own learning problems. It has given me greater insight and understanding of how others learn and, therefore, I hope has made me more aware and empathetic in my work to the different needs of others. I accept total responsibility for my own learning – if it does not happen then it is my own fault.

By the same token if I want things to happen in my life then I accept that I must make them happen and not sit around blaming others for lack of activity.

Although from an assessment point of view I say that I do not feel 'qualified' I can honestly say that a very different person left the course from the one that started it. For one thing I am no longer a down-trodden, frustrated Training Officer for I achieved my objective of becoming an independent consultant. And what's more I was able to make the final leap into the unknown with a greater sense of confidence and knowing where I was going. The outside world, when I at last stepped into it, did not seem nearly so alarming and risky as it had once appeared. I very much doubt that I would ever have made that step without having followed the programme and I also doubt that I would have completed a programme which was more prescriptive. (Atkins,[2] p. 18)

## Views of the collaborative assessment process

I have discussed with learners their views of the process. They have *all* said that this approach is preferable to any other (all of them have, of course, experienced traditional modes already, so their comparison is with those approaches). Many approach the assessment process with trepidation, but afterwards most agree that it was valuable and helpful. Some have even said that it was 'the high spot of the year' in that they could experience a culmination of their work in a context where they could get live feedback. Some specific positive points mentioned have been:

1 It gives face-to-face contact so that people are treated as human beings.
2 The person being assessed by others can comment on the judgements of others. There can be a dialogue which can resolve misunderstandings.
3 The individual has to justify his or her own work to others and confront his or her own judgement with those of others.
4 It is all open and above board.
5 When someone is presenting work which is not in the traditional mode (for example, creative work) then it can be most easily discussed in this context.

Some negative points have been:

1 It takes time to do it properly.
2 It does not necessarily reduce stress and tension. Some people still feel nervous facing their colleagues even when they have come to know them well.

## Standards

On programmes leading to a qualification, people become concerned about issues of level or standard. They want to know what makes diploma- or Master's-level work. They are concerned about equivalence. As everyone is doing different things, how can each person be measured against the same standard? Addressing this problem forms a key discussion in sets. Learners need to recognize that in traditional educational programmes there is no guarantee of equivalence and similar standards applying across all courses. In the Minutes of a meeting of the Convocation of the University of London on Tuesday, 12 May 1981, the following exchange was recorded:

> *Question*
> What are the procedures whereby it is ensured, as far as reasonably possible, that the same class of degree is granted by the University for work of equivalent quality in different faculties and subjects, both at first degree and higher levels; and how is a comparison of quality made in relation to such different disciplines as, for example, Geography and English?

> *Answer*
> While the establishment of exact equivalence of standards in widely different fields may be a matter of legitimate aspiration, the University makes no claim that its procedures can achieve it.

This is the only honest answer possible. Even in the same subject area there is no guarantee of equivalent standards in research degrees such as PhDs where each person is doing something different. So an SML programme throws up no new issues in this area. What it does, however, is to make the subjective, messy side of assessment more transparent. It is exposed to scrutiny by giving set members responsibility for assessment.

## Criteria

People normally find it difficult to come up with specific, measurable criteria by which to judge work. This is not surprising given that (a) most people have not been asked to do this before coming on an SML programme and (b) it is difficult to lay down criteria for everything one does. I think people can beneficially struggle with this issue, but sets should also recognize that some criteria will be more readily measurable than others. I do not take the view that if it cannot be measured it cannot be important. The most important things in life often cannot be measured – like love or artistic ability. We cannot expunge these from organizational life just because they cannot be neatly tied down.

# Evaluation

Evaluation is the other judgement process to set alongside assessment. Evaluation is of the worth and value of a programme or activity. SML programmes covering many hundreds of managers have been evaluated since 1980. I have, in this chapter, quoted from published comments of individual managers about the post-graduate diploma in management (by SML) at what is now the University of East London. I chose these comments because they have been published and are therefore accessible. Evaluation of SML programmes creates no different issues from evaluation in general, and I have commented elsewhere on evaluation research.[14] A model piece of research evaluating SML was carried out in British Airways.[15] (Other research is mentioned in Appendix I.) I say it was a model because the perspectives of participants, managers, HR staff and mentors were obtained, hence drawing together a wide range of views. Also, the evaluation covered recent graduates from the programme as well as those who had finished a year earlier.

This latter point is important. Often we have had evaluation reports months after a programme where managers have said that they were only just appreciating the full benefits of their learning. A contrary situation has occurred in more than one organization where evaluation was carried out in the middle of a programme. In SML this can be a disaster. If participants have not seen through their learning contract, evaluation is of limited use. It is not like a modular course where it is possible to evaluate each module in turn after it has happened.

An aspect of evaluation which is often lost is the need to evaluate at different levels. Here the U model comes into play. A programme needs evaluating as to:

● *Purposes and principles* – are they appropriate?
● *Strategies* – have they worked?
● *Tactics* – have they worked?
● *Actions* – were they as planned, and appropriate?

From a range of studies, evaluation of purposes and principles is almost wholly positive. People say that they want the autonomy of an SML programme. They welcome the chance to own their own learning. The only negative notes have occasionally come from traditional, power-oriented senior managers who are less interested in organizational performance and more interested in controlling their employees.

On some programmes there have been concerns about strategy. In one organization participants were critical of the company for not integrating the SML programme into company practice. They felt let down by senior management. However, these criticisms grow less over time as organizations start to see the merits of a more strategic approach to learning.

Tactical evaluation is usually very positive. People like the concept of sets and they usually welcome the idea of learning contracts. However, at the action level a few concerns are expressed. About 5 per cent of sets struggle and never achieve high levels of trust and openness. At assessment, around 1–2 per cent of participants have significant problems. The percentage of those who fail is higher than this, at around 5 per cent: however, only some 'fails' create ongoing difficulties (that is, that they are unhappy with the outcome). While I always hope (and aim) for zero per cent problems, I am comforted by the fact that in evaluating appraisal systems and assessment centres, the levels of dissatisfaction are typically much higher.

## Summary

This chapter has explored some aspects of typical SML programmes from a tactical perspective. I have indicated how the strategic processes in the previous chapter can be put into practice. The one area I have largely omitted is that of the role of 'staff', such as set advisers, mentors, and so on. This issue will be central to the next part of the book.

While I have made some reference to practical issues of making programmes work, Chapter 10 goes into more detail on the issue of set adviser development and also provides some pointers to newer developments such as the use of on-line sets or learning groups.

## Notes

1 Lao Tsu (1972) *Tao Te Ching* (translated by Gia-Fu Feng and Jane English), London: Wildwood House. (This is one of the most accessible translations, but there are many more.)

2 Atkins, L. (1983) 'Self managed learning at the Anglian Regional Management Centre', *Group Relations* (Winter), 7–21.

3 Clutterbuck, D. (1983) 'Cheating – and making better managers', *Observer Business* (Sunday 28 August), 16.

4 Miller, A.G., Gallanter, E. and Pribram, K.M. (1960) *Plans and the Structure of Behavior*, New York: Holt, Rinehart & Winston.

5 Lee, B. (1985) 'Learner-centred courses – a personal experience', *Management Education and Development*, **16**, 1 (Spring), 31–40.

6 Skilton, M. (1982) 'Self managed learning – a manager's

report on his management course', *LGTB Training Newsletter* (Nov./Dec.), 4.

7  Boldero, N. (1981) 'Self managed learning: a personal view', *The Training Officer* (October), 292.

8  Maher, P. (1984) 'SML: it changed my life', *ARMC Newsletter* (February), 1.

9  Knowles, M. (1986) *Using Learning Contracts*, San Francisco: Jossey-Bass.

10  Steiner, C. (1974) *Scripts People Live*, New York: Bantam.

11  Maclean, C.A. (1978) *Sets and Tutorials*, North East London Polytechnic, Working Paper.

12  Pedler, M. (1981) 'Developing the learning community', in Boydell, T. and Pedler, M. (eds) *Management Self-Development: Concepts and Practices*, Aldershot, Hants: Gower.

13  My own writing on assessment has included:

    (a)  Cunningham, I. (1991) 'Case studies in collaborative assessment', in Dove, P. and Brown, S. (eds) *Self and Peer Assessment*, SCED Paper 63.

    (b)  Cunningham, I. and Dawes, G. (1990) 'Is objective assessment rigorous enough?', Paper to Ashridge Management College Research Conference (January).

    (c)  Cunningham, I. (1981) 'Assessment and experiential learning', Paper to Fifth International Conference on Higher Education, University of Lancaster (September).

    (d)  The above paper was modified and published (with the same title) in Boot, R. and Reynolds, M. (eds) (1983) *Learning and Experience in Formal Education*, University of Manchester: Manchester Monograph.

    (e)  There is reference to assessment in Cunningham, I. (1981) 'Self managed learning and independent study', in Boydell, T. and Pedler, M. (eds) *Management Self-Development: Concepts and Practices*, Aldershot, Hants: Gower.

I would also recommend
Heron, J. (1979) *Assessment Revisited*, London: British Postgraduate Medical Federation, for an excellent theoretical analysis of assessment issues.

14  (a)  Cunningham, I. (1991) 'Action learning for chief executives', in Pedler, M. (ed.) *Action Learning in Practice*, 2nd edn, Aldershot, Hants: Gower.

    (b)  Cunningham, I. (1988) 'Interactive holistic research', in Reason, P. (ed.) *Human Inquiry in Practice*, London: Sage.

15  Fraser, J. (1988) *An Evaluation of Self Managed Learning in Practice*, Berkhamsted, Herts: Ashridge Management College.

# PART FIVE    Practice

The four chapters in this part cover some key practical issues. Chapter 9 discusses 'staff' roles and the role of assisting learning. The chapter emphasizes the role of the other person in linking with learners. Chapter 10 is new to this edition and goes into more detail on issues raised in Chapter 9, especially the role of set advisers in SML programmes. Chapter 11 discusses the learner in context. Chapter 12 concludes the book by looking at directions in strategic learning, including issues for organizations and for individuals. It also discusses directions for self managed learning.

# 9 Roles in learning and change

Introduction
Strategic learning, the development of learning businesses and the operation of self managed learning does not just happen by saying it ought to. I realize that this would be taken as obvious by most people. Yet much of the literature on learning organizations and cultural change seems implicitly to assume that change will happen because someone says it should. Books and articles say it is a good thing, and gurus exhort managers to change through charismatic performances. Yet it is not obvious that these methods on their own bring results. I am not suggesting that the analyses of theorists and the expositions of gurus are valueless. They can energize people and inspire them to want change. But something more is needed – a lot more, in fact.

One part of this 'more' is the role of people such as top/senior managers, HR/personnel professionals, management developers and consultants. Part of the change process is bringing together the strategic alliances mentioned in the opening chapters of this book. We need those

- who can
- who know and
- who care

to work together to assist change to occur. It is clear that, if one analyses the situation in organizations against the above framework, specialists such as management developers cannot produce change on their own. (The wider dimensions of managing change belong outside this book.) So let us assume that top management has agreed to a strategic learning policy and wants self managed learning programmes. (Such examples were quoted in Chapter 1.) What is now required to make it happen?

The thesis in this chapter is that specific people need to play particular roles in making it happen. These people may be all from personnel/HR departments, but this is seldom the case. The roles I shall describe could be seen as 'professional' roles and I am comfortable with the term professional if it is used in a loose way. I am not comfortable with professionalism as an élitist, closed-shop model of working. This latter model undermines strategic learning, and I shall comment on it later. Another term I have used earlier is 'practitioner'. This is looser and perhaps more user friendly.

The labels to try to describe all the roles are often inadequate, so let me, instead of labouring this, introduce the four roles that, from research[1] and experience, describe all that must be done and all that is needed to be done. These are:

- theorist
- designer
- manager
- assistant.

*Theorists* provide the theory for action.
*Designers* design programmes and activities.
*Managers* manage them.
*Assistants* assist learners to learn.

These roles can be played by one person, by small teams or by a dispersed range of people. Let me explain each in turn before returning to the overall theory.

## Learning theorist

The learning theorist role is essentially about

(a) creating and developing
(b) reviewing and synthesizing, and
(c) articulating

the theory underpinning any programme.

All programmes are based on theory – in this context theories of learning and theories of managing. (Burgoyne[2] provides a good analysis of the major schools of thought on learning which underpin management development programmes.) Often the basic theory is not made explicit, particularly in traditional management development courses. But a 'theory' is, nevertheless, there.

It is worth emphasizing that there are three aspects to the theorist role. 'Theory creating' may be, in its full-blooded sense, relatively rare. However, 'theory review' and 'theory articulation' have to be more widespread. Every planning or development team starting up a programme needs to articulate theory. For instance, in SML there is an understood theory related to learning, part of which I have indicated in earlier chapters. In traditional management courses, when people say 'We should have a session in the course on X' they are implicitly saying something about a theory of managing (for example, 'to be an effective manager you need to know X'). The problem is that 'theory articulation' is often done implicitly, and one has to dig beneath the surface statements to understand the base theory.

In SML, underlying theory is more likely to be articulated in an explicit way. Indeed, it is often argued about in great detail in planning teams.

The issue of theory links back to earlier discussions of mapping. Theory provides the basis for mapping. If an organization is serious about becoming a learning business, developing sufficient shared maps becomes important. (I say 'sufficient' because it does not need total uniformity – nor is this possible.) The theorist role is key to developing shared maps. Effective CEOs that I have studied have had clear theoretical bases to their work and have usually made these relatively explicit. They do not, however, tend to use academic language, so the point that they are good theorizers is often missed. For instance, they tend to communicate in metaphors and analogies or in visual models. A good theoretician CEO can provide a backdrop for practitioners to develop specific theories about learning and about managing. In SML programmes both are important. Managers need to develop an understanding of learning issues so they need a theory *of* strategic learning. They also need a theory *for* strategic learning, for example theories of managing.

A theory *of* strategic learning includes issues discussed in earlier chapters, such as:

- first-order and second-order learning
- theories of good learning.

Theories *for* strategic learning include:

- the U model linking purpose, strategy, tactics and action
- the triangle model linking questions of Why?, What?, How? and Who?

Practitioners such as management developers and consultants working on SML programmes need to be able to work with such theories. They need to be able to use theories and models with comfort in planning programmes and in working with managers on programmes. This is not to say that such theories have to be articulated in the way it has been done here. Each practitioner will integrate theory and practice in their own way. This is the mark of the 'centred' practitioner.[3]

## Learning designer

I take 'design' to be the process whereby the 'theory' is fleshed out in order to provide a basis for action. The learning designer role is often written about, but seldom analysed. Some of those who have commented on it usefully include Garratt, Harrison and Morris.[4]

The term is used in a metaphorical sense, since one does not literally design a product. I think this is a problem with the concept as it can give a false concreteness to the idea of 'a programme' which has been 'designed' by someone (and made by that person or someone else).

Despite the difficulties with the metaphor, I want to use it because

(a)  it is what has been used by others, and changing the
       language is a problem
(b)  I cannot think of a better term.

I want to define 'design' closer to Harrison's[4] use of the term than to Morris's[4] more restricted use. The latter talks of:

> trust-based negotiation, which aspires after the
> condition of a gentlemen's agreement, and design-
> based negotiation, which always seeks formal
> commitment on details. (It seems no accident that
> 'designing' and 'calculating' are applied to people that
> we do not feel we can trust!)

I believe that design can be a mutual activity: the staff and manager(s) can design a programme together. I do take Morris's point that tightly defined prestructured courses may be predicated on low-trust assumptions, and I am not in favour of rigid pre-timetabled designs.

However, in my wider use of the term, no matter how loose the structure of the programme, it is a design. We can have a 'non-design design' as the designer (non-metaphorical) Massimo Vignelli suggests. Even to call together a group of managers and say 'choose what you want to do' is a design. (It might be labelled a non-design design, but it is a design.)

A useful distinction might be between macro design and micro design.

Macro design is related to the totality of developing strategic learning and the structure of activities to achieve it. So practitioners in an organization could design a strategy based on the strategic processes discussed earlier, namely:

●  preparing

- resourcing
- collaborating
- judging.

The micro design of events within this overall strategy might be left more in the hands of others.

In the last chapter I have shown aspects of design such as:

- the use of sets
- the use of a learning community
- the use of learning contracts (as individual designs).

Each of these elements provides the basis for micro design work. A staff team may do this prior to launching the programme. Once the programme starts it is possible to work on the kind of trust basis that Morris suggests.

A learning contract is an example of micro design. While needing to be written in order that other set members can read it, it is very much taken on trust by each set. There is no pressure from staff for course members to produce a carefully laid-out and immutable design; rather the set to which the person belongs needs to have some idea of what the person is aiming to do, so that it can be of most help to the individual. Thus the micro design (by the learner) of a learning programme, which constitutes the contract, is seen as an attempt to think through ideas, but not as an immutable document.

In engaging in design activity, one draws on the following, in addition to theory:

- client needs
- economics – for example, cost-effectiveness
- social factors, including what is allowable in the norms of a society
- methodology available – that is, what can be done
- staff capability
- time factors

and so on. Designing requires considerable capability and wisdom, though I hope that the chapters in Part Four of this book can assist designers.

Macro design work generally tends to be done by 'professionals', for example consultants and management developers. This makes sense. Designing for learning is not usually part of the capability of a line manager, except where they are involved in micro design elements such as learning contracts.

# Learning manager

If one articulates a theory and a design which could be the basis of a programme, in order to operationalize that theory and design a programme has to be established and run. This is where the role of the learning manager comes in. I further subdivide this role into two: one I shall label 'Fronting' and one 'Back-up'. The spatial metaphor is reasonable to use if one perceives the programme as delineating a bounded 'learning experience'. It can be presented in diagrammatic form, as in Figure 9.1.

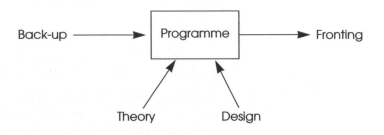

*Figure 9.1   Managing learning*

This shows that the theory and design provide the basis for the programme and fronting and back-up are in direct relationship to the programme.

'Fronting' covers the following kinds of functions and activities:

1  The initiator role, a term used in action learning; see Pedler.[5]
2  The leadership role, in terms of, say, leading a staff team which sets up a programme.
3  Most of Mintzberg's[6] ten managerial roles (liaison, figurehead, spokesman, negotiator, entrepreneur, resource allocator, disturbance handler, leader, monitor, disseminator) in so far as any of them would be relevant to a particular programme.
4  Political activity, specifically the preparational work necessary to set up a programme.[7]

Some of the above relates to setting up a programme (for example, initiating and planning), but other factors are relevant during the operation of a programme. This tends to be underestimated in the self development literature, and may be a factor in explaining why there is sometimes little follow-through of programmes (for example, they do not tend to be recorded so it is difficult to know their extent).

Another factor hindering programme efficiency is the lack of recognition of the 'back-up' role. This covers:

- administration – for example, getting material posted on time, and so on
- registry-type activity – admitting people to a programme (usually more relevant in institutional settings)
- finance/budgeting, and the like
- technical support – for example, with equipment such as VTR, computers, and so on
- premises organization – booking rooms, and making similar arrangements
- learning resource back-up – handouts, materials, library facilities, audio-visual material, computer access, and so on
- secretarial – DTP, photocopying, filing, and other functions.

Some people have assumed that an SML programme implies that the boring administration is less relevant. They equate 'administration' with 'bureaucracy', which is not necessarily valid. Bureaucracy describes a particular theory or style of organization; administration is necessary whatever organization theory one works with.

In some cases, especially in educational institutions, much of this back-up role is passed on to other staff. However, in other programmes this is not so.

Fronting has tended to be seen as the glamorous side of managing and back-up has been largely ignored in the literature. This may partly be due to the fact that it is relatively easy to see what skills and abilities are necessary to perform the back-up role. However, I think it is also related to the lower status given to non-academic/non-professional trainer staff in organizations. Hence, I suspect that some people would not even see back-up as part of SML work. Obviously I disagree with this view.

## Learning assistant

The learning assistant role is the aspect of SML work concerned with direct interaction with learners. Set advisers and mentors come within this category. When one set advises, the role is defined through interaction with learners. This makes this role different from the other three (theorist, designer and manager), as they do not require direct contact with learners. Learning theorists and designers do not have to see the learners for whom they have theorized and designed, though such theory/design activity would eventually become sterile without contact with learners. However, in relation to a *particular* programme, theorist and designer may rely on research evidence collected by others to get feedback.

Learning managers may also 'front' a programme to get it

started and provide back-up facilities, but not meet programme members. This may be especially so when a steering group has been set up to initiate a programme: not all steering group members need necessarily meet learners. So the learning assistant role is uniquely defined as requiring direct contact with learners, and, as I have defined the other three roles, at one level one can say: the learning assistant does the rest. However, before saying something about the concept as a whole, I should perhaps say a little more about the 'assisting' process, as assisting is not a readily accepted concept. I take 'assisting' as a noble, valued, time-honoured process in human communities. Parents assist their children to learn; a person assists another person with a job that is too big for them; children assist their parents with housework and gardening. Someone assisted me to learn to drive; my accountant assists me with my finances. Note that I want to define professionals in general as 'assistants', as I wish to play down the power that they have accumulated to themselves. Negative aspects of professionalization include:

1 Changing processes to nouns. So instead of 'need' being a verb it becomes a noun. People thus have 'needs' which have to be met by professionals, as in 'training needs'. In the process professionals redefine what a person wants to learn and translate it into their own language.
2 Successful clients are those who are able to satisfy the professional. In a well-known management college course participants were given a secret rating by trainers and this was put on file for future reference. This rating was linked to the extent to which participants had learned what the trainers wanted them to learn.
3 Professionals define what are legitimate problems.
4 Management educators in business schools limit what can be addressed by the subjects they are able to teach.

Functional learning assistant activity in strategic learning and SML is such that one can take categorization one stage further and identify:

● learning assistant (problem/person based), or LA(P)
● learning assistant (solution/subject based), or LA(S).

The abbreviations LA(P) and LA(S) are somewhat clumsy, perhaps, but I wanted to distinguish these two roles without putting traditional labels on them. As I shall indicate later, it is possible to see the 'P' role as similar to what people call 'facilitation' (and some organizations have used this term for this role). However, as I shall explain below, I have some concerns about how the word facilitator has come to be used. It is also possible to see the 'S' role as being like that of a teacher. Again, I think that there are problems with this label and I shall try to indicate why. So for the rest of this chapter I shall use the 'P' and 'S' distinctions and I get by with the abbreviations LA(P) and LA(S) to describe these two facets of assisting learners.

LA(P) is the set adviser-type role: the person who works with a group (but also possibly individuals) and works with them on their problems. The LA(P) is not there to teach or train in any standard sense, but to assist others with what is relevant to them, and in the process help them to learn.

LA(S) is a legitimate role. It is sometimes undervalued in the pendulum swing towards rejection of expertise. In the post-graduate diploma mentioned in Chapter 8, LA(S)s were called 'specialist tutors' and their role was to respond to the requirements of learners who wished to tap into their expertise. Thus in a set meeting a person may identify that they need to learn about accountancy. The set adviser (LA(P)) may then help them to identify different ways of learning about accountancy. These might include: reading books, watching videos/films, listening to tapes, or using a staff member to tutor them on the problems that they have identified. The learner chooses the mode they want to use (or more than one mode if needed): many choose to go to tutors to get their advice. The sequence in this is (crudely):

1 Define the problem.
2 Look for the solutions (if necessary).

At stage 1, LA(P) *assists* in defining the problem; at stage 2 LA(S) *assists* with providing solutions. LA(P)s ask questions; LA(S)s answer them (approximately). Table 9.1 elaborates on this.

*Table 9.1*   *Learning assistant: roles*

| LA(P) | LA(S) |
|---|---|
| Assist learners as *persons* to define *problems.* Assist them to change basic *patterns* and *processes.* | Assist learners to develop *solutions* to problems by drawing on *specialisms* and *subjects* or using *systems.* Learners may also learn *skills.* |

This process reverses the usual order in teaching/training, where the manager learns solutions (subjects) and then has to find problems to use them on.

In such a process one only needs one staff role, that of teacher, as learners are left to fend for themselves in finding applications for the knowledge and skills they learn.

It is worth noting that traditional teachers are well able to play the LA(S) role, but this is not traditional teaching. The learner goes to the LA(S) with their requirements, and ideally the latter responds to what the person asks for. This does not always work out, of course.

One issue to address is that of whether the learning assistant needs to have face-to-face contact with the learner. With the growth of distance learning programmes the case has been made that modern technology can replace face-to-face contact. It is certainly true that in terms of subject/solution (S) learning a great deal can be carried out via books, tapes, CDs, Open University broadcasts, learning packages, the Internet, and so on.

The problem with much of this material is that it is not very user friendly. Books are often written *about* managers but not necessarily *for* them. The growth of CD-ROMs has not necessarily created better material, especially where the 'garbage in, garbage out' syndrome is present. Too often creators of materials have been inclined to hope that glitzy technology will make up for poor content. This can also apply to web sites on the Internet – fancy graphics do not make up for sterile content and poor signposting for the user. Therefore there is often a need to help learners to make sensible choices about materials – and this usually requires human intervention.

However, the human intervention may not be face to face. A great deal can be done using flexible technologies such as the phone, e-mail and interactive Internet capabilities. I find that, for instance, I can carry out coaching-type activity over the phone. I also use e-mail to share ideas and to write joint articles with colleagues in other countries. In Chapter 10 I have described aspects of using on-line interaction for working with learning groups on the Fielding Institute MA (Organization Design and Effectiveness). This programme uses Digital's Alta Vista software to provide the facility to carry out 'learning assisting' with groups in any part of the world. At the time of writing I'm assisting groups with members in Japan, the USA, Australia and South Africa.

Allowing, though, for the value of using technology to its best advantage, there is still something about face-to-face contact which adds value. A key aspect is the ability to work quickly in the face-to-face mode and respond instantly to what learners are raising. In the fast-paced world that most managers inhabit, speed of response is often vital – and it may be unhelpful to have to wait for a response to an e-mail or a posting on an Internet site. The other key advantage of the face-to-face meeting is the opportunity for the learning assistant to read all the non-verbal messages that are missed in print or on the phone. Of course, some enthusiasts see an advantage in reducing the emotionality of the face-to-face interaction – and that can be the case sometimes. A claimed value of asynchronous communication is that it can allow a more considered response than face-to-face communication.

Some of these issues surface in more detail in Chapter 10 and the interested reader may want to look at that chapter. In summary here my guess is that the mix of technology use and face-to-face interaction will be the best in most circumstances. The ideal is to have regular set meetings with electronic and other contact in between, and as more people have access to the Internet that mode will become increasingly important as a support for learning.

In Table 9.1 I have defined roles, not persons. One person may play both roles, as long as the roles emerge roughly in the order indicated (problem to solution). In the post-graduate diploma course we had a rule that the LA(P) to a course member could not also act as that member's LA(S) (that is, in an official capacity). That does not preclude a set adviser from offering knowledge to a set member, if needed, during the process of a set. We rejected the pseudo-Rogerian mode of the LA(P), merely making reflective or process comments. If I know something, and I am asked about it, I shall give an honest answer and not deflect the question on to another staff member.

## Assisting and facilitating

Many see the set adviser as a 'facilitator' and draw on interpretations of the work of Carl Rogers to justify a particular facilitative stance in sets (and other learning environments). In its common, everyday use, or in its dictionary definitions, there is not much wrong with facilitating. Making something easier for someone seems a good activity.

However, in the training profession, facilitation has become a noun and 'facilitators' have gained a particular status. My concerns about the new profession of facilitation include the following:

1 A gross misunderstanding of Rogerianism prevails. Carl Rogers was seen as demanding therapists and counsellors

to adopt a dogmatic non-directive approach, and this was linked to his ideas on facilitating learning. Brink comments:

> In Germany, all counsellor education consists of bureaucratically controlled training in non-directive technique. Rogers' offers to meet with the leaders and participate in training seminars have been declined. It appears as though he is seen as a threat. Here, in New England, a two-year masters' program in counsellor education drills its students in reflection skills. One of their graduates, a gifted young man, unusually warm, sensitive, bright, insightful, finished the program having been stripped down to an efficient echoing device; *he* had largely disappeared. Instead of the program having been a growth experience for him, he was diminished by it as a person and as a professional. (Brink,[8] p. 32)

Rogers, in response to this, wrote:

> I totally agree with Brink in deploring the inauthentic, mechanical, wooden, dogmatic, client-centred therapist. In fact, I probably feel worse about such therapists than they do, because I feel personally offended. But I equally deplore dogmatism and rigidity in any therapist of whatever persuasion. (Rogers,[9] p. 33)

2  Facilitators may attempt to deny responsibility *to* learners. They pretend to be just one of the group and deny that they have a specific role apart from 'non-directive' 'catalytic' remarks.

3  Facilitators can get over-obsessed with group process. Sets are there to assist learners to learn what they (learners) decide. Facilitators can overemphasize the set as an entity beyond its basic role. If the set is working well, 'process comments' are not necessary.

4  Learners can get 'facilitated' whether they want it or not. The worst excesses of this include the promotion by trainers of inappropriate secondary feedback. Note the following interaction reported in Clark et al.[10] (p. 37).

> Trainer:  What are you doing, Jim?
> Jim:       (Who has been silent and looks very tense) I'm thinking.
> Trainer:  Tell me what you are thinking.
> Jim:       I'm trying to find the right words to give Peter (another trainee) some feedback.
> Trainer:  How about taking the risk of giving feedback using the wrong words?

> Jim:     OK ... Peter, I don't like you.
> Trainer: Are those the right words, Jim?
> Jim:     Yes (smiling). That's what I wanted to say.

5  Facilitators can get into 'Rescuing'. This term has a technical meaning in Transactional Analysis, developed from the work of Stephen Karpman. James and Jongeward[11] interpret 'Rescuing' as maintaining dependence under the guise of helping. Steiner[12] argues that Rescuers believe people cannot really help themselves. He suggests that Rescuing reaffirms and maintains inappropriate power imbalances. He proposed

   (a) do not help without a contract to do so
   (b) do not believe other people are helpless
   (c) assist others to find their own power
   (d) do not do most of the work (in an assisting relationship).

My own mapping of the relationship of the main approaches to helping people to learn is shown in Figure 9.2.

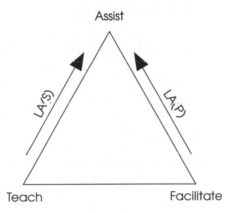

**Figure 9.2**   *The assisting role: a map*

The implication of this figure is that there are three major processes being used. I have argued in favour of assisting rather than teaching or facilitating. However, the boundaries of these processes are not neat. The teaching role shades in the direction of LA(S), as I've indicated earlier, when teachers give up teaching, in the didactic sense, and instead offer expertise and wisdom to learners in response to what learners ask for.

The facilitator role shades in the direction of LA(P) when facilitators see their role as helping learners to define their own problems and change their patterns of behaviour.

*Assisting – Who?*     Who assists learning is an open question. It does not have to be a designated practitioner. Sets encourage peer assisting. Managers, it is hoped, assist people who report to them.

*Assisting – How?*     There are many aspects of the 'How?' of assisting (for a fuller analysis see my earlier research[1]). I shall indicate a few major ones here. (The interested reader may also want to consult Chapter 10 regarding set adviser development.)

### Legitimizing

Learners need their involvement in learning legitimized. If they leave their workplace to attend a set meeting or meet with a mentor, this has to be seen as a legitimate use of a person's time. The learning assistant, whether set adviser or mentor, can legitimize such time. This is especially necessary where an organization is moving away from the dominant use of training courses to a more flexible approach. Training courses tend to be seen as legitimate: other modes less so.

### Supporting and stimulating

These two processes need to go together. There is significant research[13] to suggest that supporting on its own may lead to the learner feeling comfortable but not stimulated to learn. Stimulation only – the heavy pushing of someone to learn – can lead to burn-out, stress and anxiety. Stimulating people to learn through challenging them can develop skills and abilities, but at a cost if there is little or no support. Figure 9.3 shows, simplistically, the linkages of support to satisfaction, and stimulus to satisfactoriness.

In other words, feeling good and performing well can be balanced. Balancing in this process can assist the kind of

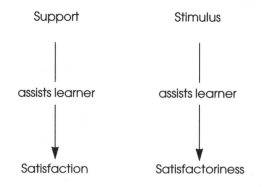

*Figure 9.3*    *Support and stimulus*

balance discussed in Chapter 5. Learners can be assisted in developing a 'both/and' rather than an 'either/or' view of the world.

## Encouraging

The assistant encourages 'good learning'. This is not imposing on the learner, but helping people to open their eyes to new possibilities and to make these new possibilities real. Learners realize that they can become more capable, more wise, more centred and more grounded.

## Modelling

The learning assistant can model 'good learning'. I am not saying that learning assistants are always capable and wise, but that they are moving in this direction. They can show that it is possible to change through learning.

## Trusting

The learning assistant needs to show appropriate trust. Set advisers need to show that they trust the set and the people in it. When they challenge learners it is not to try to take control, but to stimulate.

## Linking

A set adviser can link members of the set to other learning possibilities. Set advisers may point the way to resources. A mentor may help someone to access other people in the organization in order to further their learning.

## Intervening and responding

This is another balance. Some literature characterizes the set adviser as an 'interventionist'. The set adviser is viewed as making interventions in the set process, for example to help the set to function better. This, like 'stimulating' discussed above, is a yang activity (in traditional Chinese philosophy); it is outgoing and active. However, as Taoist Chinese philosophers point out, this needs a yin balance. Yin is receptive, and open. So intervening needs balancing with responding. This is confirmed in research. Set advisers will not just intervene, they will be asked questions and they need to know how to respond appropriately.[1]

## Guarding

Set advisers are often in the role of guarding the principles of the processes used in SML. They may need to be vigilant to watch for any undermining of these principles – for example, when inappropriate controls creep in. Also, senior managers who have promoted strategic learning may need to be continually monitoring progress and guarding against back-sliding.

### Infilling

Often the set adviser's job in a set is to do what no one else is doing. If a set is very challenging and confronting, the set adviser's first role may be to show supportive behaviour in order to develop balance in the set. Alternatively, a set that becomes too cosy may need some challenge from the set adviser. Whatever the imbalance, the set adviser has an important role in detecting such issues and helping the set to see what it may be missing.

### Befriending

When someone is struggling with difficult and perhaps painful learning, maybe all they need at times is a friend – someone to talk to; a friendly ear. It sounds a simple remedy, but it is easily forgotten.

### Meta-assisting

By this I mean assisting the process of assisting. Top managers do this when they create a culture conducive to learning, encourage senior managers to mentor their juniors, sponsor development programmes, and so on. In an ideal world they might then be able to sit back and let it all happen. Except that ideal worlds rarely exist for long. The meta-level processes need continual attention.

### Learning assistant style

Within the processes described each person has their own style of doing things. There are some common features and there are some differences. It can be interesting to study the different styles to recognize these similarities and differences. In my own research[1] I studied a number of people. In some cases I taped them talking about their style. Here are two examples for comparison.

**Example A:**

> I try to tease out the task they (the learners) are working on – and sometimes help them to be aware of it from time to time.

I risk being disliked: I'm initially tough and difficult.
I confront personal difficulties between them and me.
I try to be silent a lot of the time – but it's difficult.
I try to be patient when they're struggling.
I share my understanding of what is going on at any time – test the validity of it. I'm prepared to be wrong sometimes.
I work when and where appropriate – I'm not likely to work in contexts which don't seem right.
I work by example as much as possible.

**Example B:**

My style is my predominant manner of working – what I do without thinking about it.
In groups this is what learners would say of me:

– remotish – warming up with time
– do rough work out loud
– tend to be obscure
– romantic
– belligerent and lethargic with bouts of excitement (intellectual and emotional).

My approach is to work towards shared responsibility – organizationally and conceptually (I prefer ideas that emerge rather than what comes from me).
I can easily (unhappily) slide to being directive – however, mental untidiness and emotional unreliability saves the day – directiveness breaks down.

The two examples are edited from long tapes but they give a flavour of style issues.

Another way to explain this is through studying people who are particularly effective in certain areas, especially sport. The advantage of sport as an arena of study is that results are generally quicker and more precise than in management. I can take as an example David Leadbetter, the golf coach, because the results of his students, such as Nick Faldo, are easy to see. Here are some quotes from an article on Leadbetter.[14]

'He bases his teaching methods on the fact that no two players are identical.'

'You can't just say there is only one way to do it ... You tailor your instructions to the player' ...

'David is a very introspective person, which may be to his detriment', Nick Price says. 'But if you disagree with something he encourages you to bring it up, to give him your opinion. He listens to you, tries to understand what you're saying and then guides you into an understanding of what he is talking about.'

Faldo cites Leadbetter's ingenuity in making practising more interesting ... Leadbetter is endlessly inventive in finding devices to help his pupils understand what he is trying to get them to achieve ...

'I try to help players by getting inside their mind to see what they're thinking' Leadbetter says. 'Once you have established the ways in which you can help, the key is to explain them, give them concepts. But I always listen. I learn from these players. They are the greatest players in the world doing it under pressure. I want to know what works and what doesn't work.'

All of the above is *very* relevant to the set adviser, mentor or manager assisting someone else's learning in an organization.

## Four roles: pulling it together

Figure 9.4 shows a way of linking the four roles. The four-leaf clover shows how each leaf is part of one plant: the leaves do not exist on their own. The roles need to 'centre', that is, harmonize and balance, and then ground themselves (in values, in contexts, and so on). Figure 9.4 also shows that 'theory' and 'design' tend to be the more paper-based, cerebral, detached roles, and 'managing' and 'assisting' tend to be the more practical, active and involved roles.

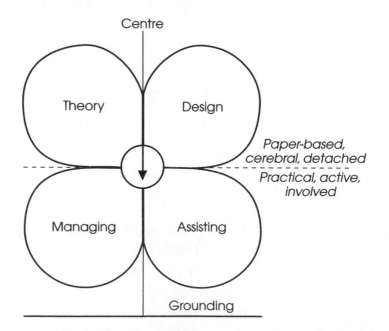

**Figure 9.4**   *The four-leaf clover*

The research evidence suggests that if the roles are played poorly then significant problems occur. Indeed, this is a major weakness of strategic learning and SML: it takes good people to make it work. It is much easier to run a learning/training activity on the reactive or bureaucratic models I discussed in Chapter 2. In standardized (bureaucratic) training procrustean tactics can force trainees into a fixed mould. Also, it is much simpler to ignore strategy and to muddle along. The challenge is that the tougher (strategic learning) route is the one that will ensure organizational survival and growth in the future.

**Four roles theory**

1 These four roles are all necessary even though some of them may be partially played out *in absentia*. This usually applies only in relation to theory and design – for example, learning managers may pick up and use theory and/or design already developed by others. However, someone will need to *articulate* the theory even if that person is not involved in its development. Hence, while someone may have done the theory *development*, if no one in, say, a planning group is able to articulate clearly and accurately the theory upon which they are working, a genuine learning programme is unlikely. (How can someone design or plan (manage) anything without having a theory to base it upon?)

2 Roles are not necessarily fixed to individuals:

(a) More than one person may be involved in playing a particular role; for example, there may be a team of LAs, a management team, and so on.

(b) More than one role may be played by the same person.

3 These roles are sufficient for SML programmes: no other roles need to be played in order to run an effective programme.

4 These roles are interdependent: they do not stand alone. For this reason it may well be desirable for people to play multiple roles in order to ensure linkages. It seems to be a feature of effective practitioners that they are able to play multiple roles.

5 The roles need to be further subdivided. Specifically in managing, the fronting and back-up roles are distinctively different. In LA, the problem-/person-based (P) role is different from the subject-/solution-based (S) role. Macro design is different from micro design.

6 People can play different roles and they can also play roles differently. The balance of roles played indicates something about macro style, and the way the person plays a role says something about micro style.

Thus one could say of someone that they are more interested and involved in theory and design issues than in managerial issues. This says something about that person's macro style. However, to define more clearly the person's style one would have to say *how* they played each role – for example, are they more theory creators (innovative, original); or more theory reviewers (good at synthesizing); or more theory articulators (good at understanding others' theories and seeing the relevance of a particular theory to specific situations); or all three?

All the above propositions are ones I have tested and they stand up.[1] The theory would need modifying or scrapping if such propositions were found to be invalid by others in future.

**Learner involvement**
Once a programme of learning has started, there is the issue of the extent of learner involvement in the four roles. Let me run through them in turn.

*Theorist*
A programme is set up on the basis of a theory, and it seems difficult for learners to be involved in altering that theory. My research indicates that practitioners often tend to be quite fixed about the theory base of their work, and some explicitly said that if learners wished them to change the theory underpinning the programme into one closer to traditional management training, they would refuse to do it. This can be a source of confusion for learners who imagine that on an SML programme everything is open for negotiation. It is not.

*Designer*
I have already stated that I think design should be relatively open for joint agreement. Learners often have problems with doing design; and in terms of design (as it affects a whole programme) I believe in joint action, where staff can contribute their expertise, but programme members/learners have some power to say yes or no.

*Manager*
The political aspect of 'fronting' a course or programme tends usually to be played by staff, though learners need not be excluded from that role. Also, learners tend to prefer much of the tedious 'back-up' work to be done by staff – for example, administrative work, resource acquisition, and so on. In the mid range between these two, our experience has been that course members can be equally involved with staff. Indeed, in terms of strategic and tactical issues it is important that course members share in major decisions.

*Learning assistant*
At one extreme there is the position which says that learners can and should do it all. Few people support this view. However, a key role for sets is to encourage learners to take on more responsibility in assisting others.

**Value of the theory**  I want to summarize here what I think is the value of the 'four roles' theory:

1  It provides a reasonably clear basis for categorizing practitioner activities.
2  It fits in with earlier theory I have discussed.
3  It does not prescribe the content of roles, as they are variable and dependent on style. However, it does provide a prescription in terms of the need to consider the four factors.
4  As a result of the above, it provides a better basis for practitioner development.
5  It has been widely tested: it is neither armchair theorizing nor the result of a one-shot case study.
6  It provides an overview from which more detailed analysis can come – for example, the subdivision of roles already indicated.
7  It shows, in the model, the interdependent links, thus avoiding the notion of four separate roles.
8  It provides a better way of characterizing the job of an academic in SML than the traditional administration/research/teaching split, for example by separating out teaching activity into LA(P) and LA(S); by showing where research (if it is for theory development) fits into the process; and by identifying 'design' as a key element.

**Summary**  This chapter has moved into the arena of implementation. It has made a specific case that four roles need to be played to make strategic learning and SML successful. It has also been acknowledged that programmes may fail if these roles are not carried out effectively.

**Notes**
1  Cunningham, I. (1984) *Teaching Styles in Learner Centred Management Development Programmes*, PhD Thesis, University of Lancaster.
2  Burgoyne, J.G. (1975) *Learning Theories and Design Assumptions in Management Development Programmes*, University of Lancaster: Centre for the Study of Management Learning.
3  See: McLean, A.J. , Sims, D.B.P., Mangham, I.L. and Tuffield, D. (1982) *Organization and Development in Transition*, Chichester: Wiley. Also, see Cunningham, I. – note 1 above.
4  Garratt, R. (1983) 'The power of action learning', in Pedler, M. (ed.) *Action Learning in Practice*, Aldershot, Hants: Gower; Harrison, R. (1978) 'How to design and conduct self-directed learning experiences', *Group and Organization Studies*, **3**, 2 (June), 149–67; Morris, J. (1980) 'Joint development activities: from practice to theory', in

Beck, J. and Cox, C. (eds) *Advances in Management Education*, Chichester: Wiley.

5 Pedler, M. (ed.) (1997) *Action Learning in Practice*, Aldershot, Hants: Gower.

6 Mintzberg, H. (1973) *The Nature of Managerial Work*, New York: Harper & Row.

7 Cunningham, I. (1984) 'Planning to develop managers', *Management Education and Development*, **15**, 2 (Summer), 83–104.

8 Brink, D.C. (1987) 'The issue of equality in the client- or person-centred approach', *Journal of Humanistic Psychology*, **27**, 1 (Winter), 27–37.

9 Rogers, C.R. (1987) 'Comments on the issue of equality in psychotherapy', *Journal of Humanistic Psychology*, **27**, 1 (Winter), 38–40.

10 Clark, M., Phillips, K. and Barker, D. (1984) *Unfinished Business*, Aldershot, Hants: Gower.

11 James, M. and Jongeward, D. (1971) *Born to Win*, Reading, MA: Addison-Wesley.

12 Steiner, C. (1974) *Scripts People Live*, New York: Bantam.

13 (a) See note 1 above.
   (b) Smith, P.B. (1980) 'The T-group trainer: group facilitator or prisoner of circumstance?', *Journal of Applied Behavioural Science*, No. 1, 63–77.
   (c) McCrone, J. (1993) 'Is there a gene for genius?', *The Independent on Sunday*, 2 May, 52–3.

14 Hopkins, J. (1992) 'The Mr Masterclass of golf', *The Independent*, 23 August, 24.

# 10 Developmental roles in practice

## Introduction

This chapter picks up some issues from the last one. It moves the discussion into areas of practical application. The four roles model is used as a start point to consider how people might need to develop their capabilities. I then discuss issues of the selection of set advisers before considering their development. The logic here is that the development work has to fit with the people selected to carry out a programme. Hence there cannot be hard and fast rules about development. However, I can indicate some of the work we have carried out in this field.

Following the discussion of set adviser development, there is a section making a link to mentoring and coaching before moving on to emerging issues such as the role of an adviser in on-line programmes. Here I shall refer to the specific example of an MA programme conducted mostly via the Internet.

## Developing from the four roles model

The first thing to say here is that whilst people in development roles need to consider all four roles and their capabilities within each, there is an important point about integrating these. Centred, grounded wisdom provides such integration. So while I shall briefly mention development under the four headings, it should be apparent that I am not implying that such development occurs in neat compartmentalized packages. If, for instance, one is developing capabilities in designing, this will tend to link to theory issues as a matter of course. It's not possible to design a programme without basing it on some theory of learning, even if such a theory is not articulated.

The development issues discussed in this chapter will initially seem more relevant to the development professional than the line manager. I would argue, though, that if organizations are serious about becoming 'learning organizations', as many proclaim, then at least an awareness on the part of line managers of these wider issues may be called for. A line manager acting as a set adviser may not need to be expert at designing, but should be aware of the basis of the design and be comfortable with the learning theory that underpins it.

The obvious baseline for anyone developing in this field is to have their own learning contract. By virtue of having to explore existing capabilities and to choose future development, this sets the ground work for future learning. So I shall assume that the rest of this discussion is based on a person having that start point – along with the kind of mapping presented in this book.

I shall make many of the comments below based on what we do in workshops. The workshop is often a core piece of work with an organization wanting to start up SML. However, there is usually a great deal of pre-work necessary before such workshops can be run, for example preparing a handbook covering basic issues. Also, there is much learning that people need to undertake outside such an environment. As it is often the most visible action, though, the workshop mode will provide a focus for many of my comments.

**Theory**  It is easy for people to overlook the need to develop in this area. Emphasis on the practical value of SML may lead the novice to assume that the theory side has little relevance. This is not so. The last chapter made a case for the importance of this factor and I will not repeat that case here.

Whilst all the standard modes of learning such as reading and attending lectures can have their place, we have found that in workshops for set advisers we have had to discuss theory issues as we go along. I say 'as we go along' because that is often the neatest way to ensure integration with other aspects of the development role. So, for instance, if we are looking at goal setting (question three in the five questions) we can add in theory about career development and how that impinges on goal setting and we can look at the research evidence on the value of goal setting and relate it to theory from, for instance, neurolinguistic programming. This integration can mean that people can learn the theory more effectively as it is linked to practical concrete issues. It is also apparent that some cultures within which we work are almost anti-theory, so any attempt to open a workshop with a theory base will be resisted. On the other hand there are some cultures, for instance academia, where the absence of an initial theory input to a workshop would be unwise.

A final point on this subject is that this book contains many references to theory which we know that development professionals and managers have found useful. I shall comment later on the value of new technology but suffice it to say here that, for instance, web sites on the Internet are a great source of information. However, as with so much of what we can access, it's often best to rely on recommendations than on random searching using search engines.

**Design**   It can seem easy for some to try to avoid learning in this area. For instance, I know that some organizations used the first edition of this book just to take ideas from directly and apply them. It's flattering that the designs discussed in earlier chapters are deemed to be so attractive. However, I worry about this strategy. Designs need to fit context. It's important to consider a whole range of factors in designing a programme. And a programme needs to fit within an overall learning and development strategy – for the organization or for the individual.

I would, though, see value in people learning how to use some of the content-free models covered earlier. One example is the U model (discussed in Chapter 7). At the very least this can provide a check on whether all the angles have been covered in a design. If the organization has particular espoused strategies for development, then the model allows for tactical decisions, such as the provision of specific programmes, to be analysed for coherence and goodness of fit with the strategy.

Following these points, then, I do see the need for people to consider how they improve their design capabilities. In workshops in organizations we have spent time on exploring how a programme can meet the criteria necessary to satisfy participants, sponsors and other stakeholders in a programme. Hence mapping out stakeholders and identifying their values and requirements is usually a key need. In development terms it's therefore important that people learn how to undertake this kind of process. This mapping then needs to be integrated with theory issues and with constraints on design. There are always constraints, so again developers need to learn how to map these and how to find ways round some and work within others. Resource constraints are, for instance, always present and have a heavy influence on programme design.

Whilst reading, research and attending workshops can assist learning, there is no way of replacing the value of direct experience. A novice designer, either of macro strategies or of micro tactics and methods, can often best progress by getting involved in design teams and in evaluating the results of design choices, so as to learn from them.

**Managing**   At one level the management of learning and development activity throws up few fundamentally different issues from any other managerial issues. Learning and development need selling and marketing (see Appendix II); they need organization and leadership, and so on. Returning to the use of learning contracts, we look to people to identify what they need to learn in this area alongside any other. However, where managers are involved as set advisers they are often already working on issues such as time management, influencing and leadership in their own learning contracts.

The major area where one might find a difference is in the management and leadership of teams of consultants or trainers. A feature which some managers who move into this area of work comment on is the problem of organizing a group of people who, in some companies, have gravitated to training because they don't fit elsewhere in the organization. This can mean that, at its best, one has a group of creative, lively and interesting people to lead. At its worst this can be a group of individuals who see themselves as subversives undermining aspects of the organization that they don't like. This can make life tricky for the leader, who may have to learn some new tactics to deal with the situation.

### Assisting

This is the area that many organizations feel that they need the most help in developing. It will therefore take up the major part of the rest of this chapter. What I described as the 'S' role in the previous chapter I will leave to one side. The 'S' role, remember, is about providing *subject* knowledge, *skills*, *specializations*, and so on. It is almost overemphasized in much of the literature on training and development. Also, at its simplest level it is more about being available to share one's expertise or skills. In SML programmes participants learn how to get the best out of experts through, for example, smart questioning.

## Selecting set advisers

In order to provide a basis for considering the development of set advisers I shall start with the problem of selection. The methods whereby set advisers are selected will vary by organization. However, I can say something from my research about some generalized criteria for selection. These need modifying to suit circumstances but they provide a good, well-researched basis for considering who will carry out this role prior to undertaking any development activity.

### Some possible criteria

I am often asked about criteria for selecting set advisers and it is clearly an important issue. However, we have worked in some contexts where we have taken risks on this front. For example, in one organization, for strategic reasons, we chose all senior managers as set advisers. We knew that some would take to the role better than others, but the decision was taken because of the strategic value of getting everyone involved. It meant that tactically we had a few problems, but in the interests of creating a better learning culture overall it clearly paid off, as evaluation results showed. However, the same evaluation also showed that some sets had a less positive experience than others.

In the example I have just mentioned you will note that I referred to managers as set advisers. The key issue here is that set advising in SML is not something that has to be restricted to development professionals. A manager who is excellent with their team and displays the qualities described below is ideal – and often preferable to a trainer who is determined to instruct people and cannot break out of a control habit.

The evidence for the criteria described below comes mainly from my PhD research,[1] which was a study of those identified as the most successful and experienced set advisers (or those who took on similar roles). At the time there was more action learning going on than SML, so the research was more oriented to that kind of work. However, in the succeeding 14 years since that research I have continued to test and modify the ideas in contexts involving many hundreds of SML set advisers (over 100 in one organization alone).

The list of qualities can look quite daunting when stated baldly. Some people will no doubt think that they could never aspire to be such a paragon. However, we have found that people can learn and improve in most areas. So there needs to be a link to the next section of this chapter on developing set advisers. Also, I have separated out essentials from desirables in an attempt to make it less challenging as a set of criteria.

Here is the list. You will note that it focuses on qualities and capabilities, in keeping with the discussion in Chapters 4 and 5. Trying to reduce these factors to knowledge and skill requirements really would make it daunting – and unnecessary. The effectiveness of the set adviser is usually governed by these qualities and capabilities and I have observed that a set adviser can get away with being inelegant in, say, their questioning, if it's clear to the set that they are genuine, caring and supportive.

*Essential*
1. *Secure sense of self* – they need to be centred and grounded as discussed in Chapter 5. They need to feel comfortable about themselves and within themselves. They need to be able to stand on their own feet and feel secure in taking decisions for themselves.
2. *Generally positive attitude* – they need to show that they believe that people can learn and change and that it's

worth working at a learning contract. This attitude may
be especially needed when people in a set feel depressed
or anxious. It does not mean that the set adviser must
always be up-beat and jolly; rather it requires a generally
optimistic attitude – getting over to people that even
when things look bad it's worth doing something. This
stance in education has been linked to what has been
called the Pygmalion effect: if you believe people can
succeed, they are more likely to do so than if you hold
the opposite view. There is solid research evidence to
support this.

3 *Tolerance of uncertainty* – what happens in a set is largely
unpredictable: the set adviser is not in control. This can
be a cause of anxiety to control freaks, such as many
trainers, as they cannot control what goes on. If they
attempt to do so, they undermine the process.

Tolerating uncertainty may also call on the set adviser
to be flexible and adaptable in the ways they behave in
the set. Note that I'm suggesting a level of behavioural
flexibility but not necessarily flexibility at the level of
values and beliefs. The set adviser usually has to hold
firm to the values that underpin SML and to believe in
the possibility that people can learn – even if the
evidence at times seems contrary to this belief!

4 *Belief in the value of learning* – set advisers quite clearly
need to accept the case made earlier in this book that
learning is a priority activity in organizations. They also
need to model this, for example by having their own
learning contract and showing that they are good
learners. In my research one person talked in even firmer
terms by saying that you need a 'passion' for this work.[1]

5 *Basic interpersonal capabilities* – set advisers should want
to relate to others and enjoy dialogue. This will include
listening to others. This is a cliché often churned out in
this context. However, I don't mean the kind of listening
that would just produce the ability to repeat back what
someone has said. It goes beyond that. It's about
entering the other person's world through hearing not
just the words but often what's behind the words.
Empathy is one term that relates to this quality.

Another important basic interpersonal capability is
questioning. Set advisers will need to ask good
questions a lot of the time. However, this is an example
of where a development programme for set advisers can
address issues of this kind. Novice set advisers may be
limited in their questioning capability but if they have
the other qualities identified here they can quickly learn
to improve.

6 *Patient* – the value of a set that meets regularly over a

period of months is that the set adviser does not need to look for quick changes in participants. Often it takes time for people to make fundamental changes in their behaviour. The set adviser needs to avoid being over-anxious to see rapid progress on learning contracts. Sometimes people struggle for months and seem to be making little or no progress but then it all suddenly comes together.

7 *Trustworthy* – this quality has a range of dimensions, from set members being able to trust that their adviser will keep confidentialities, to being able to trust that the adviser will keep to promises, for example in providing materials or arranging contacts.

8 *Sympathy with the issues participants want to address* – this does not mean necessarily agreeing with everything that people do, but it does mean being understanding about people's concerns. There needs to be a basic level of respect for set members. This also links with the set adviser developing a good level of awareness of what is going on for each person.

9 *Making time* – the set adviser needs to be able to make time for people – and not always just at set meetings. This links to the need for the set adviser to be reasonably well organized.

10 *Selflessness, no ego trip* – set advisers must accept that at times they will get no credit for the brilliant work that they do. They need to care intrinsically about what they are doing and not rely on extrinsic rewards. They also need to be prepared to be unobtrusive when necessary.

11 *Analytical capability* – this was a factor in my research observations of effective practitioners – but it tended to be something they themselves did not mention when interviewed. They seemed almost to take it for granted. It is a capability that, like others, can be developed. It is not related to some crude IQ measure; rather in my scheme of things it is closer to 'wisdom'. One dimension of this quality is being able to see the wood for the trees – sifting through a mass of talk that occurs over a day's meeting and making the best sense of it.

*Desirable*  1 *Warmth and enthusiasm* – it helps if the set adviser exhibits these qualities but it is not essential. Sometimes a cooler, laid-back style can work. The ideal is where a set adviser is able to be warm and enthusiastic but has considerable style flexibility so that they can pull back as needed.

2 *Knowledge about the kind of issues faced by set members* – this might include being aware of the things going on in the managerial world (if it's a set of managers).

3 *Rich cognitive mental map* – the set adviser should have a personal mental map that can accommodate the kinds of things participants raise. At another level it helps if the set adviser has to hand models and ways of thinking that can inform the dialogues in set meetings. This can also include the ability to link to the metaphors and analogies people use and to respond to them.

4 *Ability to locate their work in a wider context* – seeing how set advising fits into other work that they do, ideally also within a wider social framework. If they are good networkers this also helps.

5 *Able to provide useful insights* – it's valuable if the set adviser can offer insightful comments, when needed. But often set members will do this anyway.

6 *Consistency* – in my research one person said that it was important 'to maintain a consistent level of professionalism'.[1] Others in the same research acknowledged that they might stray from this criterion – and have 'off' days. They recognized, though, that they might need to retrieve the situation at a future meeting of the set.

**In-house programmes**

For programmes run solely in-house there may be some extra desirable criteria, including the one below.

*Having a 'feel' for the organization* – they don't have to know it in detail but they must be able to work within the culture, to be able to empathize with issues faced by set members. For example, it is possible for someone from the private sector to work with a public sector set so long as they understand the different issues in a non-profit environment and will go along with the concerns and problems this throws up.

# Set adviser development

One of the first things to get over to a new set adviser is the nature of the role. Figure 10.1 may help to explain this. The figure shows the relationship of a teacher to learners. In the traditional educational model the teacher may interact with a particular learner as shown by arrows A and B. In teaching B comes before A, that is, the teacher goes out to the learner – with a lecture, an instruction to write an essay or whatever – and the learner responds (A). The teacher will also, via D, relate to other learners in the same way. The relationship between learners (shown as C) is often largely ignored – or if learners help each other it's called 'cheating' and people get punished for it.

In SML the process works differently. First, A usually precedes B, that is, the initiation of learning comes from the learner. Second, the process C (the interaction between learners) is regarded as a key part of the learning process

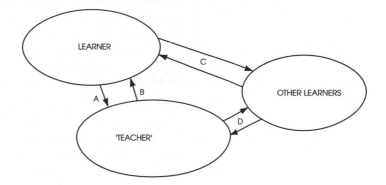

**Figure 10.1**   *Interacting with learners*

and is encouraged. The process D, with other learners, occurs in the same way.

Set advisers have to start by recognizing the different nature of SML programmes compared to the experiences that most of them have had in educational and training environments. It is then possible to move into a development process. Figure 10.2 shows a rough spectrum of choices with the least engaged and least practical on the left and the most direct and engaged on the right.

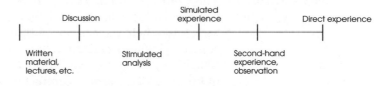

**Figure 10.2**   *Development of set advisers*

**Written material, lectures, and so on**

This has its place but is likely to be seen as a support to more practical methods of development. This book contains references to material that could be useful. The other dimension here is that handbooks created for programmes provide an important source of material for someone coming new into a programme. Also, workshops are best supported with handout material and I shall show one example below.

**Discussion**

In providing workshops, this can encourage discussion about issues, and can be useful up to a point. However, I would distinguish between *discussion* and *dialogue*. Discussion is about ideas and issues 'out there'. It may engage the intellect but not the emotions. It is about generalizations and opinions – often detached from anyone in the discussion owning the problem under discussion. So in this context it's possible to have a generalized discussion about the nature of set advising. People can swap ideas and opinions. If they have had any experience of the role they may swap 'war stories' ('Well, if you think that participant was a problem wait until you hear about this one').

This can be useful – but limited. Dialogue has a different quality. It engages people in a real issue that is owned by someone in the group. Sets exemplify this kind of interaction – and workshops on set advising need to have significant time in dialogue modes that have some of the quality of a set meeting (without being a set, of course).

**Stimulated analysis**   The idea behind this approach is implied in the title. It is to provide material which can stimulate the person to undertake analysis. We recognize that this analysis is not a substitute for actual experience (see later) but it provides a gentle introduction to set advising for total newcomers. It also engages the person to a greater extent than just discussion processes. Hence this approach is useful early on in a workshop.

Below are described four examples of methods – three to use early on in a workshop (typically on the first day of a two-day event), and one to use near the end of the second day.

*Mock learning contract*   This exercise involves producing a mock draft learning contract and then asking participants how they would, as a set adviser, help the person to improve it. Typically I ask someone in the organization to write a pretend contract which they know is flawed. They will answer all five questions in the learning contract model and in the process provide enough background for this to be a realistic task for workshop participants. This mock contract is then copied to make it available to workshop participants.

I usually suggest that individuals make notes for themselves on the mock learning contract and then work in trios to compare ideas. This starts to move the process from a purely analytical one into one that encourages dialogue. The trios then report on their views in a larger group meeting.

This exercise gives a good opportunity to coach participants in questioning methods as well as to raise many issues about the operation of SML programmes, such as

● how the set adviser can help people to develop realism in their contracts
● how organizational and personal goals might be integrated

- how short-term job development needs to be linked to longer-term career issues
- the importance of doing the first two questions well, in order to provide a basis for the other three
- the difficulty of answering question five, that is, providing criteria and measures
- and so on – the kinds of issues raised depend on the group, the programme, the organization, and other factors.

*Vignettes*  The method we use a great deal is to give people short vignettes or mini cases of what can happen in a set and ask them what they would do about it. This material is best created from events that have actually taken place in that organization. However, if that is not possible, for example with a totally new programme, then we have some standard cases of what has happened in sets in other organizations.

The task for individuals, presented with the vignette, is to make notes on what they would do. (The kind of cases we give people vary from practical issues such as a person continually turning up late to set meetings to more rare problems such as a person crying in a set meeting.) After people have made notes on their own, they are split into trios and again encouraged to dialogue with their colleagues. We especially recommend that they don't compare answers in a competitive way but rather seek to enlarge their own repertoire of possible behaviours through sharing ideas with colleagues.

In order to extend this latter process we give out what we have called 'Indicative Answers'. These are not meant to be model answers but rather they show a range of choices, with the theoretical underpinnings for each. This can assist people to explore even more options and feel more confident about the choices open to them as set advisers. What we steer clear of is any notion that there is one right way of doing things. We can be clear about what is bad practice (for example abusive or oppressive behaviour), but good practice has many facets. It's also apparent that people need to work within their own comfort zones when they start work as set advisers, so we don't encourage a style of working that is too demanding.

*Video tape*  I have made video tapes of myself acting as a set adviser with simulated sets. One of these has a commentary with it of what I was thinking during the piece on the video. This has meant that anyone could view it at their leisure and analyse my behaviour and my thinking. If I am working with a specific organization I might run a simulated set in the workshop, have one of the participants video it and I review the tape with the group. What is important is the talking through. Most of what you do as a set adviser is invisible to set members. It's about all the internal processing you do in deciding whether to do anything – and if so, what. Novice set advisers quickly see that the adviser is working hard most of the time – even when apparently sitting quiet doing nothing.

*Preparation for acting as a set adviser*

The following is an exercise that is useful for people to do near the end of a workshop. It is one that is valuable for people to discuss in trios and share ideas. It is also extremely useful if two people are going to co-set advise (that is, work together as a set advising pair). The sharing of this information in a pair that are going to work together in the same set is invaluable in avoiding misunderstandings.

(*Note:* In the material below, I have reduced the spaces between questions to avoid leaving lots of white space on the page.)

### PREPARATION FOR SET ADVISING
The following questions are designed to help you to plan/prepare for set advising. Please take some time to go through these and make notes on each in the space provided (or on a separate sheet).

It can be most useful to discuss your answers with others in order to clarify your thinking. Such a discussion should not be on the basis of comparing and seeing who has the best answer. The objective is to develop your thinking – not for you to copy someone else.

### BACKGROUND
How have you come to be taking up set advising? Why are you doing it?

What have been the influences on you in the way you think about learning? How do you think people learn best?

What do you hope people will get from the set with which you will be working?

What other activities will you be engaged in during the life of the set which might affect how you play your role as a set adviser (for example, work pressures, particular projects, home circumstances, and so on)? If there are any of significance, how will you handle these?

### ETHICS
How will you handle issues of confidentiality? What will you do with information you glean in the set, for example as it affects the organization?

How will you handle any difficult personal issues (among participants) that might come up?

EXPERIENCE
What experiences have you had which will help you to be effective in the set; for example, experience of being a set member?

METHODS/PRACTICE
What might the set adviser need to do at the start of the first set meeting?

What is your view on the best way to structure a set meeting; for example, do you prefer a fixed time for each person, or for each person to bid for time?

What is your view on the best locations for set meetings?

How will you model best practice in the set; for example, regarding questioning, supporting others, challenging others?

DEVELOPMENT
How will you continue with your own learning and development in this kind of role? How will you review your own performance as a set adviser?

ARE THERE ANY OTHER ISSUES FOR WHICH YOU NEED TO PREPARE?

**Simulated experience**
The methods discussed above are ones that are more engaging for people than lectures and discussion. But they stay at an analytical level. The use of a video tape, as indicated in the previous section, can result in participants in a workshop going in front of a camera themselves. The method we use avoids the great artificiality of a role play with a created script. Rather we ask that one participant acts as the set adviser starting off a set. The other participants behave as if they were forming a set – and they are asked to be themselves (it's not play acting).

Hence it is, of course, artificial in that it is not a set that is going to carry on meeting. But everyone is being themselves so that a video playback can focus on relatively real issues. These simulated sets can provide further opportunity to explore issues such as

● how to start a set
● how to sort out ground rules for working
● how to question people
● how to choose what to question
● how to balance support and challenge in a set.

The playback of a video tape will, then, usually take two or three times as long as the original event that was taped. And even then one might not have gone into depth on all the issues raised in the tape. One thing that can be done is to let the person who acted as set adviser keep the tape so that they can review it later.

**Second-hand experience, observation**

Being a set member is the most obvious way of being able to observe a set adviser at work. In running workshops where everyone has already been a set member I typically start by asking people about their experience of seeing someone else carry out the role. Often people have observed problems in the way the set adviser worked and this can provide a good jumping-off point in a discussion of the role and what it means to carry it out effectively.

There is no doubt that it is much easier to take on the role of set adviser if you have already been in a set, written a learning contract, and so on. The experience of being in a set helps people to see some of the difficulties of carrying out the role well. At the same time it gives reassurance that it is possible to carry out the role and that sets can be effective even if the set adviser makes mistakes at times.

**Direct experience**

I mentioned above the idea of a pair of people co-set advising. We have used this as a valuable development mode. Ideally an experienced set adviser is paired with someone new to the role and they agree to work together over a defined period. The pair need to agree to consult each other before a set meeting to agree their own mode of working and to avoid problems such as 'over-advising' (two people working together should not produce double the set adviser air time, so some way of handling this has to be agreed). The preparation exercise covered above is a useful tool in this context.

Also, a co-set advising pair need to agree a time to meet after each set meeting to review their performance. Especially with a novice, such meetings are essential to ensure continued learning.

One way to enhance review meetings is to audio tape set meetings (or part of them). Assuming that set members agree, this is a valuable development aid. It can also be used solo. I have found it valuable to tape set meetings when I have been working alone and then get someone else to transcribe the tapes so that we can go over what happened and how I operated. I have found that it is more useful to engage in a dialogue with someone else rather than just try to make sense of the tapes on my own. An outsider can ask different questions than I would ask myself, for instance.

Note that I'm suggesting here audio tapes rather than video tapes. Audio is quite unobtrusive whereas video is the opposite. Video is fine for a workshop environment but not for live situations.

**Workshops in practice**

I have mentioned a great deal about using the workshop mode as a development approach. Here is a typical agenda for a two-day workshop – it is taken from one used with Arun District Council for developing some of their senior managers as set advisers.

OUTLINE OF SESSIONS/TOPICS TO COVER

- Opening – introductions, expectations, administration, agreeing agenda.
- Clarifying SML and the role of the set adviser, especially in the context of the Arun programme. Issues of responsibility.
- Learning contracts – questioning a contract (including questioning skills and the use of dummy contracts), developing outcome statements, criteria for good contracts, and so on.
- Sets – structure of meetings, ground rules, and so on.
- Set advising – the concept of the 'learning assistant', exercise using critical incidents.
- Models used for set advising.
- Starting a set – practice sessions.
- Own contracts as applied to set advising.
- Review and next steps.

**Workshop design**

One thing that will be apparent in the above is that there are no times allocated to topics. We prefer to keep workshops quite open (and sometimes, if we are allowed to by the client, have no agenda at all). We expect that the agenda will be modified in the light of expressed needs from the opening session anyway. We argue that if people want the security of a rigidly timed event they are probably unsuited to set advising.

Another preference we have is to feed in ideas and information as we go along but then have a fall-back, at the end of the workshop, of a summary of issues about set advising. The following is a typical handout used at this stage. I will elaborate the points a bit in places beyond what is normally given out as a kind of reminder handout (as on the handout the points are made rather tersely).

NOTES ON SET ADVISING

- The role of the set is to help people to learn – it is not a team/'groupy group'/syndicate group or the like. (The point here is to remind people that set advising is not, for instance, group facilitating in the way that some trainers might have been taught.)

- Its efficacy is to be judged by whether people learn (or not). So good set advising is related to how well you assist others to learn – not because you are a 'clever facilitator'.

  (I find that this is reassuring for managers – and helpful in reminding trainers not to get too 'trainery'.)

- It isn't necessary that the set is always a comfortable/nice place to be (it may at times be undesirable for it to be too comfortable).

  (Again this is reassuring to novices – and it reminds people that the main objective of a set is to foster learning, not to be purely a support group.)

- Each person is responsible *for* their own learning – you are responsible *to* them to assist as appropriate.

  (This responsibility distinction is not always easy for people to understand initially but usually by the time this handout is used they've got the message.)

- Support set members in their learning.
  Challenge behaviour appropriately.
  (RULE: Support being
  Challenge doing
  – and not vice versa).

  (The trite distinction I make is that the set adviser may need first to show that they care about the person and because of that they want to raise concerns about some aspect of their behaviour. This shows support for the person as a human being, whilst challenging their behaviour as part of that support. The theory is that if you really want to help someone you are not doing them any favours by letting them carry on behaving inappropriately. This would contrast with bad practice where the set adviser might say 'That was a wonderful piece of work you've done there: I don't know how a little idiot like you could do such good work!' That would be an example of 'support doing, challenge being' – and it's obviously wrong when presented as baldly as that.)

- Check any question: Is what I am about to ask going to assist the other person's learning?
  (The key here is to get people to avoid asking questions just out of curiosity. They must have a purpose.)

- Helping set members to help each other can be a key need. This may mean encouraging people to challenge each other, especially through questioning each other.

- It is easier if people ask for help than if it is imposed on them. However, people may need encouragement to do this.

- Assume set members are sensible people who do want to learn to be better – even if the evidence appears to be the contrary!
  (I often link this to the issue of patience; sometimes it takes time for people to get into a self managing mode – and the set adviser has to 'hang on in there'.)
- Do not do all the work in the set – get set members to take appropriate responsibility; for example, for fixing venues, for asking for what they want.
- You are an important model for appropriate behaviour.
- But you don't have to be perfect – it's important that the set recognizes you as another human being!
- Developing trust in the set is important. But it isn't something that can be artificially created – you have to be genuine and sincere in what you do in order to facilitate the growth of trust.
  (This is another attempt to get trainers to avoid doing artificial exercises to develop trust, for example 'blind walking', and so on.)
- You may be able to help people with activity outside the set; for example, by pointing them to resources that they may not know about.
- Avoid advice of the kind: 'If I were you I would . . .' You are not the other person and never can be.
- However, if the person is searching for information which you have, it would be silly not to provide it for them.
- You have a key role in maintaining the principles of the programme – you can't police people but you can confront them if they seem to have trouble 'playing by the rules'.
- It can be best if the set handles issues for itself – you may find that if you give people time, they will tackle problems that you see ahead of them (but if you intervene too early they will not learn to solve the problems themselves). However, if no one does pick up on an issue, you have a role in pointing it out.
  (This links to the idea of the set adviser as 'infill' – discussed in the previous chapter.)
- At the start of a set you need to put energy into learning about the set members. You can only help them learn if you have first learned from them.
- Primary feedback – the evidence of your eyes and ears – is usually more reliable than secondary feedback (interpretation of what has happened).
- It is important to establish at the start that you have your contract with your own set and not with the set you are advising. One value you bring is as a neutral who does not have a vested interest in the set's work.

(This is of course a key argument as to why set advisers are important.)

- In preparing for a set meeting it can be useful both to prepare 'mechanically', that is, plan how to get there or re-read contracts, and to prepare 'mentally', for example by thinking about each set member as a person, visualizing them, and so on.
- Even if you did little or nothing in a set, your role would be valuable. The set needs some way of marking its role as a context for learning. The set adviser symbolizes that. Also, it is not possible not to behave – you will find yourself being very active just listening to people. (And novice set advisers often say how tiring it is to do this!)
- Set advisers may need to help the set to avoid appearing as a deviant or unserious activity. For instance, sets are free to meet where they like. However, if they choose locations away from the office (for example in people's homes), they may need to be sensitive to the image this might engender if such decisions are communicated internally in an inappropriate way. The set adviser may need to warn set members of this.
- Add your own ideas below – set advising is what you make it. If you genuinely care about helping set members to learn, what you do is probably of benefit.
  (This last heading is important and in a workshop we might discuss what else could be added.)

## Coaching and mentoring

In the above I have deliberately focused on the set adviser role as it's the one that people raise most often as an issue of concern. However, the danger in this is of under-emphasizing other roles. For instance, self managing learners can be helpfully supported by one-to-one assistance in the mentoring and coaching mode. This is not the place to go into detail on this role and the interested reader can follow up material both on the idea of coaching and mentoring, and practical ways of improving practice, in other texts.[2] However, a simple point to make here is that if individuals learn to be effective coaches and mentors, they can find it much easier to learn to carry out the role of set adviser.

I would go further and say that in today's climate (see Chapter 1) *all* managers need to learn to be effective coaches – and that if an organization is serious about being a learning organization then it must invest in the development of all its managers to help them to be effective in this role.

## The development adviser role

There is emerging, in organizations such as Birmingham Midshires Building Society and KPMG, a role best described as 'development adviser'. John Bailey, in KPMG, acts as a development adviser (with this title) in one part of this firm's operations. He was trained as an accountant and then moved within the firm into training and development. His latest move has put him into a different role. He can be observed providing what looks like straight coaching to managers and partners – and he's very good at it. But more importantly, he is focusing not just on individual needs but on developing the effectiveness of the whole of this part of the firm.

John Bailey has a strategic role to see that the capability of people matches the demands of the business – and this can require him to call on the whole panoply of training and development provision to support such needs. He is at times an internal consultant, a facilitator, a broker and resource finder, a diagnostician, a confidant to partners – and more. This role is played out a great deal in one-to-one relationships – but it differs from the pure coach or pure mentor role. Coaches in the past have tended to be largely tactical, focusing on specific short-term performance problems. Mentors, on the other hand, have tended to be seen as more strategic, concentrating on the career needs of individuals. The development adviser needs to have these capabilities to hand – but to take them further. It needs a strategic integration and an awareness of how the culture of the organization is evolving.

This strategic perspective fits with the case made in earlier chapters. The development adviser role is a trend which needs to grow. But it needs people with the ability to understand business imperatives and hold these in mind when working with an individual on seemingly micro level concerns.

## On-line working and technology

Another clear trend is using modern technology effectively, especially the computer. Let me take the case of the Fielding Institute's MA in Organization Design and Effectiveness. This programme requires participants to attend a residential period of three days twice a year. The Institute is in Santa Barbara, California, but these events could be held anywhere accessible to an airport – because the people on them come from Europe, Japan, Australia, Canada, Alaska, South Africa, and so on. Also, after forming learning groups, similar to sets, the rest of the time participants work together via the Internet and the server at Fielding, using Digital's Alta Vista software.

The programme is based on the American course model

(participants take two courses per term over five terms).
Appendix III contains my leadership 'course' for the first
term. The design is an SML design (though I have left out
much detail, for example on the mapping of the literature). I
hope, however, that my edited version of the course gives a
flavour of how it operates.

The keys to making the course work include

- ensuring a strong bond between learning group members
  at the start (during the three-day 'orientation session')
- using the technology to encourage dialogue between
  participants
- being very organized as a group adviser – you have to log
  on to the system twice a week to keep up with what is
  going on
- creating a good basic design at the start – and then
  modifying it as you go along
- being very clear about your own learning theory so that
  you have a firm base for action on the above.

These criteria can be recognized as exemplifying the four
roles model discussed in the previous chapter. The different
mode of communicating still requires these roles to be
carried out effectively. However, the roles are clearly
manifest in a different way on this programme.

There are many positive features of the Fielding MA, but I
suspect that in the medium term we will see more use of the
Internet as a support for learning groups but not the main
communication channel. My aim in getting involved in it
was to see how far you can push the at-a-distance mode. My
current conclusion is that more face-to-face contact would
be valuable (and participants are tending to say that). Also,
other technology such as video conferencing may become
more important as a way of creating immediate
(synchronous) dialogue to balance the asynchronous
Internet mode.

These and other issues have been taken up by other writers[3]
in relation to similar programmes at UK universities such as
Lancaster.

## Summary

This chapter has taken the ideas raised in the previous
chapter and explored some practical implications. I have not
attempted to be encyclopedic, but rather to show a range of
concrete ways of addressing such matters as the
development of set advisers. The chapter has also pointed to
some trends such as the concept of development advisers
and the use of technology.

Notes 1 Cunningham, I. (1984) *Teaching Styles in Learner Centred Management Development Programmes*, PhD Thesis, University of Lancaster.
2 Cunningham, I. and Dawes, G.D. (1998*) Exercises for Developing Coaching Capability*, London: Institute of Personnel and Development; and Cunningham, I . (1992) 'Someone to watch over me: the meaning of mentoring', *Human Resources*, **39** (8), Winter, 39–42. There are also commercial providers on the Internet, for example the Coach University at www.coachu.com has quite an interesting site.
3 See Burgoyne, J. and Reynolds, M. (eds) (1997) *Management Learning: Integrating Perspectives in Theory and Practice*, London: Sage, especially chapters by McConnell and by Hodgson.

# 11 The learner in context

## Introduction

This chapter focuses more on the learner. First, I shall say something about the self managing learner, and then discuss issues of difference and diversity among people, specifically as they affect learning issues.

## Self managing learner

Umberto Eco,[1] in his essay *Reflections on 'The Name of the Rose'*, discussed how he came to write his famous novel *The Name of the Rose*, and his choices in the way he wrote it. He commented on the first 100 pages of the novel, which many readers had found tedious. These pages set the scene for the book's story of murder and intrigue in a monastery in the Middle Ages. Eco said that he wrote these pages in the way he did so that the reader could read what follows in the appropriate way. He wanted the reader to have to go at the pace of the monastery and to get into the spirit of the times. In short, he wanted to create a reader who could read in the way necessary to get the most from the book.

Eco's idea of 'creating a reader' has great relevance to our concerns here. In order to make strategic learning work we need to 'create learners' who can learn in appropriate ways. Learners who are comfortable with change, welcome it and see it as an opportunity to learn: learners who enjoy difference, like to visit other countries, welcome visitors from different cultures and like diversity in their organizations. Learners who can take calculated risks, but not stupid risks. Professional gamblers are those who know when to risk and when not. They prefer limited risks.

It is desirable to develop this learning pattern as early as possible in people's careers. A problem is that many graduates come from university with characteristics that make them poor learners in business settings. They have learned the ways of a distorted academia which values detachment, analysis, individualism (but not individuality), conformity and dependence.

I shall take as a text a paper by Indrei Ratiu[2] as this links to the other part of this chapter. He based his research on how

251

international managers learn, and conducted an elegant study which is relevant to more general learning issues. His first step was to identify managers who seemed to be more 'international': people who were more interculturally adaptable. His study identified those people who were seen as particularly adaptable, flexible and open-minded in intercultural working. He then studied these exceptional performers especially from the point of view of key learning experiences.

This produced evidence of *patterns* which particularly distinguished international managers. These included:

- their views of what is 'international'
- their assumptions about the world and themselves
- their ways of dealing with stress
- their ways of making sense of new experiences.

The most international managers tended to talk of relations with individual people rather than with cultures. They took a micro view. They learned from experience through modes that were identified as intuitive, empirical, relational and immediate. Less international managers learned in ways that were described as analytical, conceptual, theoretical and withdrawn. You will note here that this latter learning style is closer to that valued in academic settings, and is characteristic especially of new graduates. (Ratiu's research is supported by others – for example, Harrison and Hopkins,[3] who provide an incisive critique of university training in the cross-cultural arena.)

The more involved, personalistic style of good international learners correlates with effective learners in general managerial situations. My own research on CEOs produced results which support Ratiu.

Ratiu's research also showed that international managers worked on a subjective view of the world. They did not assume that they could find fixed, true knowledge. They were, in my terms, good cartographers. They went into new cultures with a rough map which they modified as they went along, responding to new information all the time. Less international managers had either fixed views which remained stable or poor maps which might stay that way.

Cross-culturally able managers seem to concentrate a lot on the need to map. They focus on *what* is going on in a new environment, and they assume that they will have to modify their maps accordingly. Less cross-culturally able managers are more concerned with *why* questions. They tend to lose sight of the data around them and perhaps reach premature conclusions. They are also less likely to deal well with their emotional responses to situations, perhaps by making judgemental remarks such as blaming others for problems.

The kind of research I've mentioned is consonant with evaluation studies of SML programmes. Managers learn how to learn better by integrating data and feelings, by developing wisdom and capability, by becoming more self reliant *and* more able to assist others in their learning.

Self managing learners are not 'perfect' individuals. Rather, they see the value of changing; of re-patterning their existing abilities as well as adding new ones. Their continued desire to learn is because they recognize that there are still things to learn. They make mistakes – and use them as data to be addressed, not explained away in rationalizations and excuses.

Self managing learners tend to *reduce* secondary feedback in order to allow them space to receive primary feedback. They are less interested in the opinions of others and more concerned to get close to situations and learn from sensory-based data. At the same time they want to balance this with feelings and values. Among other features:

- They are active learners – seeking new learning, asking questions of others, learning from unusual circumstances (they may get insights into new ways of thinking from almost anything that happens to them in a normal day).
- They use formal situations for their own benefit. Self managing learners may go to lectures but they will do so with clear objectives or from a serendipitous perspective. Poor learners either take no notes or try to get the lecturer's ideas on to paper. Self managing learners note what they want in relation to their own maps, values and requirements.
- They translate learning across contexts – but only if it does translate. They will test and modify as they go along.
- They take responsibility for their own actions, their own feelings, their own learning.
- They prepare for new circumstances through learning.
- They are strategic – linking big picture with little picture and macro with micro.

Much of what has been indicated above has been discussed earlier, so I shall not labour the points. Rather I want now to move away from universal and shared factors to the differences between managers, and diversity among people in organizations.

# Difference and diversity

There are at least five ways of thinking about the process of managing:

1 *Universalist*   This assumes that all managing is very much the same the world over. Or if it is not, it ought to be. This assumption has been the basis for much of the work of consultants going from rich countries to poor countries to offer advice. Poor countries are seen as 'underdeveloped' and in need of developing to be like rich countries. A similar view underpins the work of the majority of consultants and developers going from North America and Western Europe into Eastern Europe. Simple messages such as privatization are seen as part of a universal requirement for good management.

2 *National cultural relativism*   Writers on cross-cultural issues base their work on the assumption of large, possibly unbridgeable, differences between national cultures. They may suggest that theories developed in the USA have almost *no* relevance elsewhere, that almost *all* US writing is ethnocentric and culture bound and that *no* methods developed in the USA should be translated directly into another culture.

3 *Organizational cultural relativism*   Just as the above view has become increasingly prevalent in Europe, this third perspective has become a key feature of US literature. The argument is that organizations vary widely and that we may not be able to translate ideas from one organizational culture to another. As with 2 above, in the extreme some writers suggest that there are no universals, because each organization is so different.

4 *Individual particularism*   This position argues that every manager is different, so we should stop generalizing. Psychological literature is used to show large-scale differences between individuals, for example through psychometric tests.

5 *Subgroup diversity*   In this stance subgroups in society are identified as a source of difference (and often disadvantage). These include:

● women
● black people
● disabled people
● gay men and lesbians
● older people
● working-class people.

It is argued that people within each group will have something in common which also creates a difference from other people. As indicated in Chapter 3, a learning business would welcome difference and diversity. A strategic learning approach recognizes the value of balancing all five perspectives. There are universals – such as the need for learning; there are national and organizational differences which must be accommodated strategically: each person is different and needs treating as such; and there can be sources of disadvantage which need to be tackled directly.

In Part Two of this book I discussed organization culture, so that issue will not be considered here. I shall begin with the issue of disadvantage and then move to national culture. SML addresses individual differences, as discussed in Part Four, so that will be taken as a baseline for moving into these other domains.

## Diversity and disadvantage: strategic learning issues

Most management development activity in North America and Europe is designed on the assumption that the customers (course members) are white, able-bodied, middle-class, heterosexual males aged about 25 to 45. In the UK, this group is less than 4 per cent of the population;[4] in the USA it is an even smaller proportion.

Some of the simple ways in which these assumptions create problems for those outside this privileged group include:

1 If there is a social function to which partners/spouses are invited, how is the situation handled by gay people?
2 Courses tend to rely on visual communication. What does this mean for people with sight difficulties?
3 Cocktail parties and many group exercises can create problems for some people with particular hearing problems.
4 Tiered lecture theatres can create difficulties for those with mobility problems.

These are all practical issues which can be addressed in practical ways. More profound difficulties come in the course curriculum where, say, case studies assume that managers are within the privileged group. This can alienate others. Even in flexible programmes which encourage people to discuss their own issues, black people, women and gay people comment that they find it difficult to raise issues of concern to them when they feel they are the only ones in the group who face particular problems. A black manager, for instance, had just experienced some racist attitudes before coming into a group. This deeply affected him and he underperformed in the group. He did not, however, feel able to say this to his all-white colleagues.

The latter example raises the problem of denial. There is an expectation in many organizations that managers will deny aspects of themselves if they do not conform to the requirements of white, able-bodied, middle-class, heterosexual male society. A successful managing director of a factory in the north of England was required by his chairman to attend a course 'to polish himself up' and rid himself of his blunt, northern, working-class ways. Women are expected to join in with men on a course, and deny any differing perspectives on managerial issues. Gay managers are expected to keep quiet about their sexuality. A lesbian training manager was reprimanded for going into the company shop with the child of her partner.

In SML we expect to be able to address factors of difference and diversity in a positive way. The design of programmes helps, but there is also a premium on learning assistants, such as set advisers, in recognizing and dealing with problems. There are certain aspects of SML *designs* that help these situations.

**Sets**  Sets provide a base for people to talk personally about themselves. Where a difference is visible (for example, if someone is black or in a wheelchair) a capable set adviser can play a key role in creating an environment in which these factors can be discussed. But some differences are not necessarily visible, for example if someone is gay. We have found, however, that a gay person has valued a 'set' environment where they could open up. I have seen heterosexual managers benefit greatly from this, as often they have never had to talk openly with a gay colleague about sexuality issues. Many 'straight' men initially find it uncomfortable but gradually see this as part of their learning – their need to develop wisdom.

Although sets are of great value, we have, as staff, often encouraged women managers and black managers to form support groups to discuss issues of common concern. This itself can initially feel threatening in a learning community, but again the white males can gradually adjust to the situation and see that their feelings of being threatened are something to address for themselves.

**Learning contracts**  Learning contracts provide a basis for anyone on an SML programme to create a curriculum to suit themselves. A woman of 50 commented:

> The course is excellent for a middle aged woman like me. I have realized that I could create a new future for myself – even at my age. I ceased to feel stuck and now I feel I'm escaping from stagnation. It's an amazing relief to feel young again.

However, this is also an example of the need for a set adviser to support difference. A Chinese manager, on the post-graduate diploma course mentioned in Part Four, expressed an important formulation of the problem. As she saw it, there was a danger in a set that white managers expected her to conform to their expectations of a good contract. This would also have affected assessment as she was going to have to present her self assessment to her set for confirmation and approval. She characterized the potential problem as in Figure 11.1.

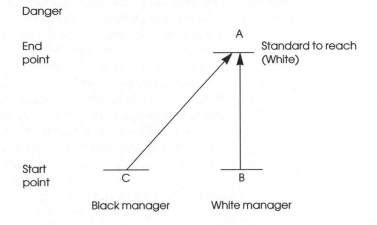

Path to travel for black manager (CA) is longer than for white manager (BA)

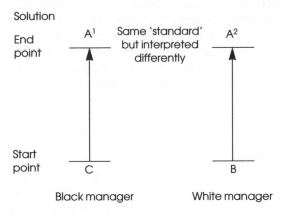

$CA^1$ and $BA^2$ are the same length – therefore 'fair'

*Figure 11.1* *Levels and differences*

Her concern was that she would have to conform to an end-point level that was inappropriate for her as a Chinese manager (managing a Chinese centre in London). She felt that the set needed to understand that she could develop a parallel track based on the requirements of her own culture. This needed the set adviser to assist her in raising these issues in an appropriate way in the set, and getting other set members to appreciate the problem. On the same programme a number of black managers put issues in their learning contracts that, to white managers, raised political matters. Again, this had to be worked through so that white managers could see these concerns, and learning needs, as legitimate.

**Learning assistants**

Learning assistants can play a key role, as already indicated. Mentors in organizations can be of great value. Many women on SML programmes have chosen women mentors to provide the support that they have felt was lacking from their male manager and/or their husband. Another way of addressing this issue has been to bring managers and husbands/partners into the programme. We have often found that men have no desire to be explicitly unsupportive of a woman's learning; rather they have not recognized what was required and, with some guidance, began to see ways in which they could be of more help. The balance in a learning assistant team can be important. One cannot cover all the alternatives, but by being sensitive to the male/female, black/white balance in a staff team one can go some way towards modelling not just a respect for diversity but a positive valuing of difference.

**Learning community**

Learning community processes and structures can help to create a culture which supports difference and addresses disadvantage. The openness and trust that can be created in such contexts can provide the one place in which managers can really feel that they can be themselves without having to deny aspects of themselves. Men can also allow themselves to open up about issues they cannot raise in their day-to-day work. They can stop feeling the need to be macho and show other sides of themselves.

**Strategic approaches**

Strategic approaches show the need to address issues of the contexts of a development programme. For example, selection issues are important. Often they subtly discriminate against people, and development programmes end up with an imbalance of privileged white middle-class males. A strategic perspective requires programmes to be created in context, and these contextual factors to be addressed, such as: how do imbalances occur? and how can the problem be solved?

# Cross-cultural issues

Some of the points made above can assist strategic learning

(a)  to be relevant to managers from different national cultures and

(b)  to assist managers from different cultures to learn well together.

Indeed, with the globalization of management we have no option but to consider how learning can occur across cultures.

Ratiu's research, discussed earlier, gives us pointers. He, and Harrison and Hopkins, show that learning to work across cultures cannot be carried out in standard classroom-based courses. Managers need to become self managing learners to work cross-culturally. And the obverse applies. By working cross-culturally, by travelling and by experiencing other cultures, people become better self managing learners.

However, all of this may need assistance – and we are back to staff/practitioner/professional roles and the need for good designs for strategic learning. We have found that managers from a wide variety of cultures can come together in sets and use SML methods. I have worked with managers from Europe, America, Africa and Asia, and SML programmes are starting to develop in a variety of countries. They, of course, have different styles and outcomes in different cultures. In the USA the natural tendency to self reliant optimism has meant that managers easily pick up the basic ideas. Learning contracts have been used in the USA for a long time, though not necessarily in the SML mode. Sets can, however, create a new challenge, especially for very individualistic managers who need to learn to support others in their learning.

In Asian countries there can be the opposite situation. In many cultures, which could be labelled more collectivist, the supportive environment of the set comes as second nature. What surprises some managers is the opportunity to develop their own curriculum, and this can feel strange initially. However, SML has drawn on Eastern thinking, so that the basic ideas can make sense in Asian countries. An Indian professor, who is keen to develop SML in India, wrote to me saying: 'India is the land of Buddha, Upanishads and Krishnamurthi – SML will have its followers!' He recognized the links with Indian philosophy and saw the possibilities for an Indian style of programme. One of his colleagues also commented that 'traditional Indian teaching modes have something to contribute'. I agree.

I could go on at length, referring to different cultures and their response to strategic learning and SML, but that would be tedious. As a generalization I have found that SML challenges different cultures in different ways, in terms of its *processes*. (In terms of *content* there is no issue, as the content of SML programmes is driven by managers themselves, hence immediately overcoming one of the problems in transferring standardized training courses across cultures.) An example of a process challenge is between high-context and low-context cultures.[5] High-context cultures are those where verbal communication is more implicit as the context provides the basis for understanding messages. To quote Hall:

> high context communication is one in which most of the information is either in the physical context or internalized in the person, with very little in the coded, explicit, transmitted part of the message. In low context communication 'the mass of information is vested in the explicit code'. (Hall,[5] p. 91)

Yamaguchi used Hall's ideas in her research on Japanese and American managers. She comments:

> In a High Context (HC) society, people tend to rely on the context in communication. They are expected to understand what one intends to mean although very few words have been said. On the other hand, the people from Low Context (LC) society try to look for every word related to the content to read the speaker's intention. Thus, in conversation with people from an HC communication society, people from a Low Context society will struggle with ambiguity while the people from an HC society may be sick of verboseness.

> The differences in American and Japanese rhetorical styles are derived from context differences as follows: In a 'low-context' culture ... like ... the United States, the lack of shared assumptions requires the American speaker to verbalize his or her message to make his or her discrete intent clear and explicit ... By contrast, Japanese is a typical 'high-context' culture ... the Japanese speaker tends to minimize extra- and paraverbal aspects of communication. (Yamaguchi,[6] pp. 25/26)

It is clear from Yamaguchi's research (and that of many others) that Japanese–American communication can be difficult, and that if Japanese and American managers are in a learning context together there can be problems. However, Yamaguchi shows that these problems are soluble through managing 'context' (in Hall's use of the term). She suggests that context should at the start be low or zero and then be built up through shared language, tasks, rules and working principles. This is how good learning communities and sets work, and it again shows how important the learning assistant is in handling these issues. (Appendix III outlines a programme designed to work on a global basis.)

Summary In this chapter I have explored strategic learning from the perspective of the self managing learner and from the point of view of individual, cultural and other differences. I have not made an exhaustive survey of the issues, but rather shown how SML approaches can work to address some thorny ones.

Notes
1 Eco, U. (1985) *Reflections on 'The Name of the Rose'*, London: Secker & Warburg. Also: Eco, U. (1983) *The Name of the Rose*, London: Secker & Warburg.

2 Ratiu, I. (1983) 'Thinking internationally: a comparison of how international executives learn', *International Studies of Management and Organization*, **XIII** (1/2), 139–50.

3 Harrison, R. and Hopkins, R. (1987) 'The design of cross-cultural training: an alternative to the university model', *Journal of Applied Behavioural Science*, **III** (4), 421–60.

4 It is difficult to be more exact than 'less than 4 per cent' as the statistics are open to interpretation. For instance, the boundary between disabled and not is open to differing perspectives. Also, the statistics on the percentage of the population who are gay are controversial. However, I have erred on the cautious side in my figure of 4 per cent.

5 Hall, E.T. (1976) *Beyond Culture*, Garden City, NY: Anchor Press/Doubleday.

6 Yamaguchi, I. (1988) *Communication Skills Between Japanese and American Managers and Subordinates in a Japan–USA Cross-Cultural Corporation*, MA Thesis, University of Hawaii.

# 12 Conclusions and directions

## Introduction

This chapter rounds off some issues. One way of being clear about an idea is to define it by what it is not. In Chapter 2 I suggested that strategic learning can be understood in part by recognizing that it is not an approach characterized by apathetic/antagonistic, reactive or bureaucratic styles of working. Here I want to say something about approaches to learning that are not SML – but which attempt to masquerade as SML. I shall also indicate some myths about SML (which are myths in the pejorative sense) as well as some real problems with the approach. Finally, I shall suggest some directions in terms of desirable actions for the future.

## Not self managed learning

I want to outline here approaches that I see as outside the boundaries of SML. In some respects this is the easiest way to define SML. It will, I hope, provide a clearing of the ground and put in perspective earlier comments on SML. I shall move rapidly through a series of headings which exemplify some issues, but this is not meant to be encyclopedic or comprehensive.

## 'Participative' pseudo-learner-centred courses

Reynolds[1] has commented on this phenomenon. 'Participative' is regarded as an 'OK term' to attach to a course, but participation in what is rarely specified. The 'participation' is almost always only in highly tutor-controlled case studies and simulation exercises: the course members do not participate in decisions about content, timing, location, learning objectives, and so on.

A number of people feel they have moved beyond this by asking learners as a group to say what topics they want to cover (within boundaries preset by tutors). However, the tutors are still in charge of the class, as, of course, they control final assessment. Even this extended participation seems too limited to me.

Lee was honest enough about his experiments in learner-centredness to say:

Evaluation mechanisms are crucial to 'learner centredness'. At the end of the day I awarded the grades, and I suppose it was awareness of the power this gave me which allowed me to delegate other aspects of the course and not worry too much about potential anarchy, absenteeism, apathy or other problems. (Lee,[2] p. 38)

**Curriculum separate from learner**

This is a major problem with independent study programmes where learners write out a plan of study and then have it approved by the institution. I have been Degree Committee Chairperson for an individualized MA student of Antioch University. They used this approach. The problem is that the 'degree plan', as it is called, was expected to be judged separately from the person. Antioch's requirement was that the degree plan should be written as a curriculum such that another person could come along, carry out the plan and get an MA.

This seems to be too tied in with an 'objective knowledge' model as it assumes that a curriculum can exist separately from its designer. It attaches a false concreteness to a process, for which we use the metaphor 'plan'.[3] In SML we do not swing to the other extreme and assume that what we call a 'contract' is a totally personal document. We expect that it should be understandable to others, but we do not expect it to exist as a disembodied entity. The contract comes out of the subjective experiences of the person and is meaningful only in the light of that person's experience. And as we are all to some extent unique, even if another person tried to carry out the 'degree plan', that individual would not do it in the same way as the person who designed it.

**Oxbridge tutorial system**

Sometimes when I have tried to describe what we do to someone with an acquaintance with the English higher education world, they have said: 'Ah! What you mean is something like the Oxbridge tutorial system' or, more patronizingly, 'Well, of course, Oxbridge have been doing this for centuries with their tutorial system.' It's nonsense, of course. The Oxbridge tutorial system is linked to a tightly controlled process where, despite some openness of relationships, the learner is still controlled through an imposed assessment process.

**Impotent Rogerianism**

Carl Rogers was not actually 'Rogerian' in the way the mythology has grown up (that is, solely supportive and non-directive). There is evidence of his behaving in quite 'un-Rogerian' ways; for instance, he could be quite structured and confronting. Be that as it may, there certainly is a view about non-directiveness, and from my own research I have a nice quote which sums up one person's changing perspective:[4]

> I created uncertainty and turbulence through Rogerian non-directiveness. I refused to respond to direct requests for assistance, e.g. if they actually asked you what your solution was you'd say 'Well, I think I'd like to think that through', hence increasing turbulence and uncertainty.
>
> Previously people asked for help and I copped out – I assumed it as a sign of dependence and therefore refused to help.
>
> I now disagree:
> I don't see it as dependency (to ask for help) – I am prepared to share my experience/expertise.

**Darwinian élitism**   This term was used by someone in my research to define approaches which glorified tough individualism. This could be a problem with some organizations' approaches to action learning where they see it as a way of sifting out potential top managers (by choosing those who cope best with certain kinds of 'hairy' project). As action learning can veer towards overly individualistic programmes, this seems a genuine concern (especially when the set is played down and the project exaggerated).

**Open learning/ distance learning/ computer-based learning/ independent study/project-based learning**   I have deliberately put together here a conglomerate of currently fashionable labels. Predefined packages (which underpin much open learning/distance learning/computer-based learning) cannot be adequately responsive to learner needs; they cannot be holistic; they can rarely be action based. Hence, on their own they are limited. That does not preclude learners on an SML programme choosing, as part of the programme, to use packaged material. My concern is only with courses which are built around such packages (even if they add on a residential weekend here and there as the Open University does). Project-based approaches also do not guarantee an SML approach.

**Intrusive desire to apply one's own skills/knowledge**   In one programme for which I was a 'hired in' outsider, one of the internal set advisers created many problems in the set to which he was attached, because he saw his role as a 'counsellor' and insisted on counselling people whether they liked it or not. Others have pet theories or ideas which they insinuate into set meetings inappropriately. They usually get found out. Genuine SML accepts the group's right to refuse such intrusions.

**Predefined model of ideal process**   Some set advisers have an idea of how a set should 'ideally' progress and try to bend the set in that way. They may have a view, for instance, that the set 'has to work through dependency/counter-dependency issues' (a common view of some T-group trainers). My experience (and that of others) is that sets do not *have* to work through any phases: it is a trite truism, I know, but each set really is different and one can presuppose no necessary similarities with any other set.

### 'Guess my list' games

In an effort to be 'learner centred' the trainer may refuse to teach, but instead sit and ask questions of 'his or her group', carefully writing up, on the board or flipchart, answers that conform to what he or she wants to hear. The trainer only accepts what is part of his or her own 'map', ignoring the views of learners that do not fit.

### Cutting off

Richard Bandler, one of the developers of neurolinguistic programming, was once asked in a workshop if he worked with blind people and he replied: 'All the time.' Some trainers do not seem to want to *see* (or *hear*) what is going on around them. It is not that they are unable to see or hear, but they do not know how to respond, or they feel anxious about their ability to deal with problems being raised. The easy answer is to 'cut off', perhaps through mental or emotional withdrawal. Effective practitioners seem to 'hang on in there' even if they do not always know what to do.

### Not pre-negotiated

Sometimes trainers try to change a course in mid-stream. I have encountered many who have complained that they started with a standard, trainer-controlled course that was not working too well. Then they read an article or talked to someone and had a 'Road to Damascus' experience. They saw the light. In mid-course they stopped standing at the front of a classroom teaching and instead handed over the course to the participants. The trainer would explain that they were not going to teach any more, but instead let participants do as they liked.

The general result of this was mayhem, and anger from participants. The trainer would see this as a necessary counter-dependence and struggle on until they had to admit defeat.

One of the problems with this approach is that it was not the basis on which the course was set up. It is important in SML to tell people about the design and the principles of the programme in which they will take part. Being up-front is crucial. Participants on a programme will still not understand it fully from a pre-programme briefing, but at least they will know it is not like a traditional type of course, and hence recognize that it is something different.

### Messy, unplanned programmes

Another fault with the situation described above is that the trainer may not provide sufficient help in structuring the programme. SML can easily degenerate if staff do not take seriously (a) structures and (b) their own roles. The following consequences can occur:

1 Assessment is not taken seriously – people are allowed to assert that they have learned something without providing evidence of learning.
2 Contracts become loose statements of intent, which are allowed to become mere background documents.
3 Support for learners is reduced – sets meet less often and are sloppy, easy-going affairs.
4 If there is a learning community it degenerates into endless discussions of internal procedures and loses sight of its role in assisting learning.
5 Staff, for example set advisers, turn up late for meetings, demonstrate their ignorance of learning issues, refuse to take on responsibilities and refuse to learn to be better.

## Degeneration into control

This, in some respects, is the opposite of the above. An example was a programme a colleague and I developed for a large international manufacturing company that had restructured its organization and dispensed with the role of supervisor, replacing it with the enlarged role of 'team leader'. The team leaders had increased responsibility and reported directly to shift managers. The company wanted a course to train the new team leaders (mostly promoted supervisors). We first had a one-day event where we explored the concerns of team leaders and ascertained what they wanted to learn. We brought in their shift managers in the afternoon and shared with the latter the views of their new team leaders. We obtained the shift managers' general support for the issues. Then we had each shift manager meet with the team leaders who reported to him and who were coming on the course (one or two per shift manager). They negotiated in detail learning objectives for the team leaders. These were set down in mini learning contracts, and my colleague and I then designed a one-week course on the basis of these precise learning objectives.

The team leaders largely managed their own learning in the course. Near the end of the week the shift managers attended the course to discuss its progress with team leaders and to plan further development for each individual team leader. The training manager was present throughout the course, and in post-course evaluation proclaimed that he was delighted with the results. He therefore decided that the content of this course would now be the content of all future courses for team leaders. He also dispensed with the one-day planning event. As far as we were concerned he had missed the point of why the first course was a success. Participants and shift managers 'owned' it, and it integrated with ongoing needs. The design we had produced allowed participants to drive the learning, and to feel a real sense of control over it. This was lost in the new trainer-controlled course.

In general, some of the problems that can occur when SML is tightened up and becomes trainer controlled include:

- mapping becomes fixed as a curriculum for all to be taught
- staff control events and learners become more apathetic
- staff deal with personal anxieties and with course problems by blaming learners
- contracting becomes perfunctory or non-existent
- the organization says it wants more structure: in reality it wants more control.

## Self managed learning going wrong

The reasons why SML programmes sometimes don't work well include some of the misinterpretations already discussed. However, there can be other reasons for problems, some of which are discussed below.

### Roles are not carried out effectively

The roles of theorist, designer, manager and learning assistant are crucial in SML. It's clear that some programmes have struggled when there has not been a good balance of these roles. If theory is poorly understood and not explained, for example to participants on programmes, this can cause misunderstandings. If designs do not fit the culture of the organization, the resources available and so on, then there can be problems. If management is inept, this undermines SML programmes. Such problems might be at the level of poor marketing and leadership (the 'fronting' role) or at the level of poor administration and resourcing (the 'back-up' role).

The most visible cause of problems can be at the level of the learning assistant (set adviser, mentor or coach) – and some of these problems have already been mentioned. However, we have found that getting the other three roles right makes it very much easier for a set adviser – to the extent of coping with less-than-ideal set advisers. Hence if a programme has a well-articulated theory, is carefully designed and efficiently managed, one can cope with set advisers who may not fulfil all the criteria discussed in Chapter 10.

### Tactics, not strategy

SML courses may be run as one-offs. They can become interesting side shows from the main business of running standardized training activity. This may not be a total disaster for participants but it can create the notion of a deviant subculture – and this is usually disastrous in the long term.

**Personal development plans only** Organizations can feel that sets are an unnecessary luxury – or that personal development planning alone is all that is needed to foster learning. The evidence is that the results of this approach are usually so variable and unreliable as to make one doubt the cost-effectiveness of these schemes.

**Sets only** Sets can be of some value without the use of learning contracts. However, over time they become more like support groups and they lose their edge and rigour. They also tend to have more of a tactical problem-solving focus. The value of a set with learning contracts is the strategic backcloth to its work. The ideal is not to solve a particular problem but to assist set members to learn to be effective problem solvers (and more).

## Bandwidth

SML operates within a band of possibilities. This is indicated in Figure 12.1, which shows three options.

To the left are the messy, unplanned programmes I have referred to, and to the right the controlled, curriculum-led programmes. SML can operate across a band between these, but there is a definite 'flip' in crossing either boundary. This is especially recognizable in the role and behaviour of staff on programmes. (This factor was discussed in Chapter 9.)

## Myths about SML

These myths[5] are based on typical questions and concerns raised by organizations or academic critics as to why they should not develop SML programmes. Some are genuine and reasonable concerns which need serious attention from SML practitioners. Others are excuses based on spurious arguments.

**SML is an alternative to mainstream management education and training** It seems evident that, long ago in history, even before the concept of 'management' was systematized, effective managers took charge of their own learning. The people who succeeded as managers had no courses to go on, no business school professors at whose feet they could sit, no prestigious institutions of management education to attend, no management books to read. Only in recent times has the idea emerged that 'management' is a subject to study in

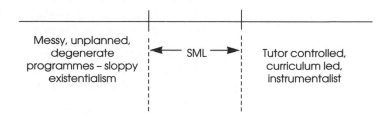

*Figure 12.1* *SML bandwidth: spectrum of possibilities*

isolation from the work of managing. (Revans[6] has chronicled historical perspectives in many of his writings on managerial learning.)

What I find interesting is how the educational and training worlds have succeeded in developing an aberrant alternative to traditional management development. A charitable explanation would be that there has been an attempt to improve the way managers learn by teaching them in the classroom, and in the process hoping to accelerate what can be learned at work. There are various uncharitable explanations, including allegations of status seeking and job creation on the part of academics, trainers and consultants. (Revans[7] is, again, an important commentator on such matters.)

There is a danger in polarizing our perspectives on management development. In some circles there has been a debate between proponents of traditional mainstream work-based approaches (such as action learning) and defenders of the modern alternative mode of taught courses. It is clear that most managerial learning is in the traditional mode (see, for example, Livingstone[8]). Experienced senior managers typically report that the main things they have learned (that are useful to them) have come from their experiences at work (this includes observing and learning from others with whom they work). A major problem occurs because most people who write about or talk about management development are professors, lecturers, trainers and consultants (managers actually *do* it). Those who are course providers tend to believe that what they do is the mainstream and that activities where managers take charge of their own learning are the alternatives.

When I was involved in developing self managed learning programmes in a college – *because* these programmes had no predefined curriculum, *because* they were designed to respond to the precise needs of managers, and *because* staff did not impose a rigid timetable on learners – the programmes were labelled as 'an experimental alternative' to 'proper management education'. It speaks volumes for the power of articulate but misguided management educators that they are able to get away with such a stance.

At one level, however, management educators do not control what managers learn on courses, even though they try to. As Postman and Weingartner[9] point out (in quoting Earl Kelley),

> Now it comes about that whatever we tell the learner, he will make something that is all his own out of it, and

> it will be different from what we held so dear and
> attempted to 'transmit'. He will build it into his own
> scheme of things, and relate it uniquely to what he
> already uniquely holds as experience. Thus he builds a
> world all his own, and what is really important is what
> he makes of what we tell him, not what we intended.
> (pp. 94–5)

These authors go on to say:

> In other words, you end up with a student-centred
> curriculum, not because it is good for motivation but
> because you don't, in fact, have any other choice. (p. 95)

So we find that in terms of the individual manager and their
learning, there can be little need to polarize the two kinds of
'learning situation' (work or course). Managers learn what
they choose to learn in both contexts. The trouble is that
both work and taught courses can be extraordinarily
inefficient. Many managers learn little from work
experience if they are just left to it without any assistance
(for example, if they get poor feedback). Also, we know that
managers are dissatisfied when they are instructed to attend
course sessions that they regard as irrelevant to their
requirements.

One of our motives in developing self managed learning as
a formalized approach to management development was
our desire to address these issues. It does seem that off-the-
job learning can have something to offer: managers do not
necessarily learn all they need to learn solely from work
experience. However, the taught course mode on its own
has not delivered the goods.

**SML means
messy,
unstructured,
chaotic
programmes**

This has already been addressed: SML has significant
structuring. In the hands of poor practitioners the
programmes can, of course, degenerate. In some respects
the standardized training course can be an organized mess:
a goulash of unconnected sessions masquerading as order
by virtue of rigid timetabling.

**SML is resource
intensive – with
standardized
training it is
possible to have
large numbers of
trainees being
taught by one
trainer/teacher**

There are a number of responses to this:

1 The large lecture model can be low in cost but also low in
effectiveness. People may learn little that is not in
textbooks – and buying and reading the books could be
even cheaper.
2 In SML, by dispensing with lectures, we free staff to be
able to work with learners in small groups.
3 If course participants are given the budget, they can (and
do) work out the most cost-effective ways of learning.
They might ask for lectures (but rarely do). What we do
see is learners using budgets that might have been spent

on expensive glossy courses in a much more practical and focused way.

4 SML taps untapped resources, especially of existing expertise in organizations. In one company, a junior manager needed to learn about some legal issues. He asked to go on a law course. It was pointed out to him by his mentor that there was a legal department in head office, and he learned all he needed by asking them. He saved a great deal of money, not just in course fees but also in productive time that would have been lost had he gone on a course. (He learned all he needed *and* stayed in his job.)

5 Senior line managers can act as learning assistants. We have trained hundreds of managers to act as set advisers and mentors. They say that they also get a great deal out of taking on these roles. They improve as managers by learning more about how to develop their own staff, and they contribute to wider strategic learning initiatives.

6 We have run programmes for many hundreds of people in organizations such as PPP healthcare, Sainsbury's and the NHS. It works.

**People do not know what they do not know and cannot, therefore, draw up meaningful learning contracts**

Responses to this include:

1 Thousands of people have been through SML programmes, and *all* of them have drawn up learning contracts. They vary in rigour and planning, but that is to be expected. But individuals can *all* say something about themselves and what they want to learn.

2 Mapping processes help choice.

3 Sets provide support and challenge to help people develop meaningful learning contracts. Mentors and learning communities also help.

4 Some trainers and educators put this up as a spurious item because they feel threatened by their loss of control over learners.

**Learners will set easy goals in SML programmes so it will be just a soft option**

This rarely happens, and if it does, sets challenge people. Indeed the peer group is usually more challenging than managers are in appraisals. The most common problem is that people set objectives that are too demanding, and they have to be helped to develop realism about what can be achieved in specific timescales.

**Individuals may want to learn things that are not in the organization's interests**

This always strikes me as a strange objection. If someone is being employed by an organization, the organization has to trust that individual to talk to customers in the right way, not to steal from the organization, and so on. If people breach such trust, they are presumably disciplined for it, but we know that people cannot be policed every second of every day. Senior managers cannot listen in to every phone conversation to check if the person is letting the organization down or not.

As Postman and Weingartner commented, people make their own choices anyway, no matter what teachers or trainers do. If someone is sent on a course, they could be asleep at the back all the time as far as the organization is aware. There is the bizarre myth that what is taught equals what is learned, so fixed curricula are assumed to control learning. This is just not true.

In SML, on the other hand, learning contracts can make explicit what the person plans to *learn*. These can be discussed and negotiated, so that there is integration between individual learning and organizational requirements. Deviations can of course occur, but they are *less* likely than with traditional training courses.

**Individuals cannot assess themselves**

1 People assess themselves constantly – for example, when they apply for a job they have to assess whether or not they meet the requirements. The fact that people often do this badly shows that they need assistance to develop this ability. SML does this.
2 People do it in SML programmes and in appraisal schemes based on self assessment. It is not always easy but it happens. On SML programmes for qualifications – for example, the post-graduate diploma, an SML Master's programme, and so on – there are external examiners who check the process of assessment. They all comment favourably on the rigour and the quality of assessments carried out – and these are professors in business schools who can compare the assessments with traditional academic-controlled methods.

**SML is too radical for conservative organizations**

I have worked in classic government bureaucracies as well as fast-moving market-led organizations. Issues that arise are different and SML designs need to respond to these differences. However, in terms of acceptability, I have been pleasantly surprised by seemingly old-fashioned conservative organizations. There is a recognition now that they have to change: there is a genuine move away from the tightly controlled bureaucracy and a realization that members of the public have to be treated differently. SML fits where organizations want to move to TQM, empowerment and customer care.

# Real problems

Despite my comments above, I recognize that there can be real problems in moving towards strategic learning and learning businesses and the implementation of SML programmes. These include:

1 It does require high-quality people to implement the ideas. This quality is expressed not just in terms of capability but also in the personal security that people in senior positions need to feel. There are many disturbed people who get into powerful positions – the Robert Maxwells of this world – and they are not likely to find these ideas congenial.
2 Distortion and back-sliding can occur. Many people feel comfortable with existing ways: change is unpleasant to them and they would rather do the wrong thing that they know than something new that they do not fully understand. Lecturers get used to lecturing, and giving it up is not easy.

## Directions

There is an urgent, desperate need for change towards more strategic approaches to learning. The world grows in complexity. The naïve optimism of those who thought that the demise of communism and of the USSR would produce an easier, safer world has been shown to be unfounded. Wars and suffering continue because people have not *learned* to live in peace. It is a learning issue. The exhortations of politicians will not help. The kind of learning needed has to be bone-deep, second-order learning; the kind that develops unshakeable commitment to ideals, and the capability to deliver on them.

These learning issues move, then, beyond the needs of companies. In many societies there are crises in healthcare and in education. Organizations that deliver these services are in need of strategic learning.

Research in England[10] has shown that at least one-third of 16-year-olds have truanted at some time or other in the last half term. At least one in ten is playing truant more than once a week. This situation has been known for a long time. Reports on truancy a decade ago gave the same picture – a massive rejection by young people of the way schools are organized and the way they are treated. However, teachers' union officials are reported as dismissing this evidence. They do not recognize the massive professional failure that teachers are presiding over. Their need to learn is enormous, but largely unrecognized.

Those who see the problems, and care, have opportunities to act. We have to avoid Utopian dreaming on the one hand and pessimistic depression on the other. Marien[11] calls for 'pragmatic maturity' and argues for a Taoist integration of some paired approaches, such as

● *Inspiration and Perspiration*: We need to be creative and inspiring *and* we need to work hard at the issues.

- *Realism and Idealism:* We need to keep our feet on the ground *and* leap into the air.
- *Intellect and Spirit:* We need a new rationality that recognizes the non-rational – a kind of meta-rationality that is able to reason about reason and acknowledge its limitations.

Marien closes his proposals by suggesting that if you aim high you will not shoot yourself in the foot. I would go with that.

## Notes

1 Reynolds, M. (1980) 'Participation in work and education', in Beck, J. and Cox, C. (eds) *Advances in Management Education*, Chichester: Wiley.

2 Lee, B. (1985) 'Learner centred courses: a personal experience,' *Management Education and Development*, **16**, 1 (Spring), 31–40.

3 This issue of the nature of plans is discussed in Cunningham, I. (1984) 'Planning to develop managers', *Management Education and Development*, **15**, 2 (Summer), 83–104.

4 Cunningham, I. (1984) *Teaching Styles in Learner Centred Management Development Programmes*, PhD Thesis, University of Lancaster.

5 Many of the myths here come from discussions with Deborah Booth and Stephanie Elkin, with whom I worked on the SML programme in British Airways. I would like to acknowledge their contribution to these ideas. Also, they were clear, as British Airways HR staff, that the myths could be rebutted in the way that I have done here.

6 Revans, R.W. (1977) 'Action learning and the nature of knowledge', *Education and Training* (Nov./Dec.), 318–22.

7 Revans, R.W. (1980) *Action Learning: New Techniques for Management*, London: Blond & Briggs.

8 Livingstone, J.S. (1971) 'The myth of the well-educated manager', *Harvard Business Review*, **49** (Jan./Feb.), 79–89.

9 Postman, N. and Weingartner, C. (1969) *Teaching as a Subversive Activity*, London: Penguin.

10 O'Keeffe, D. and Stoll, P. (1993) *Truancy in English Secondary Schools*. Report, quoted in *The Guardian*, 26 June, p. 3.

11 Marien, M. (1983) 'The "Transformation as Sandbox" syndrome', *Journal of Humanistic Psychology*, **23**, 1 (Winter), 7–15.

# Appendix I
# Research into SML

The following is a summary of some of the research carried out to evaluate the results of self managed learning programmes. This appendix does not attempt to cover all the research evidence. The aim is to provide a supplement to the main text. Many studies have already been referenced in the text, along with articles written by participants on programmes.

## Published papers – a selection

1 Webster, J. (1995) 'Self managed learning in Cable and Wireless', *Croner's A–Z Guide for HRM Professionals*, Issue 6, 6–8. This provides a brief summary of a longer internal evaluation report produced from evidence from programmes in Europe, the USA and the Middle East.
2 Broscomb, T. (1994) 'Induction and change through self managed learning', *Purchasing and Supply Management*, March, 35–8. Again this is a shortened version of an internal report in Shell, produced by Arjan Overwater and Mike Saker, based on the work done on Shell's programme for purchasing managers across Europe.
3 Jackson, S. (1993) 'Learning to learn in Lewisham', *Organizations and People*, **1** (4), 22–4. This is another short summary of their own evaluation studies.

All the above report positive results, many of which have been covered in the main text.

## Evaluation reports of specific programmes

1 Cooper, J. (1988) *Evaluation of Young Professionals Programme in British Airways*.
   Jane Cooper's report provides evidence from participants on two programmes, from line managers, from HR staff, from mentors and from set advisers. The overwhelming evidence was positive, with some criticisms of operational issues. Even those participants who had concerns said that they would not have wanted a standard training course – they agreed with the principles of SML.
2 Bennett, B. (1994) *Evaluation of Consortium SML Programme, Strategic Developments International*.

Ben Bennett's report evaluates the 1993/94 programme, with participants coming from the following companies: Barclays Bank, Ladbroke Group, Norwich Union, Bowrings, EMI, Amersham International. The report is based on interviews with participants. Again the responses were highly positive with much evidence of pay-off to the participating companies.

The above report is available from the Centre for Self Managed Learning, 'Ellerslie', 23 Western Road, Abergavenny, Mons. NP7 7AB. The Centre's newsletter has contained summaries of evaluations carried out in Arun District Council, Cable and Wireless, PPP healthcare and Sainsbury's.

## Studies internal to organizations

The following have carried out their own evaluations (but the information has not been published in full): Allied Domecq, BBC, KPMG, St Helier NHS Trust, South West Thames Regional Health Authority.

## Higher degrees

A number of master's theses have referred to SML. Julia Ross's MSc has already been referenced in the text. There are at least two studies going on at present on SML.

## Related studies

1 Lancaster University, Centre for the Study of Management Learning (now Department of Management Learning), conducted a comparative study of a range of programmes including the Post Graduate Diploma in Management (by SML) at North East London Polytechnic (now University of East London).
2 My PhD thesis (*Teaching Styles in Learner Centred Management Development Programmes*) covered the issue of the role of staff in SML programmes.

# Appendix II
# Selling SML

There are a number of issues to address in getting buy-in for a self managed learning programme. However, at one level one can just see it as drawing on any standard selling methods. On that basis, those who are good at selling will have already spotted how to sell SML from what is in the text. Chapter 12, especially, offers guidance on dealing with some misunderstandings about SML – and some more are explored below. For those who would like further help on selling (and we get asked to provide advice on this at many workshops on SML), here are some additional possibilities.

## Dealing with misunder-standings of SML

The following are some standard misunderstandings that may need to be tackled in getting others in the organization to understand SML as we mean it. Their understanding is a prior need before any other action can be taken.

- *SML is anything vaguely to do with self development.*
  I hope that the main text has dealt with this – it is a common problem and it is growing because more and more providers of training and consultancy are finding the term self managed learning one that appeals to their clients.

- *SML is the same as self directed learning.*
  Again, the text shows how to distinguish what has been a relatively unstructured approach to learning (SDL) from SML.

- *SML is the use of personal development plans (without any collaborative learning structures such as sets).*
  This can seem an attractive option, especially where individuals in an organization refuse to collaborate with their colleagues in sets (or any other kind of group). I can see that if the latter is the case and the organization accepts the situation, it should at least cease to try to be a learning business, in the way I've described it. It is possible that this issue will be resolved in organizations that move to having a core of employed people and draw

on self employed individual contributors or outsourced companies. (Those who will not collaborate with their colleagues may still be able to offer useful services as outside providers, but I can't see why they should be employed in the core group.)

● *SML is the use of sets/learning groups (but no learning contracts).*
This is less of a problem than the one before, in that people can still get a great deal out of a set. However, there are then issues of how the learning can be evaluated and why the organization should fund unplanned learning.

● *SML is the same as open learning.*
There are still managers who say 'We do SML because we have an open learning centre.' Such centres are valuable but we know that they are usually under-used and poor value for money unless there is some structure like SML to focus learning and to give people a compelling reason to go into such a centre. Other open-learning-type approaches include the use of rigidly structured handbooks or workbooks masquerading as SML.

● *SML ideas can be incorporated into other programmes – SML becomes just another influence on course design.*
This was addressed early on. It is a danger when organizations have tried to copy what is in this book without, say, developing set advisers or creating a good design. Hence the programme comes off the rails. The tendency is then to blame the looseness of the approach and introduce more controls, including taught elements. This often only makes things worse and so, in the downward spiral of problems, SML gets a bad name.

● *SML is a variant of action learning.*
This has caused some organizations to rename sets, for example as learning groups or development groups. This seems a good solution if there is a danger of confusion.

● *SML as tactics: SML is sets and contracts but other learning is outside SML, for example courses, workshops, reading, and so on.*
This is an attempt to box in SML and see it as a purely tactical approach. It makes a mockery of using learning contracts as strategic documents which need to cover the range of learning approaches the person is using and which can provide a longer-term view.

**Research**     Some people want research evidence, as they may claim that the approach is unproven. Appendix I addressed this factor. However, there are many who claim to be interested in research evidence but who will still reject it when they see it.

# Users of SML

Some people are more convinced of the value of SML if they can see that it is widely used. Here is a list of organizations that have made use of SML either for in-house development or as part of an SML consortium. The list excludes the many organizations that have sponsored people for SML diploma and master's programmes.

Abbey National
Allied Domecq
Amersham International
Arun District Council
Barclays Bank
BBC
Birmingham Midshires Building Society
BP
British Airways
Cable and Wireless
C.T. Bowring
Electrolux
EMI
Finnish Post
GKN
KPMG
Ladbroke Group
London and Edinburgh Insurance
London Borough of Lewisham
Mid-Essex District Health Authority
Nestlé
Norwich Union
PPP healthcare
Prudential
RCO Support Services
Rothmans
St Helier NHS Trust
Sainsbury's
Scottish Health Service Centre
Shell (UK and Netherlands)
SOK (Finland)
South East Thames Regional Health Authority
South West Thames Regional Health Authority
W H Smith

This is not a complete list, as the above are just the organizations known to the Centre for Self Managed Learning.

# Why the above approaches may not work

Chapter 3 discussed the problem that many leaders of organizations are not as interested in the performance of their organizations as their rhetoric would imply. Figure A.1 shows diagrammatically the balance of influences on leaders of organizations. The problem is that while the arguments against using SML can appear rational, they are more likely to be emotional or political. SML can feel threatening to those who like to feel that they are in control and insecure leaders can feel nervous about embarking on something new like SML.

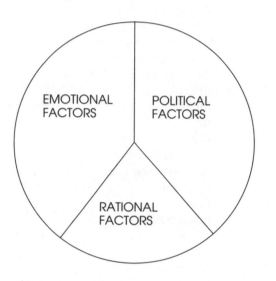

*Figure A.1    Factors affecting leaders' decision making*

It can therefore be important to recognize these factors and to try to address fears and uncertainties. Of course there will be some situations where these attempts might not work. Some leaders will never budge. We have been very successful in a variety of organizations, but I would not have liked to try to sell these ideas to a Hitler or a Stalin. Mercifully leaders like this are few and far between.

# Conclusion

This appendix has only hinted at the options available for selling. We usually find that we have to tailor our strategies to the precise context within which we are working. The above provides a few generalized ideas but there is nothing to beat a specific plan of action to suit the circumstances.

# Appendix III
# The Fielding Institute
# MA

This is an abbreviated version of my course for the Fielding Institute MA in Organization Design and Effectiveness. The programme is designed for people who are not able to attend an educational institution, but want an interactive learning experience rather than one that is based on packaged distance learning. It seems especially valuable for people in dispersed locations who want to learn how to work in globalized contexts (I have group members in Alaska, Tokyo, Sydney and South Africa). I have left detailed information, such as dates, in the text in order to show how the course has worked in practice. In subsequent terms the dates have, of course, been different.

**Course 301 – Human development and leadership**

COURSE OVERVIEW

The course will use leadership as its focus. Issues of 'human development' will spin off from this, as will other factors such as the role of technology, aspects of diversity, and so on. The style of the course will allow you to develop your thinking and ideas in areas relevant to you.

I take the view that no course can be objectively true in its content. If you look at how leadership is taught across the world there are huge differences in the content of these courses. It's a controversial and tricky subject – and people have varying biases and perspectives. So I'll start with my biases.

The start point to my perspective on knowledge is the need to integrate three basic dimensions – the first, second and third person. What I mean by this is that the first person perspective is about 'me/I' – it's about self knowledge. This is often tacit, not explicit (see Nonaka and Takeuchi, 1995, in the reading list). In simple terms this means that tacit knowledge is not available to others (or even yourself) – it's the taken-for-granted internal knowledge you often use unconsciously. Explicit knowledge is out there and shared. One aspect of this course will encourage you to make more explicit some of your tacit knowledge about leadership and human development.

Second-person knowledge is about 'you', that is, the people around you, the others you relate to. People 'know' all sorts of things about these others. In this context you may, for instance, have views about others who have led you, others you have observed taking a lead, others you lead. This all comes under second-person knowledge. Again this is often taken for granted – and in this course we want to explore some of that.

Third-person knowledge is what, in some people's eyes, is the only legitimate knowledge. It is about 'them/it' – it's the world of theory and generalizations. It's what dominates textbook knowledge, especially in much of the traditional psychological literature. It has its place – and I worry about people who come to take too sceptical a view of received wisdom and reject it all. My view is that we need to integrate the three dimensions. This is to be a good scientist – compare theory with evidence/experience. If the theory doesn't match the evidence, modify the theory and/or check your evidence.

One starting point for us will be to consider, in relation to this area:

- what you know you know
- what you know you don't know
- what you don't know you don't know.

You will need to initiate exploration under the first two headings. The job of myself, your colleagues and the literature will be to help in the third heading. In the process this should cause you to modify what you have identified under the first two headings (as you'll either realize you already know something or you now know that you don't know it). This process is called 'mapping' as it allows you to make better choices on your learning journey, if you have a more sophisticated mental map.

COURSE DESIGN

The course is in three phases (times in brackets):

1 Mapping and contracting (5 weeks: 29 April – 3 June 1998)
2 Implementation (4 weeks: 3 June – 1 July 1998)
3 Assessment (2 weeks: 1 July – 15 July 1998)

Each phase is explained below. One aspect of the design is that you will need to carry out phase 1 in order to get a basic foundation in the field and then carry out activities in phase 2. Assessment (phase 3) will be collaborative, that is, you will need to assess your own work, get the judgements of others on it and make judgements about others' work. I will be part of that judgement process as another judge as well as umpire/referee, if needed.

One principle of the design is that the process should mirror the issue under examination. Leadership requires leaders

● to understand themselves and the people around them
● to set goals and initiate actions to meet these goals
● to make things happen in real time and in the context of limited resources
● to judge their own performance and that of others
● to assist others in their learning and development.

All of these will be required of you in the process of this course. Phase 1 will set the basis for this: hence the need for it to take up the largest time period.

PHASE 1 (29 April – 3 June 1998)
Components of this phase will be as follows:

1  You will need to carry out a repertory grid exercise to explore how you see leadership (material for this was given to you at the orientation session). You will need to get in the results of this exercise by midnight GMT, 6 May. Please keep to about 2 pages maximum in the final posting.
2  You will need to interview at least one person whom you regard as a leader – and report on what you found – by midnight GMT, 13 May. The report can be a series of bullet points on the qualities, capabilities, skills, and so on that you identified (it is not required at this stage to write a lengthy essay; again keep it to a maximum of 2 pages if possible). I provided guidance notes for interviews, at the orientation session, but you should also be guided by what you get from the repertory grid exercise and from your reading.
3  You will need to undertake reading in this field in order to get a sense of the third-person knowledge. Reading material is discussed below, as it could be germane to phases 1 and 2. There is no time limit on this activity.
4  You will need to produce a learning contract by midnight GMT, 27 May. This will answer five questions, namely:

  ● Where have I been? What's been my past experience of leadership (being led and being a leader)? What have I learned from this?

- Where am I now? What leadership capabilities, skills, knowledge, and so on do I now possess? What's my current perspective on leadership?
- Where do I want to get to? What are my goals for this course? What are my longer-term goals in terms of leadership? If I want to be a leader, what kind of leader do I want to be? If I want to act as a consultant to leaders, what will that mean for me?
- How will I get there? What do I need to do for the next four weeks to meet my goals for this course? What other actions will I undertake that will contribute to my longer-term development?
- How will I know if I've arrived? What criteria will I set in order for my work in the next four weeks to be judged? What evidence will I produce for my colleagues so that they can judge my work effectively?

*Note:* All the above can be in the form of bullet points. Also, it makes sense to test drafts of each of these questions well before the deadline date. The trickiest question is the last one – so you may need to put time and energy into that one – but that question can't be answered effectively without doing justice to the other four.

In answering the second question, you should, if possible, include data from a psychometric test or instrument. At the very least you probably ought to know what tests like Myers-Briggs or FIRO-B bring to the field.

5  The last week of this phase will be given over to agreeing the contracts and completing feedback on all the pieces of work. The learning contracts are contracts with all the group and everyone has to get involved in agreeing them. This is non-negotiable.

PHASE 2 (3 June – 1 July 1998)
This is the time for you to complete your contracted work – which must be posted by midnight GMT, 1 July. There should be NO new work posted after this date, so if you want comments on drafts and so on these need to be posted at least a week before. Since this work is not predictable ahead of time, the only thing to say here is that everyone in the group is expected to support their colleagues in their learning. Also, during this phase we will need to tidy up any details on assessment so that we can minimize problems in phase 3.

PHASE 3 (1 July – 15 July 1998)
This is assessment time. You are expected to assess your own work and post your own judgement with your work by

4 July. This judgement should include the work you did in phase 1 also, though you may want to give less weight to this than work in phase 2.

You then have a week to respond to others and to give your own judgements on their work, that is, by 11 July. Between 11 July and 15 July we will need to decide on grades.

RECOMMENDED TEXTS

The literature on leadership is huge. Below are some of my selections for reading, but you may have your own favourites. However, I've tried to identify below the key names of people you ought to know something about. As most of you will be working in the USA, I've kept the majority of the recommendations to US texts. However, if you take the work of people like Hofstede and Trompenaars (see below for references) seriously you should be aware that most of such texts are culture bound, that is, they may only be helpful in thinking about leadership in US organizations and they may not be so good on leadership in the rest of the world.

For busy people like yourselves you may find it most useful to start with some of the texts immediately below, which I've identified as good for mapping. They are either a quick read (the first one) or have a range of chapters by big names, so that you don't have to go to the originals if you don't need to (and they can be dipped into easily).

(There then follows an annotated bibliography with my personal comments on each text.)

# Index

Acceptance 146
Action Learning 21, 87, 132–3
Agreement 146
Allied Domecq 6–11, 16
Antioch University 264
Appraisal schemes 71–2
ARBS Model 13 –16
Argyris, C. 82, 107, 147
Arun District Council 137,
    243
Aspin, David 126–7
Assessment (*see also* Judging)
    159, 197–200
Autonomy 126–8

Baba Ram Dass 5
Balance 65, 108–11, 220–21
Bandler, Richard 266
Bartolomé, F. 105
Bateson ,G. 32, 48, 97
BBC 66, 124
Benne, K. D. xiv
Bennis, W.G. xiv, 103
Berne, E. 107
Best, George 33
Bettelheim, Bruno 77
Bio-rhythms 106
Birkbeck model 66
Birmingham Midshires
    Building Society 15–16,
    247
Boyatzis, R.E. 89–90
Bramley, W. 104
Branson, R. xvi, 80, 127
British Airways 54, 86, 94, 127,
    201, 277
Brown, J. S. 52
Buddhists/Buddhism 105–6
Burgoyne, J.G. 208
Business makers 57
Business Schools 104–5, 110–11

Cable and Wireless 277
Capability 89–96

Career guidance 67
CEOs 209
Centred/Centring 107–9,
    113–14
Certificate in Management
    Studies 174
Change 28–31
    and learning 38–40, 80–82,
    ease of 147–8
    first order/second order (*see
        also* Learning, second
        order) 32–6, 59–60
    managing 38–40
Chaos Theory 32, 62, 95
Chernobyl 114–15
Chin, R. xiv
Chitty, Jim 137–40
Chuang Tzu 84
Clarks 57
Claxton, G. 96–7
Cleveland, H. 98
Cloke, D. 11
Coaching 246–7
Collaborating 161–3
Competence and competences
    42, 90–94, 175
Competitive advantage 23
Communism 84–5
Communities of practice 51–4
Confluent education 136
Connectedness (and
    connection) 106, 113–14,
    162–3
Contracting (*see* Learning
    Contracts)
Corrall, S. 124–5
Cross cultural issues 251–5,
    256–60
Culture 7, 11, 18, 65–6, 92
    and Learning Business 58–9

Day, M. 93
Design/Designing (*see also*
    Learning designer) 172–4

Development (*see also* learning)
  adviser 247
  focused 73
Diagnosing and diagnosis
  157–8, 177
Digital Equipment Company
  37, 58–9
Diploma of Higher Education
  131–2
Diploma in Management
  Studies 130
Distance learning 19, 136, 265
Diversity 61, 95, 254–8
Dixon, Mike 103
Drucker, P. 47–8
Duguid, P. 52
Dynamic (from Pirsig) 62–5,
  110

Eco, Umberto 251
Eliot, T.S. 99
Emotional learning (*see*
  Learning and emotions)
Environment design 67, 69
Equipment design 67, 69, 70
Ethics 114–16
Evaluation (*see also* Judging)
  10–11, 13, 201–2
Evans, Gil 93
Evans, Judith 17–18
Evans, P. 105
Experience, 110–13
Experiential Learning 134–5
Extrapolation 31
Extrovert 108–9

Facilitating 217–19
Faldo, Nick 223–4
Feedback 36–7, 165, 253
Fichant, René 3
Fiedler, F.E. 113
Fielding Institute 216, 247–8,
  283
Fiol, M. 110
Forecasting 29–30
Freire, P. 84

Galagan, P. A. 51, 52
Gallwey, W.T. 89
Gibran, K. 104
Good
  learners 79–80
  learning (*see also* learning)
  89
Goodwin, L.R. 126
Grabowski, Richard 115
Griffiths, I. 38
Grounding 113–14

Hall, E.T. 260
Handbooks 177
Handy, Charles 55
Harmony 107–8
Haste, H. 116
Hiram Walker 6
Hofstede, G. 83, 92
Holistic education 136
Hot action vs cool action 34
Hysteresis 41–2, 66, 69

IBM 3, 37, 58
Independent Study 131–2,
  265
Individuality 84
Institute for Research on
  Learning 51, 53
Internet 216–7
Introvert 108–9, 247–8

Japan
  and learning 47–8, 54, 83
  and USA 260
James, M. 219
Job design 67, 68, 70
Johnson, M. 85
Jongeward, D. 219
Judging 163–6, 264

Karpman, Stephen 219
Keeney, B.P. 97
Keutzer, C.S. 103–4
Kidder, Rushworth 114
Kirk, P. 56
Kirkegaard, S. 3
Knowledge 98–9, 283–4
  management 50–51
Knowles, Malcolm 179
Kolb, David 134–5
KPMG 247

La Bier, D. 105
Lakoff, G. 85
Law of Revolutionary Ideas 4
Leadbetter, David 223–4
Leadership 113
  strategic 40–41
Learners
  involvement in programmes
  226
  self managing 251–3
Learning
  and change 38–40, 80–82
  and collaboration 83–5
  and emotions 103–96
  and ownership 94
  and working 170–71
  assisting (*see also* Set

advising) 196–7, 213–24,
232, 258
budgets 161, 181–2
community 194–6, 258
curve 48
designer 210–11, 231
experiential (*see* Experiential
learning)
focus of 20
levels 4–5
manager 212–3, 231–2
resources (*see* Resourcing)
second order 35–6, 48–9,
59–60, 135
self managed (*see* Self
managed learning)
strategic (*see* Strategic
learning)
theorist 208–10, 30–31
who learns 82–83
Learning business 49–50, 54–61,
72–3, 121
Learning contracts 7–9, 17,
121–3, 138–40,
158–61,177–80, 264, 272
and difference 256–8
on the Internet 285–7
Learning
organisation/company 49
Learning sets 8–10, 12, 17,
122–3, 132–3, 182–94
and difference 256
Lebas, M. 110
Lee, B. 177–8, 263–4
Lewisham London Borough
277
Local Authority – example of
integration of needs 70–71
Luck 33–4
Lupton,T. xiv

MacLaurin, Ian xiv, 79–80
Management Charter Initiative
(MCI) 92, 93
Manz, C.C. 126
Mapping 37–8, 149–56, 209
in SML 175–7
for cross-cultural managing
252–3
Marien, M. 274–5
MBA 81–2, 89, 104, 166
McLean, A.J. 108
Mead, Margaret 99
Mentoring (*see also* Learning
assisting)
and difference 258
Merton, T. 83–4
Metafeeling 105–6

Metaphor 85–9, 159–60
and mapping 155
Methods design 68, 70
Michelin 3
Miller, A.G. 176
Mintzberg, H. 212
Models, 38
'nested' 176
Money makers 57
Morality 114–16
Morgan, G.M. 85
Morris, J. 210–11
Murdoch,Iris 116

National Health Service 11, 55
National Union of Students 129
Neill, A.S. 130
Networking 196
New towns 59–60
Nichol, Sir Duncan 55
Nonaka, I. 51
North East London Polytechnic
131

Ohmae, K. 83
Open learning 136, 265
Order – and disorder 59–61
Organization culture (*see*
Culture)
Organization design 67–8
Organization development 50,
56
Organizational capability 22
Organizational types 61–5
Organizations
apathetic/antagonistic 13–14
bureaucratic 15–16
chaotic 62–5
learning 4
'palm tree' vs 'redwood' 33
pendulum 62
pressures on 49
organic 62
reactive 14
static 61–2
Oxbridge 264

Patterns 35–6, 135, 157, 252
Pedler, M. 135–6, 195, 212
Personalism 84–5
Peters, T.G. 37, 62
Pirsig, R. M. 62–6
Planning learning 158–60
Player, Gary 33–4
Polarities 108–11
Porter, M. 54
Postman, N. 108, 270–71
Potter, David 42

Power seekers 56–7
Practitioners/professionals 209–10
Preparational planning 31–2
Preparing 149–61
Proactive 108
Problems/solutions 111–13
Projects 132–3, 265
Psion 42
Psychotherapy and learning 77

Ratiu, Indrei 251–3
Reactive 108
Recruitment 67
Reframing 35
Regional management centres 130
Renio, A. 89–90
Rescuing 219
Resourcing 161, 180–81
Responsibility (for learning) 124–5
Revans, R. 21, 38, 53, 81, 133
Rewards systems 68–9, 70–71
Reynolds, M. 263
Rogers, Carl 133–4, 217–8, 264–5
Rogers, Will 34
Role design 68
Ross, J. xvii
Rover Learning Business 55–6
Royal Society for the Encouragement of Arts, Manufactures and Commerce (RSA) 90

St Helier NHS Trust 12–13, 16
St Thomas Aquinas 98
Sainsbury's 17–18, 144–5
Sathe, V. 58
Schön, D. 107
School for Independent Study 131–2
Schumacher, E.F. 98–9, 151
Schwartz 32
Selection 67, 70
Self control 125–6
Self development 20, 135–6
Self directed learning 133–4
Self managed learning 7–11, 12–13, 17–18, 20–23, 43, 120–25, 136–40
  Centre for Self Managed Learning 277
  going wrong 268–9
  myths about 269–73
  not SML 263–5
  programmes 169–74

strategy 143–8
users 281
Senge P. M., 95
Set advisers (*see* also learning assisting) 8, 17, 132
  co-set advising 242
  development of 236–46
  selection of 232–6
Sets (*see* Learning sets)
Shaw, George Bernard 79
Shell 174, 277
Squires, C. 84
Stacey, R. D . 32, 95
Static/Systematic (from Pirsig) 62–5, 110
Start-up events 174–5
Status seekers 56–7
Steiner, C. 179–80, 219
Stephen, John 36–7
Stewart, R. 128
Strategic excellence 42–3
Strategic learning xi, xii, 6, 13, 15–23, 43–4, 148–50, 169, 225
Strategic planning 29
Strategy 143–8
Stress 113
Summerhill School 130
Szent-Györgi, A. 98

Tactics 143–8
Takeuchi, H. 51
Taoism/Taoists 61, 83, 96, 109, 170
Teams 50
Tesco 79–80
Theory/theorist role (*see* Learning theorist)
Time 157
Toyota xiii
Training, 130
  courses 14–15
  and development 27–8, 66–7
Training and Enterprise Councils 54
Transactional Analysis 107, 188–9, 219
Trompenaars, F. 92
Tutorial 188–90

U Model 143–8, 201
University of East London 131, 201

Vaill, P. 30, 87
Values 41, 51, 114
Virgin Atlantic Airways 80
Vision 5, 41

Walzer, M. 83
Waterman, R.M. 37
Weingartner, C. 108, 270–71
Weyrich K.D. 89
Wisdom 51, 96–9

Wittgenstein, L. 93

Yamaguchi, I. 260
Yin-Yang 109

# Developing Corporate Competence

## A High-Performance Agenda for Managing Organizations

William Tate

In most organizations there is a striking difference between what managers are capable of doing, and what managers choose to do and are allowed to do. HRD specialists often devote themselves to developing individual managerial competence with little regard to the context or the organization's side of the bargain.

In this challenging book William Tate shows how to link management development with the culture and problems of the organization to generate performance-enhancing action. Mr Tate shows how to treat the organization as a partner in the development process, integrating capability with a receptive organizational climate which encourages and applies learning. He offers both ideas and practical strategies, supported by illuminating case studies. Like his companion volume, *Developing Managerial Competence*, this engages the reader through activities, checklists and 'tips', helping him or her to think through the issues and plan appropriately. He stresses throughout the benefits of a value-driven model based on openness.

This is a radical, hard-hitting but above all practical approach designed to place the organization's purpose at the heart of the management development process. It will be welcomed by HRD practitioners and senior managers alike.

# Gower

# The Excellent Manager's Companion

## Philip Holden

This is for every manager who aspires to excellence in everything they do, but wonders how they'll ever find the time ...

With *The Excellent Manager's Companion* in your desk drawer you'll be equipped with succinct guidance on today's most talked about business issues. And you'll be able to pepper your conversation with pertinent quotations, and even know which books to turn to when you really do need more detailed guidance on a specific topic.

Twenty-one chapters look at key topics, ranging from corporate culture to customer orientation, and from innovation to influencing people. Each chapter is organized around standard sections, which makes dipping into the book quick, easy, and rewarding.

Sections are:

- questions for self-analysis
- a step-by-step guide to best practice
- the 10 'don'ts'
- pertinent quotations
- summaries of key books and articles
- a case study
- a glossary of terms.

Philip Holden's lively *Companion* combines expertise with entertainment, with a supporting cast that ranges from Walt Disney to Confucius, and from Dilbert to Drucker. Guaranteed to appeal to busy managers in all sectors.

# Gower

# The Gower Handbook of Management

## Fourth Edition

### Edited by Dennis Lock

*'If you have only one management book on your shelf, this must be the one.'*

Dennis Lock recalls launching the first edition in 1983 with this aim in mind. It has remained the guiding principle behind subsequent editions, and today *The Gower Handbook of Management* is widely regarded as a manager's bible: an authoritative, gimmick-free and practical guide to best practice in management. By covering the broadest possible range of subjects, this handbook replicates in book form a forum in which managers can meet experts from a range of professional disciplines.

The new edition features:

- 65 expert contributors - many of them practising managers and all of them recognized authorities in their field
- many new contributors: over one-third are new to this edition
- 72 chapters, of which half are completely new
- 20 chapters on subjects new to this edition
- a brand new design and larger format.

*The Gower Handbook of Management* has received many plaudits during its distinguished career, summed up in the following review from *Director*:

*'... packed with information which can be used either as a reference work on a specific problem or as a guide to an entire operation. In a short review one can touch only lightly on the richness and excellence of this book, which well deserves a place on any executive bookshelf.'*

# Gower

# Gower Handbook of Management Skills

## Third Edition

### Edited by Dorothy M Stewart

*'This is the book I wish I'd had in my desk drawer when I was first a manager. When you need the information, you'll find a chapter to help; no fancy models or useless theories. This is a practical book for real managers, aimed at helping you manage more effectively in the real world of business today. You'll find enough background information, but no overwhelming detail. This is material you can trust. It is tried and tested.'*

So writes Dorothy Stewart, describing in the Preface the unifying theme behind the Third Edition of this bestselling *Handbook*. This puts at your disposal the expertise of 25 specialists, each a recognized authority in their particular field. Together, this adds up to an impressive 'one stop library' for the manager determined to make a mark.

Chapters are organized within three parts: Managing Yourself, Managing Other People, and Managing the Business. Part I deals with personal skills and includes chapters on self-development and information technology. Part II covers people skills such as listening, influencing and communication. Part III looks at finance, project management, decision-making, negotiating and creativity. A total of 12 chapters are completely new, and the rest have been rigorously updated to fully reflect the rapidly changing world in which we work.

Each chapter focuses on detailed practical guidance, and ends with a checklist of key points and suggestions for further reading.

# Gower

# The Learning Organization in the Public Services

Edited by Janice A Cook, Derek Staniforth and Jack Stewart

The learning organization is an idea now informing management strategy in all sectors. And much of the pioneering work has taken place in a public service context. This challenging book brings together the experiences of a wide range of people engaged in developing and applying the relevant concepts.

Part I introduces the theoretical background and examines some current issues, including transferability and community learning. Part II presents case histories drawn from a variety of organizations, among them central and local government departments, a national charity, a fire brigade and a police force. Each chapter is contributed by someone personally involved. They show what worked - and what didn't - and what the main benefits and drawbacks proved to be.

With its combination of analysis and practice, this unusual book will provide both information and inspiration for anyone concerned to improve efficiency, raise morale, enhance the quality of performance, design new ways of managing or simply create a more rewarding place to work in.

# Gower

# Towards a Competent Workforce

Bob Mansfield and Lindsay Mitchell

For over a decade the UK has been engaged in a radical reform of its vocational education and training. As part of that process new methods have been devised to analyse and describe the outcomes which people are expected to achieve at work - which are called occupational standards. This book contains the first comprehensive description of Functional Analysis, the method developed to define occupational standards and National Vocational Qualifications. It also discusses changes in contemporary work patterns, arguing that a new model of occupational competence is needed - the Job Competence Model. The authors have both been closely associated with the methods and models described in the book and their personal insights add enormously to the value of the material.

The text is in four parts. The first argues for a more strategic role for vocational education and training - to develop a competent workforce able to meet the challenges of changing economic needs. Part 2 charts the development of models of occupational competence which reflect these changing needs. Parts 3 and 4 together constitute a manual on how to use functional analysis to develop and define the occupational standards which describe the performance characteristics of a competent workforce.

Anyone involved in vocational training or professional development will find this book invaluable both as a source of information and as a guide to action.

# Gower